A BRIEF HISTORY OF NOBLESVILLE

A BRIEF HISTORY OF NOBLESVILLE

PAULA DUNN & NANCY A. MASSEY

THE History PRESS

Published by The History Press
Charleston, SC
www.historypress.net

First published 2018

Manufactured in the United States

ISBN 9781625858917

Library of Congress Control Number: 2018948034

CONTENTS

ACKNOWLEDGEMENTS

The authors gratefully acknowledge the following people and institutions. Without their assistance, this book would not have been possible.

Marilyn Conner, Conner Prairie Interactive History Park, Sid Davis, Bob DuBois, Sherry Faust, the First United Methodist Church, Jane Cullen Gawthrop, Tonja White Goodloe, Susan Lucas and the Hamilton County Historical Society, Hamilton East Public Library, Michael and Nicole Kobrowski, Evelyn Lees and the staff of the Noblesville City Clerk's Office, Garrick Mallery, Nancy and Ross Natoli, the Noblesville Fire Department, Noblesville Masonic Lodge No. 57, Trudy Pickett, Fred Swift, Rick Taylor, Tim Timmons and the Westfield Washington Historical Society.

1
BEGINNINGS

The story of Noblesville, the county seat of Hamilton County, Indiana, actually begins about four miles south of the site on which the town was founded. It was there, on the night of August 12, 1802, that central Indiana's first permanent English-speaking settler, William Conner, put the finishing touches on a double log cabin. Over the next several years, that cabin would serve not only as his home and trading post but also as the principal gathering place for both Native Americans and the white settlers who arrived later.

Conner and his brother, John, had come to the Indiana Territory from Michigan two years earlier to trade for furs with the Native Americans who lived along the West Fork of the White River. A list of old Indian traders in the January 25, 1858 *Daily State Sentinel* shows the Conner brothers were licensed to do business with the Delaware Nation at the villages of Buckengelaus and Petchepencues as of November 30, 1801. "Buckengelaus" was undoubtedly Buckongahelas's Town, the easternmost Delaware village on the White River, near present-day Muncie. Petchepencues has never been positively identified, although Charles N. Thompson suggests in *Sons of the Wilderness: John and William Conner* that it may have been the Hamilton County village known as Upper Delaware Town.

Initially, the Conners lived with their Delaware trading partners—John in Buckongahelas's Town and William probably in Anderson's Town (present-day Anderson, Indiana.) Having grown up among Shawnee and Delaware Indians in Moravian missionary towns in Ohio and Michigan, the brothers were familiar with the Delaware language and customs, and blended comfortably into the native society. Both men took Delaware wives, William marrying Mekinges, the daughter of Chief Anderson.

In 1802, William left Anderson's Town and moved downstream to a large prairie opposite Upper Delaware Town. There, according to an article in the May 11, 1881 *Indianapolis News*, Conner—aided solely by an unidentified French Canadian—finished the roof of his cabin on a "beautiful moonlight night."

Conner would later describe the region in which he settled as "the loveliest land he had ever laid eyes on." Certainly, it was a good place to conduct fur trading. It was home to a wide variety of fur-bearing animals: beavers, otters, foxes, mink, muskrats, skunks, wildcats, fishers, deer, panthers, bears, wolves and the most abundant prize of all, raccoons. Wild game was plentiful, and nearby White River teemed with fish, as did the Cicero and Stony (sometimes spelled "Stoney") Creeks, which fed it.

The area was densely forested, but a series of fertile prairies, some of which had already been farmed by the Indians, dotted the countryside along the river. The largest prairie in the Noblesville area was the one on which Conner established himself. It became known as Conner's Prairie. About two miles to the north, on the opposite side of the river, lay Horseshoe Prairie, named for the horseshoe-shaped bend the river made as it turned east. Directly north of Horseshoe Prairie on the river's east side was a prairie white settlers would later call Plum Prairie for the wild red and yellow plums that grew there.

A prairie of a different sort, one not nearly as friendly, was located around three miles north of Plum Prairie. Fox Prairie was (and is) a peat bog, created thousands of years ago by a retreating glacier. In modern times, it's been a useful source of peat and humus for gardeners, but in Conner's day, it was a potentially deadly obstacle to travel, with sections where man and beast could easily be swallowed up and never seen again.

The mineral springs that flowed throughout the countryside were another feature of the local geography. The best known of these was located on the east bank of White River about one hundred feet south of today's Conner Street bridge in downtown Noblesville. Native Americans reportedly came from miles around to drink and bathe in the healing waters of this spring long before the white settlers arrived.

In 1803, John Conner left the native life behind and opened a store near what is now Cedar Grove in Franklin County. John's store provided William with goods to trade with the Indians, and in return, William sent

LLEWELLYN SPRING

After the Indians left, the old spring was largely forgotten until Noblesville jeweler Joseph Morse revived its reputation in 1874. Morse, a relative of Samuel F.B. Morse, the man credited with developing telegraphy and the Morse code, had been, in the words of the July 9, 1875 *Noblesville Ledger*, "pining away to the lean proportions of a worm eaten and shriveled chestnut fence rail." After a few months of drinking water from the spring, however, Morse regained his health and set out to spread the word about the spring's beneficial properties.

Originally referred to as the "Medical Spring" or the "Indian Spring," it came to be called Llewellyn (or Luellen, or Lewellen, spelling being rather flexible in those days) Spring, after a man named Llewellyn, who lived next to it.

During the summer of 1875, as news of the spring spread, hundreds of people, including some of Noblesville's most prominent citizens, lined up to take in the healing water, claiming it relieved everything from dyspepsia to weak and inflamed eyes. To accommodate the large crowds, several improvements were made to the site. An iron spout was installed to pipe the stream into a stone basin, a breakwater was constructed, the surrounding ground was leveled, and a floor and stairway were added for easier access.

That September, there was a movement to create a park at the spring. The county actually owned the land, but the Board of County Commissioners issued an order allowing the parcel to be conveyed to the corporation of Noblesville, or to an organized group of citizens, provided the city or group would maintain a free public park there. There's no evidence the offer was ever accepted, however, and by 1925, the spring was gone—either dried up or redirected elsewhere. By the late 1930s, the site was being used as a dumping ground.

John the furs he acquired along the White River. Both goods and furs were transported over an old Indian trail sometimes called the Conner Trail. The track angled northwest from John's store to Anderson's Town, then followed White River south to William's trading post, traveling through dense forests, lowland swamps and rugged countryside.

This was the trail that brought the first settlers to the Noblesville area after 1818's Treaty of St. Mary's opened central Indiana to colonization. Under the terms of the treaty, the Delawares living along the White River

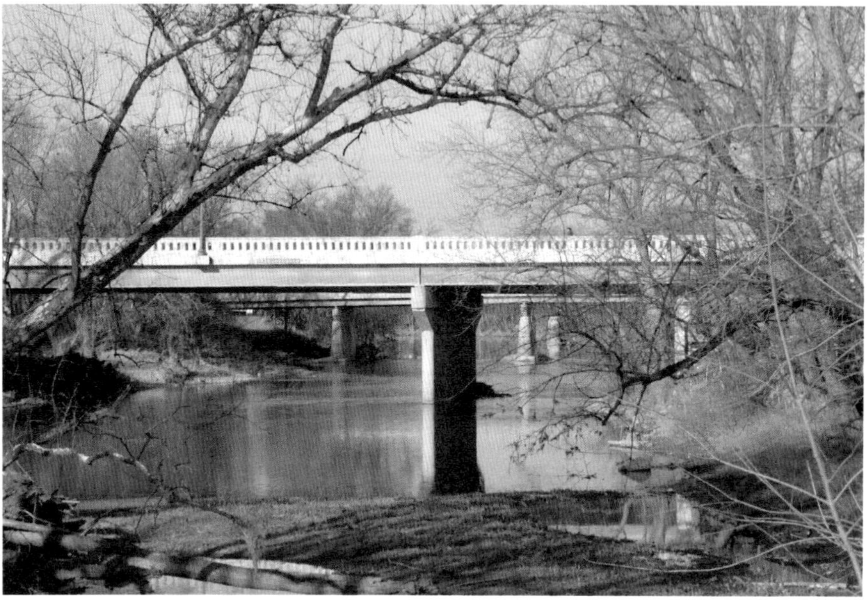

White River looking north to Conner Street bridge. Approximate location of Llewellyn Spring is to the right. *Michael Kobrowski.*

renounced all claims to their Indiana land in return for land west of the Mississippi and certain other concessions. They were given three years to prepare for the move.

The ink was barely dry on the agreement before George Shirts and his family left the Connersville area and joined William Conner in March 1819, becoming the first white settlers in the "New Purchase," as the newly acquired territory was dubbed. Shirts soon journeyed back to Connersville. On his return to the New Purchase, he was accompanied by Charles Lacy. Unlike Shirts, Lacy came alone, intending to build a cabin and plant a crop of corn before subjecting his family to the rugged journey.

The following month, the first large group of pioneers braved the hazards of the trail to settle on Horseshoe Prairie. In this band were Solomon Finch, his wife, Sarah, and four of their children; Israel and Aaron Finch, sons of Solomon's brother, John Finch; Amasa Chapman, John Finch's stepson; William Bush and his two sons; and James Willison.

An account of their journey and their life at Horseshoe Prairie, written by Solomon Finch's son, James G. Finch, appeared in a five-part series that ran in the *Noblesville Daily Ledger* in March and April 1969. By Finch's description, the trail, which was challenging for the Conners' packhorses, proved hellish for the pioneers. One or two of the men had to travel ahead to clear logs and brush so the wagons could get through. Bears, timber wolves, wildcats and venomous snakes were constant threats. Even the weather didn't cooperate, first pelting them with snow, then soaking them with heavy rain, which swelled creeks and rivers, making passage difficult.

Life didn't get any easier after they finally reached their destination. A tree limb blown down during a storm broke nearly all their dishes—a serious loss since the only source of replacements was Connersville, some sixty miles away.

Yet the community continued to grow. In July, Israel Finch, William Bush and James Willison returned to Connersville to fetch their families. The following month, John Finch arrived with additional families, including his own.

The newcomers made it to the prairie just in time to be laid low by a malaria-like illness sweeping through the area. The malady hit everyone at once, leaving no one person well enough to care for the others. By the time the illness had run its course, Amasa Chapman, one of the Finch children and George Shirts's wife were dead.

Around that same time, the settlers' provisions ran out. They managed to survive by buying corn from William Conner and baskets, moccasins, venison and dressed deer hides from nearby Indians. Later that winter, the Indians showed the settlers how nettles growing along Cicero Creek could be processed like flax. By the following summer, everyone in the settlement was wearing clothing made from nettles.

The first African American on record in Hamilton County lived with one of the Delaware families. George Shirts's son, Augustus Finch Shirts, refers to him as "Pete" and "Smith" in later newspaper articles, but Robert B. Duncan, whose family was living on William Conner's land at the time, remembered him as "Bill Allen."

Whatever his name, he was well liked by the pioneers. James G. Finch later wrote how his mother, Sarah Finch, once set her only pair of shoes outside their cabin door on a warm June day while the Indians were visiting. After the Indians departed, she discovered her shoes were gone. Her loss was mentioned to the young black man, and the next time the Indians dropped in, the shoes reappeared by the door, as if they'd been there the whole time.

The young African American eventually left the Indians and went to work for William Conner, which proved to be his downfall. A slave trader saw him on Conner's farm and returned a few months later to haul him off to slavery in Kentucky, despite the young man's protests that he'd never been a

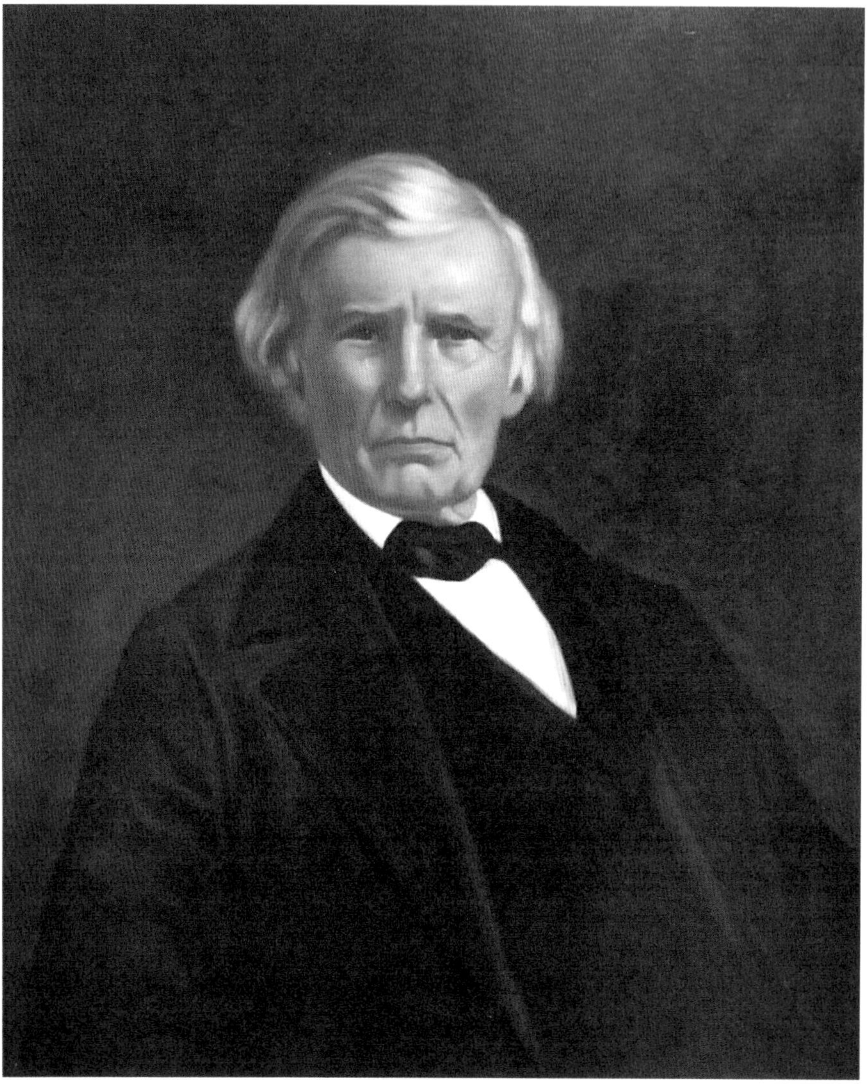

William Conner (1777–1855), co-founder of Noblesville. *Conner Prairie Interactive History Park.*

slave. With their hands legally tied by the Fugitive Slave Law, the Horseshoe Prairie settlers were unable to help him.

The following year, 1820, was an eventful one. In the early part of the summer, the commissioners charged with selecting the site for Indiana's new state capital met at William Conner's home. July saw the settlement celebrating its first Independence Day with singing, dancing and a reading of the Declaration of Independence. (There being no musical instruments available, the music was performed a cappella.) In September, the ague returned and claimed the lives of more settlers. Also that fall, the Delawares gathered on Conner's Prairie to begin the trek to their new lands in the west. William Conner's wife, Mekinges, and their children left with her tribe, as did John Conner's half-Indian son. A few months later, at the end of November, William Conner married John Finch's stepdaughter, Elizabeth Chapman.

The year also brought new arrivals, among them teacher Curtis Mallory. Mallory organized the first Sunday school, which was held in the same building in which Sarah Finch taught the settlement's children during the week.

Like those already living at Horseshoe Prairie, the newcomers were squatters. All the Horseshoe Prairie settlers built their cabins before the land they'd chosen to occupy was officially theirs—a common practice at that time. There was an unspoken understanding that, after the territory was surveyed and the land offered for sale, the pioneers would be given the opportunity to buy the land on which they'd settled.

Unfortunately for them, when the Horseshoe Prairie land came up for sale at the Brookville land office in 1822, John Conner got there first and bought up nearly the entire prairie. The settlers didn't learn of their loss until they were served with eviction notices. To add insult to injury, Conner refused to pay them for the improvements they'd made. He contended that the sawmill, gristmill, carding machine and distillery he planned to construct would more than pay them back for their cabins, fencing and the hard work they'd done to clear the land.

Conner did move to the prairie, and he built the improvements he promised, but that did little to ease the hard feelings of the settlers. Some of the families bought their land back from him. Others simply moved elsewhere. By 1837, most of Horseshoe Prairie's original inhabitants were gone, some of them relocating to the new town two miles to the north that William Conner and Josiah Polk had laid out in 1823, Noblesville.

2

NOBLESVILLE IN THE NINETEENTH CENTURY

The survival of the Horseshoe Prairie colony opened the door to more settlement in the area, but growth was slow at first because many people chose to wait to move to the New Purchase until the government put the land up for sale. Before that could happen, however, the territory had to be surveyed. One of the men hired for this task was a young lawyer from Maryland's Eastern Shore who was destined to play a pivotal role in Noblesville's early history.

Josiah F. Polk arrived in Indiana in the spring of 1821, having just finished his second term as a member of the Maryland General Assembly a few months earlier. Over the next two years, he surveyed land in Carroll, Delaware and Randolph Counties.

It's not known exactly how, or when, Polk made William Conner's acquaintance, but the two men became good friends, and at some point around 1822 or 1823, Polk moved into the Conner household. Years later, when Conner's widow, Elizabeth, attempted to claim bounty land the government owed her husband for his guide service during the Black Hawk War, Polk confirmed her identity in a letter to the U.S. Commissioner of Pensions. In the letter, Polk described himself as an "intimate friend of William Conner for several years" and stated that "for the greater part of two years I was a member of his family."

By 1822, the population in the Horseshoe Prairie area had grown sufficiently to allow the creation of a separate county. The following year, the state legislature signed a law splitting Hamilton County off from

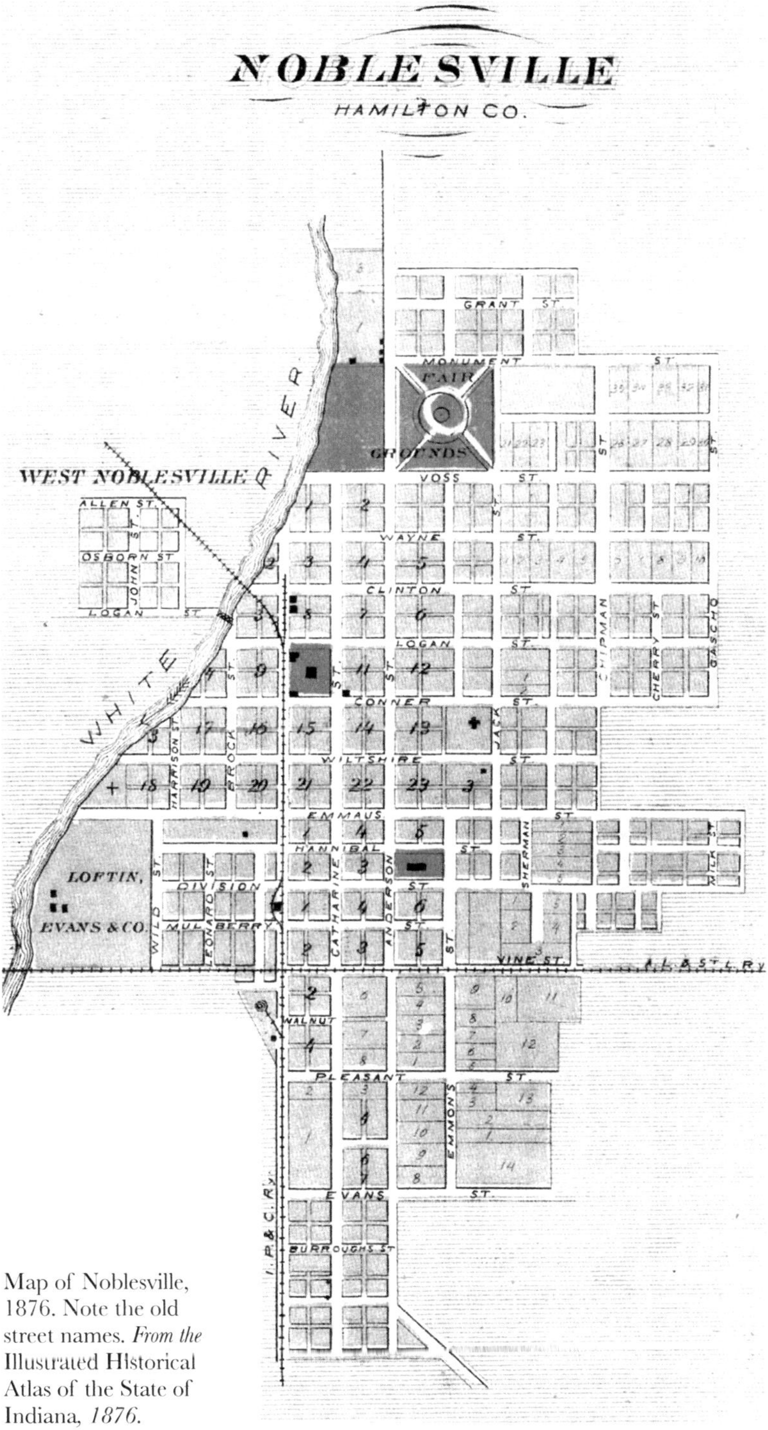

Map of Noblesville, 1876. Note the old street names. *From the* Illustrated Historical Atlas of the State of Indiana, *1876*.

Marion County, effective the first Monday in April. Anticipating the need for a seat of justice for the new county, Conner and Polk bought land along the White River and laid out the town of Noblesville in January 1823. Their gamble paid off. In March 1824, the commissioners appointed to select a site for the new county seat determined that Noblesville best met their needs. Not only was it the most central location proposed, but Conner and Polk also offered to donate half of the lots they owned for the construction of government buildings.

The new town of Noblesville consisted of about seventy-five acres, bounded on the north by present-day Harrison Street, on the south by present-day Cherry Street, on the east by present-day 11th Street and on the west by the White River.

Although the boundaries of the new town were clearly drawn, the origin of the name, "Noblesville," is a bit murky. According to a popular legend, Polk named the town for his fiancée, a Miss Noble, and as proof of his devotion, he arranged the vegetables in his garden to spell her name. Far from being impressed, Miss Noble was offended and broke off the engagement.

The Miss Noble in the tale is often identified as Lavina Noble, the sister of Indiana senator James Noble and Indiana governor Noah Noble. However, in 1926, William Conner's great-nephew Dr. William W. Conner told the *Noblesville Daily Ledger* that Polk's "special friend" was Catherine Noble, the daughter of Governor Noah Noble; that Catherine Street (present-day 9th Street) had been named for her; and that the town had been named for Governor Noble.

This simply shows how far a story can be stretched. There is ample evidence to show Polk was acquainted with some of Lavina Noble's brothers at a later date, but while he was surveying land in Indiana in 1821 and 1822, Lavina was a teenager, presumably still living in the family's Kentucky home. To date, no documentation has been found proving the two were ever in the same place at the same time, let alone engaged. Noah Noble's daughter, Catherine, is an even less credible candidate since she was born in 1823, the year Noblesville was established.

It's far more likely the town was named in honor of Senator James Noble. Not only was Senator Noble a more appropriate choice, but at the time Noblesville was founded, William Conner also was seeking the senator's help to get a bill passed in Congress that would give him a clear title to his land.

As the new county was organized and its government officials appointed, Josiah Polk was named the agent for Hamilton County and was charged

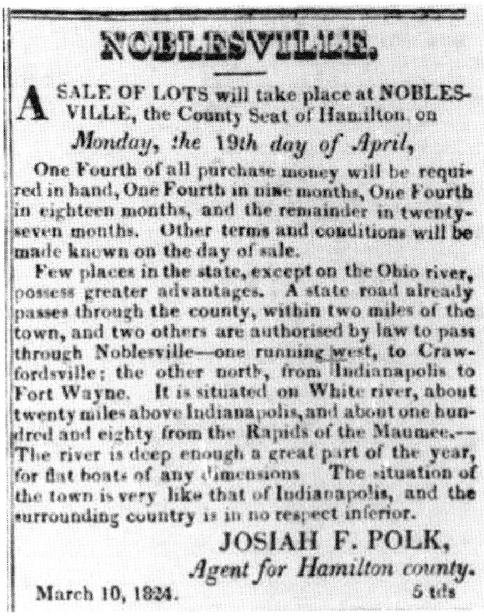

NOBLESVILLE.

A SALE OF LOTS will take place at NOBLESVILLE, the County Seat of Hamilton, on *Monday, the 19th day of April,*

One Fourth of all purchase money will be required in hand, One Fourth in nine months, One Fourth in eighteen months, and the remainder in twenty-seven months. Other terms and conditions will be made known on the day of sale.

Few places in the state, except on the Ohio river, possess greater advantages. A state road already passes through the county, within two miles of the town, and two others are authorised by law to pass through Noblesville—one running west, to Crawfordsville: the other north, from Indianapolis to Fort Wayne. It is situated on White river, about twenty miles above Indianapolis, and about one hundred and eighty from the Rapids of the Maumee.—The river is deep enough a great part of the year, for flat boats of any dimensions The situation of the town is very like that of Indianapolis, and the surrounding country is in no respect inferior.

JOSIAH F. POLK,
Agent for Hamilton county.

March 10, 1824. 5 tds

Josiah Polk's ad brought many settlers to Noblesville. *Public Ledger Volume 1, Number 6, 17 April 1824 p. 3 Hoosier State Chronicles.*

with selling part of the county's Noblesville lots. An advertisement he posted in the April 17, 1824 *Public Ledger* (Richmond, IN) included this description of the new town:

> *Few places in the state, except on the Ohio River, possess greater advantages. A state road already passes through the county, within two miles of the town, and two others are authorised* [sic] *by law to pass through Noblesville—one running west, to Crawfordsville; the other north, from Indianapolis to Fort Wayne. It is situated on White River, about twenty miles above Indianapolis, and about one hundred and eighty from the Rapids of the Maumee.—The river is deep enough a great part of the year, for flat boats of any dimensions. The situation of the town is very like that of Indianapolis, and the surrounding country is in no respect inferior.*

Polk's ad did its job. Those first few years brought many new residents to Noblesville. Among the newcomers were some of the town's future leading citizens, men such as John D. Stephenson, the county's first clerk, auditor and recorder; Judge Jonathan Colburn; Dr. John Finch, the county's first physician; Dr. Haymond W. Clark; and Canadian businessman Francis B. Cogswell.

A post office was established in 1824, with Josiah Polk serving as the first post master. That same year, Polk also was responsible for the construction of the first government building, a log jail located just north of Riverside Cemetery. The first county courthouse, a temporary structure of logs, was built in 1826.

Among Noblesville's earliest businesses were Francis B. Cogswell's tannery, William Conner's store and Joseph Willison's blacksmith shop. George Shirts left Conner's Prairie and moved to Noblesville, where he not only became the town's first shoemaker, but he also opened Noblesville's first tavern in 1827. Shirts's second wife, Solomon Finch's daughter Rebecca, became renowned for the corn pone she served at the tavern.

In 1837, William Conner left his magnificent brick home on the prairie and moved to Noblesville, where he continued to exert an influence on the town he co-founded until his death in 1855. Josiah F. Polk, on the other hand, disappears from the Hamilton County history books in 1825. For years, nothing was known of his fate, but recent research has disclosed that he actually continued to lead an active and very public life—he simply led it elsewhere.

Over the next several years, Noblesville continued to grow. In 1837, the town's first newspaper, aptly named *The Newspaper*, observed that, although "Noblesville as yet numbers but seventy-five smokes," over thirty new buildings had been erected the previous summer and twice as many were likely to be constructed in the coming year. By the end of the 1830s, the town was so well established that it managed to survive the collapse of the Central Canal project when many other communities along the canal's proposed route didn't.

The burning social issue in the years prior to the Civil War was, of course, slavery. Although no homes in the Noblesville area are known to have been involved in the Underground Railroad, in 1843, Noblesville was chosen as the site of one of the New England Anti-Slavery Society's Hundred Conventions, a series of speaking engagements designed to stir up antislavery sentiments.

Two groups of the society's agents actually visited Noblesville. The first company, which included African American orator, author, statesman and abolitionist Frederick Douglass, arrived in September. The speakers were forced to flee without delivering their message after word reached them that the violence they'd recently experienced in nearby Pendleton might be repeated in Noblesville.

The second set of speakers fared better. Sydney Howard Gay reported in the October 20, 1843 issue of the abolitionist newspaper *The Liberator* that he and his companions managed to attract a crowd of 150 to 200 people to

JOSIAH F. POLK'S LATER YEARS

Why Josiah F. Polk decided to abandon the town he helped establish is a mystery, but the rest of his life is fairly well documented. After leaving central Indiana in 1826, he spent some time teaching, and studying the language and traditions of Ottawa and Potawatomi Indians at a mission near Grand Rapids, Michigan. He returned to the East Coast in 1827 and spent the remainder of his life in Washington City, as Washington, D.C., was then called.

In 1829, he became an agent of the American Colonization Society, an organization that promoted the idea that free African Americans should be repatriated to Africa for the good of all concerned. For ten months, he traveled through Indiana, Illinois, Tennessee and Alabama, lecturing and helping establish local chapters of the society. While in Indiana, he visited Noblesville one last time to conduct some business at the courthouse.

Upon his return to Washington, he took a job as a clerk in the office of the Second Auditor of the Treasury. During James K. Polk's administration, he held the position of chief clerk of that office, a promotion undoubtedly due to the commonly held, but mistaken, belief he was related to President Polk. (DNA tests on modern Polk descendants have proven otherwise.)

Never shy about wielding a pen, Polk edited a monthly periodical devoted to religion, science and literature called *The Investigator* while working at his government post. He also wrote many pamphlets and books, some of which promoted the anti-Catholic and anti-immigrant views of the American Party, a nativist political party sometimes called the "Know Nothings."

When Polk's involvement with the Know Nothings led to his dismissal from his Treasury Department position in 1855, he resumed practicing law. During his final years, he helped revise the code of laws for the District of Columbia and served as a trustee of the public schools. He died in 1860 and is buried in the Congressional Cemetery in Washington, D.C.

the county courthouse. Their address was disrupted by hickory club–toting demonstrators who objected to the courthouse being used for an antislavery lecture, but the local sheriff stepped in to mediate. Through his efforts, the abolitionists were allowed to leave the building unmolested and simply finished their lecture elsewhere.

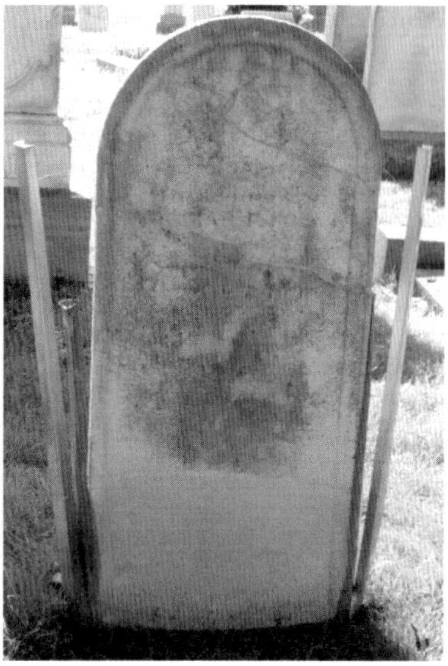

Tombstone of Josiah Polk in Congressional Cemetery, Washington, D.C. *Paula Dunn.*

The year 1851 proved to be a significant one for Noblesville. Not only was it incorporated as a town, but travel to and from the area also became considerably easier with the arrival of the Peru and Indianapolis Railroad, the state's second railroad.

Growing unrest in the country over the next several years prompted Noblesville's John D. Evans to organize a military company during the winter of 1860–61. The Hamilton Continentals, the only such unit in the county at that time, conducted weekly exercises at first, but increased the frequency of its drills after Abraham Lincoln was elected president.

In April 1861, following the bombardment of Fort Sumter, a throng of people gathered on the Hamilton County courthouse square to hear the latest news, only to learn Noblesville's telegraph office wasn't working. Evans and a few other Hamilton Continentals refused to wait for the line to be repaired. Borrowing a handcar from the Peru and Indianapolis Railroad, they headed to Indianapolis, where they promptly volunteered their services to Indiana's governor, Oliver P. Morton.

Morton accepted their offer, informing them they were the first company in Indiana to come forward to fight for the Union cause. He then instructed Captain Evans to return home to prepare his men. Evans's response, according to the September 26, 1890 *Hamilton County Ledger*, was "Dam [*sic*] it, Governor, we are ready now."

A few days later, Evans and his men reported to Indiana's adjutant general, Lew Wallace, at Camp Morton in Indianapolis and were mustered in as Company I of the Sixth Indiana Regiment of Volunteers.

Among the many Noblesville men who served in the Union army during the Civil War were two who would be responsible for what could be called Noblesville's first suburbs.

William Garver, a colonel with the 101st Indiana Infantry who later became a judge of the court of common pleas and a state senator, laid out a plat map for Garver's Village in October 1873. The community was located across the White River from Noblesville, between today's Lakeview Drive and Forest Park, in the general vicinity of Legacy Christian School.

One month earlier, Captain John B. Jackson of the 136th Indiana Regiment and John W. Wilson had platted West Noblesville a little over a mile south of Garver's Village. This area is presently bounded by Allen Street on the north, Nixon Street on the east and Conner Street on the south, with the western boundary a block west of John Street. (Interestingly, today's Osborn Street appears as "Osbon Street" on the West Noblesville plat.)

While Garver's Village has disappeared, West Noblesville still exists but is better known as Federal Hill. According to the May 7, 1951 *Noblesville Daily Ledger*, the new name came from Captain Jackson's young neighbor Luther Swain. Upon learning that Jackson hadn't named his property, Luther, who happened to be a fan of songwriter Stephen Foster, suggested it be called Federal Hill, after the plantation that supposedly inspired Foster's song "My Old Kentucky Home." Federal Hill stuck and eventually replaced West Noblesville in common usage.

In 1887, Noblesville officially became a part of the region's gas boom when the first commercial gas well in the county was drilled on the southeast corner of 11th and Pleasant Streets. Most of the buildings on the courthouse square today were constructed during the prosperous era that followed the discovery of the gas.

Among the gas boom–era buildings in the downtown area are several that still bear the names of the fraternal organizations that once met in them—the Bernice Lodge of the Knights of Pythias on the north side of the square, the Independent Order of Odd Fellows (IOOF) on the south side, the Masons on the southeast corner of 9th and Logan Streets and the Cherokee Tribe of the Improved Order of Red Men (IORM) on the northwest corner of 10th and Logan Streets.

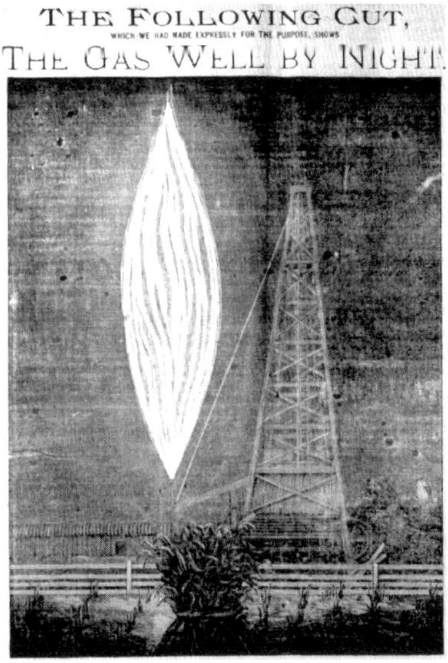

This cut of the gas well from the *Ledger* was in so much demand by readers that extra copies were published. *The* Ledger, *Friday, 4 February 1887, p. 8.*

Fraternal organizations played an important role in the lives of nineteenth-century Noblesville residents, providing

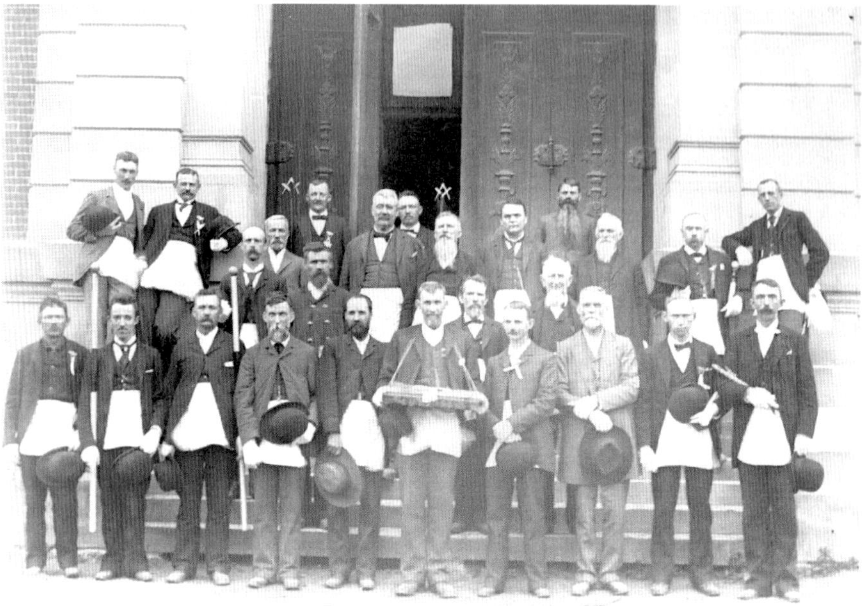

Masons gathered in front of the courthouse for the funeral of Jonathan Colborn in May 1891. Note the courthouse doors behind the Masons. They were part of the original courthouse, but major renovations in 1903–4 replaced them because the doors did not open or close properly. *Noblesville Masonic Lodge No. 57.*

both a means of social networking and an organized channel for helping their fellow citizens. Of the lodges established in Noblesville during this period, the Masons are the oldest, dating back to 1828. The Odd Fellows came next in 1853, followed by the Knights of Pythias in 1884 and the Red Men in 1890. Others include the Knights of Honor (1878), the Modern Woodmen of America (1896), the Knights of the Maccabees (1895), an African American Knights of Pythias lodge (1898) and a women's auxiliary of the Knights of Pythias, the Daughters of Rebekah (1853).

When the call went out for volunteers to fight in the Spanish-American War in 1898, the young men of Noblesville answered, but most of them spent the duration of the short war in stateside camps and never saw combat. One Noblesville soldier who did participate in the fighting was African American Charles Dempsey. Dempsey served with the Twenty-Fourth Infantry, a black unit that took part in the charge up San Juan Hill.

Hamilton County's only fatality during that war was a young Noblesville man, Richard L. "Moxie" Hinds, who died from typhoid in a Virginia camp. The local Spanish War veterans' post was later named in his honor.

Before embarking on a new century, Noblesville underwent one more significant change. Sometime in the 1890s, many of the original street names were replaced with new ones. Clearly, the town fathers wanted to make the north–south streets numbered streets, but several east–west streets, such as Emmaus and Wiltshire, also acquired new names, for reasons unknown today.

Street Name Changes

Original Street Name	Current Street Name
Harrison	5th (north of Cherry Street)
Brock	6th (north of Cherry Street)
Leonard	6th (south of Cherry Street)
Wild	Seventh (between Hannibal and Division)
Railroad	8th (different period)
Polk	8th (different period)
Catherine	9th
Anderson	10th
Van Buren	11th (north of Clinton)
High	11th (from Clinton to Conner)
Emmons	11th (south of Cherry)
Jack	12th (north of Conner)
Grant	12th (south of Conner and north of Division)
Sherman	13th (south of Cherry and north of Division)
Filmore	13th (south of Division)
Chipman	North 14th
Cherry	15th (between Clinton and Conner)
Gascho	North 16th
Milk	South 16th Street (between Cherry and Division)
Wiltshire	Maple Avenue
Evans	Plum
Burroughs	Chestnut
Emmaus	Cherry
Voss	Harrison

3

NOBLESVILLE IN THE TWENTIETH CENTURY

The arrival of the twentieth century saw Noblesville's population hovering around 4,800—well over twice that of Hamilton County's second-largest community, Sheridan—and the city continued to grow. The March 4, 1901 *Indianapolis News* reported that Noblesville was poised to undergo a building boom, the likes of which had not been seen for a number of years. Not only were several new business buildings planned, but over one hundred residences were in the works as well.

Also new was the electric railway, the interurban. It reached Noblesville in 1903, providing residents with a means of traveling to every corner of the state.

One thing that didn't change with the dawn of the new century was the struggle of the temperance forces against the sale of alcoholic beverages. That battle had been going on in Indiana ever since the state was founded, but it really began to gather steam in the early 1900s. Noblesville figured prominently in two cases concerning liquor sales brought before the Indiana Supreme Court.

In 1901, Edward Harrison built a new saloon on the corner of "Court" and "Newman" Streets, the two alleys behind the Wild Opera House. Harrison had arranged for the city council to give the alleys street names in an attempt to circumvent a law stating that saloons must face a public street. When the court issued the opinion that alleys lacked certain characteristics that allowed them to be considered streets, Harrison was forced to move his building to 8th Street. It was the first brick building ever moved in Noblesville.

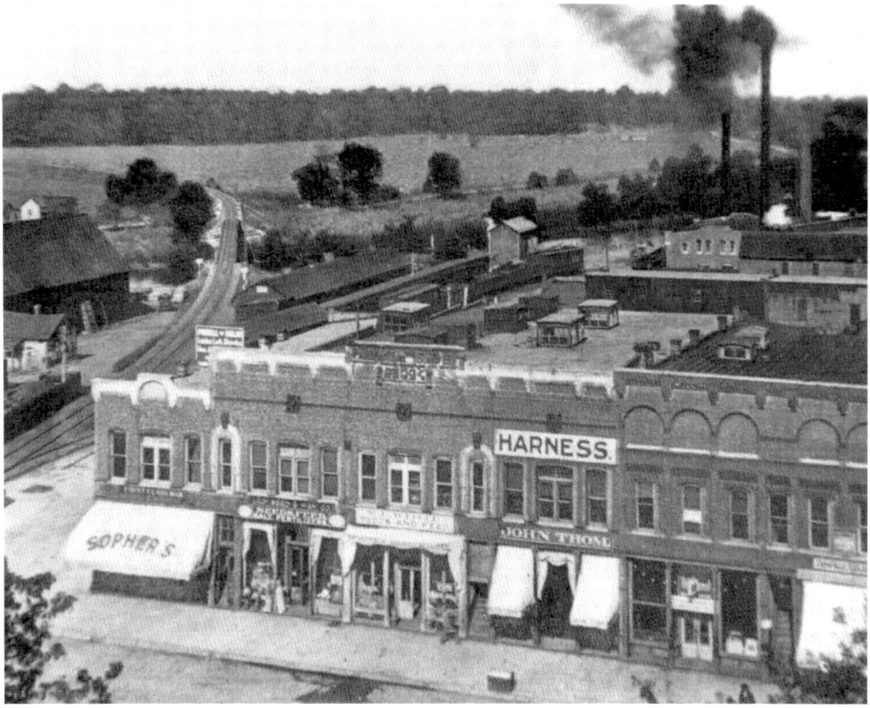

Early 1900s view of the northwest side of the square taken from the top of the courthouse. 8th Street is on the left side running past Sopher's saloon (now Syd's Bar). Logan Street runs in front of the buildings. The Noblesville Heat, Light and Power plant with the smokestacks sits in the background. The railroad bridge crosses the White River. Stores shown are Sopher's saloon, Lacy Feed and Seed, M.L. White Feed and Seed, John Thom Harness Shop, E.M. Carter and Sons (grocers) and Griffin Bros. Hardware (now Kirk's Hardware.) *Hamilton East Public Library, Joe Roberts Collection.*

Six years later, Edward Sopher, who owned a tavern on the corner of 8th and Logan Streets, became the defendant in a test case seeking to prove that saloons were a public nuisance and Indiana's issuance of liquor licenses was unconstitutional. The court ultimately ruled in Sopher's favor, although it did him little good. In 1909, both Sopher and Harrison were forced to close their doors when the entire county voted to go dry.

Things didn't turn out quite as the temperance supporters hoped, however. Far from resolving matters, the lack of legal liquor sales merely created a slew of bootleggers and blind tigers (establishments selling illegal liquor) that plagued local law enforcement officials throughout Prohibition and beyond.

In the meantime, Noblesville's Commercial Club sponsored a slogan contest in 1914 to promote the town's more legitimate economic interests.

Reverend Frank P. Miller of the Presbyterian Church received five dollars in gold for his winning entry, "Work With a Will for Noblesville." It was hoped local merchants would popularize the slogan by including it in their advertising, but the phrase never seemed to catch on (nor did "Capital Convenience—County Seat Charm," which won a similar contest in 1965).

Over the next few years, area residents watched nervously as World War I spread across Europe. After the United States entered the conflict on April 6, 1917, Noblesville's mayor, E.C. Loehr, issued a proclamation calling on the people of Noblesville, and all other Hamilton County residents who were able, to meet at the courthouse square on April 13 to demonstrate their patriotism by marching in a parade: "Let there be no floats, no cars, no banners, no delegations only people carrying flags, marching shoulder to shoulder and heart to heart, in this simple and impressive way, to show their devotion to their country."

On the day of the parade, downtown Noblesville was awash in red, white and blue flags and bunting, and all businesses, factories and schools closed. Nearly three thousand men, women and children participated in the march, accompanied by two drum corps, the Noblesville Military Band and an operator from the Lake Erie depot dressed as Uncle Sam.

During the war, Noblesville's residents supported the troops by buying Liberty Loan bonds and by contributing to the YMCA, the Salvation Army and other service organizations. Local Red Cross volunteers made up countless comfort kits, and collected bedding and other items for hospitals, while everyone cheerfully endured inconveniences such as gasoline-less Sundays and the rationing of flour and sugar.

The announcement of Germany's surrender was greeted with so much shouting, automobile honking and other noise that a November 8, 1918 *Noblesville Daily Ledger* article observed that the dove of peace was "probably going around today with cotton in its ears." On the evening of November 11, the day the armistice was signed, thousands of people once again gathered in downtown Noblesville to show their patriotism by building bonfires and marching around the square.

The decade following the war was an eventful one.

A small change in Noblesville's daily routine, but one with a lasting effect, was the reorganization of the town's street addresses in 1922. Prior to that, homes and businesses had been assigned addresses with numbers beginning at 9th Street and continuing either east or west. Afterward, all structures were numbered beginning at the White River and going east.

In 1923, the joint centennial of Noblesville and Hamilton County was observed with yet another big parade and other events.

During the first half of the 1920s, the Ku Klux Klan maintained a visible presence throughout the county, especially in Noblesville. The city would play a pivotal role in the Klan's demise in Indiana, however, when the murder trial of the state's Grand Dragon, D.C. Stephenson, was held in the Hamilton County courthouse in 1925.

In 1922, Alexander R. Holliday, the president and general manager of the Noblesville Heat, Light and Power Company, and Samuel B. Mott, the superintendent of Noblesville's power plant, constructed a dam and small hydroelectric power plant, Holliday Station, on the White River, about four miles north of Noblesville near the community of Clare. The wide, placid area the dam created in the river was perfect for fishing, boating and swimming and inspired Holliday, Mott and a few others to form the Riverwood Company to develop a resort community. They platted two hundred lots across the river from Clare for the construction of summer homes. When Riverwood opened in June 1923, it had a restaurant, a bathing beach and bathhouse, and rental boats. Over time, however, the summer cottages were gradually converted into year-round homes.

By 1929, the Riverwood area boasted a resort hotel, Lagoon Lodge, just north of Clare. The structure, which was originally the summer home of a railroad executive, possesses a rather checkered history. Periods of respectability were interrupted during the 1920s and '30s by rumors of gangsters, prostitution and bootleg liquor. Hidden compartments in the floors of two upstairs rooms seem to indicate the lodge may indeed have been a blind tiger at one time. Today, the building houses the office of River Bend Campground.

A similar resort hotel, Horseshoe Lodge, had opened south of Noblesville about fifteen years earlier. It was located on 160th Street, near the site of the original Horseshoe Prairie settlement. Horseshoe Lodge's reputation was initially built on its chicken dinners, but by the 1940s, it was better known for the gambling raids conducted there.

From June 1933 to July 1934, John Dillinger captured headlines in many U.S. newspapers and sparked innumerable sightings—both real and imagined—in several states, especially his home state of Indiana. While the infamous bank robber isn't known to have spent any time in Noblesville during his year-long crime spree, one of his automobiles did.

In the early hours of April 7, 1934, Dillinger and a companion were involved in a collision on the Range Line Road (today's U.S. 31), just north of State Road 47 (236th Street), as they were returning to the Dillinger family home in Mooresville after a trip to Ohio. When Hamilton County sheriff Frank Hattery was called to investigate an abandoned 1934 Hudson sedan at that location, he immediately suspected the car belonged to Dillinger. Not only had no one returned to claim the vehicle, but the license plates and most other means of identification had been removed, and a machine gun and ammunition had been left inside.

The damaged Hudson, which was indeed Dillinger's, was driven to Noblesville and stored in the Forsythe garage at the corner of 10th and Conner Streets, where it drew hundreds of curious spectators before being auctioned off to the highest bidder.

On December 7, 1941, the citizens of Noblesville, like the rest of the country, were horrified by the news of the Japanese attack on Pearl Harbor. The following day, people in every home and business in town paused in whatever they were doing to listen to President Franklin D. Roosevelt deliver his famous address to Congress describing the "date which will live in infamy."

Over the next few weeks, Noblesville's residents geared up for war. The sale of new automobile tires was halted, banks and the post office were designated as stations for the collection of funds for the Red Cross and a drive for scrap iron was planned. There was also a county-wide campaign to encourage people to buy defense bonds and defense stamps.

As the war progressed, everyone pulled together to support the troops. There were drives to collect newspapers, aluminum cans and grease, and the Red Cross conducted blood drives. The Girl Scouts knitted squares to be pieced together to make afghans for injured soldiers in hospitals. Necessities such as coffee, sugar, lard, gasoline and tires were rationed. Air raid wardens made sure everyone kept their lights off during practice blackouts. Businesses closed on Wednesday afternoons so everyone could tend their victory gardens, helping ensure that servicemen fighting abroad had plenty of food.

Not everything was grim, though. The USO periodically held dances at the Forest Park Inn to entertain soldiers temporarily stationed at Fort Benjamin Harrison.

Local reaction to the surrender of Germany in May 1945 was subdued compared to 1918's noisy festivities. Conscious of the war still being waged with Japan, Mayor Emmet Fertig recommended citizens refrain from gathering together to celebrate. The Allied victory over Germany was marked simply and quietly by special prayer services at all the churches, the closing of the town's taverns and a showing at the high school of *The Immortal Sergeant*, a movie starring Henry Fonda.

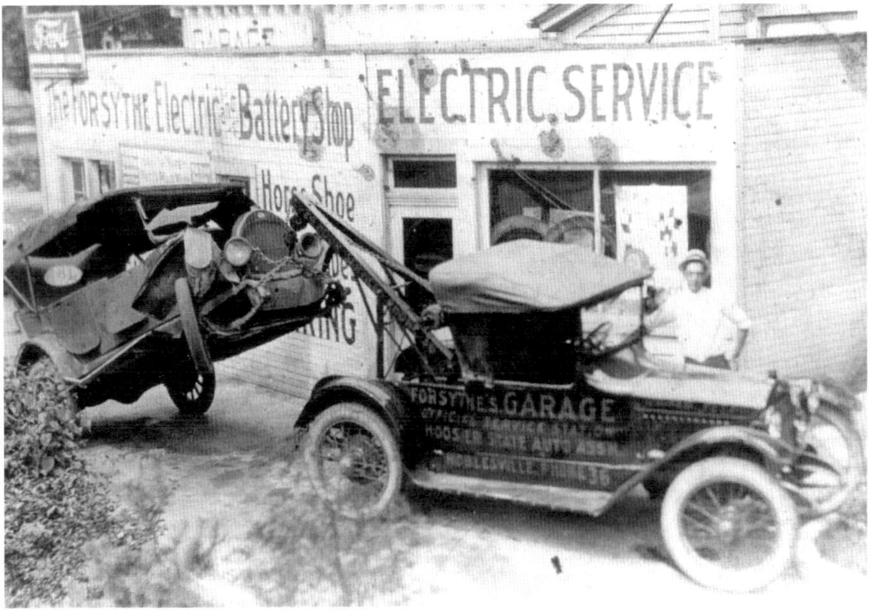

Forsythe's garage, located at 10th and Conner Streets. Harley Forsythe stands by his wrecker. When the police impounded John Dillinger's abandoned 1934 Hudson, the car (not pictured) was taken here. *Hamilton East Public Library, Joe Roberts Collection.*

The real celebration came a few months later when Japan surrendered. The August 17, 1945 *Noblesville Morning Times* compared the pandemonium created by the news of Japan's defeat to the festivities surrounding the Indianapolis 500 and noted, "Firecrackers, pistol shots, dinner bells from farm homes, big trucks, a bass drum, tin cans, whistles, hand-cranked sirens, auto horns and hoarse human voices" combined to create a joyous din as the streets around the courthouse square became clogged with automobiles and people.

World War II would prove to be the last time the community as a whole was actively involved in a war effort. Later wars tended to be experienced on a more individual level.

The end of World War II meant construction materials were once again available, and over the following decade new buildings, both commercial and residential, began to pop up in Noblesville. In 1951, a new county hospital was constructed west of town on Federal Hill and named Riverview because it overlooked the White River. Four years later, the old city hall on 8th Street was torn down and a new one built on the same block.

Another significant event of the 1950s was the opening of Morse Reservoir in 1955. The lake formed by damming Cicero Creek soon replaced Riverwood as the area's favorite spot for fishing and water sports.

The early 1960s saw the construction of Noblesville's first shopping center, Noblesville Plaza, on Conner Street near State Road 37. It was followed by two more strip malls west of the river on Federal Hill—Western Plaza, built around 1974, and Noblesville Square Shopping Center, which opened in 1980.

The new shopping centers marked the beginning of a change in direction for business in downtown Noblesville. Previously, the stores around the courthouse square had catered to the everyday needs of county residents. By the end of the century, however, most of those businesses had either closed or moved to other parts of town, prompting the city's downtown to reinvent itself as an area of restaurants and specialty shops. To further encourage people to shop downtown, most of the city's parking meters, first installed in 1948, were removed, granting visitors free parking for two hours at a time.

In the early 1970s, the Indianapolis Water Company decided to open the shores of Morse Reservoir to real estate development and established a subsidiary, the Shorewood Corporation, for that purpose. South and North Harbor, the first subdivisions to be constructed on the reservoir, ushered in a period of unprecedented population growth for Noblesville.

The last decades of the century saw several new public buildings constructed—a jail, a library, a post office and a city hall. When the old Hamilton County courthouse proved inadequate to the demands of the county's growing population, the structures on the west side of the courthouse square were torn down and replaced by the Hamilton County Government and Judicial Center.

The twentieth century also saw the establishment of some of Noblesville's most prominent and long-standing clubs and organizations.

Of the fraternal orders found in Noblesville during the previous century only the Masons remained. In place of the lodges lost, the city acquired the Elks (Lodge No. 576, organized in 1900), the Eagles (Lodge No. 450, organized in 1903) and the Moose (Lodge No. 548, organized in 1915). That Moose lodge closed in 1933, but was replaced by a new one, No. 540, in 1946.

Two veterans' posts were established in Noblesville during the twentieth century. The Frank E. Huntzinger Post 45 of the American Legion was chartered in 1919 and named in honor of the first soldier from the Noblesville area killed during World War I. The Ralph Lehr Post 6246 of the Veterans of Foreign Wars (VFW) was organized in 1946. Lehr was the first Noblesville resident killed during World War II.

Several national service clubs formed local chapters in the city. The oldest of these, the Kiwanis Club, was founded in 1920. The Lions Club was established in 1942 and the Rotary Club in 1955.

In 1915, the Beta Epsilon chapter of Tri Kappa was organized in Noblesville. During its long history, this service sorority, unique to Indiana, has provided assistance to local residents and others in need through its many charitable projects.

The Hamilton County Extension Homemakers clubs, several of which are based in Noblesville, have supplied educational opportunities for their members and volunteer support for their community since 1933.

The local 4-H clubs, also sponsored by the County Extension Service, are even older, dating back as far as 1928. Originally based in the township and intended for rural youths, urban clubs were eventually added.

Noblesville's first Boy Scout troop was established as early as 1915 and the first Girl Scout troop by 1919.

The Noblesville Boys Club (known as the Boys and Girls Club after 1990) was organized in 1951 to provide local boys with a place to participate in activities outside of school. It was first housed in a building on the courthouse square, but later moved into the old Noblesville High School on Conner Street. In 2018, a new facility opened on the site of the former Conner Elementary.

The Blatchley Nature Study Club, one of Noblesville's oldest organizations, was founded in 1922 by local dentist and naturalist Dr. Earl Brooks to promote appreciation, preservation and respect for the environment. It was named in honor of the most prominent Indiana naturalist of that day, W.S. Blatchley. Early meetings were held in members' homes, but in 1963, the club acquired a permanent sanctuary on the White River near Potter's Bridge.

Although a county-wide organization, the Hamilton County Artists' Association is headquartered in Noblesville in the former First Baptist Church. The group, established in 1951, operates the Birdie Gallery in the old church and supports local artists and art education in all types of media.

Following pages: 1940s aerial of Noblesville shows the Conner Street bridge, the Logan Street bridge and the railroad bridge across the White River. The buildings between Conner and Logan Streets east of the river were demolished to make room for the Hamilton County Judicial Center in the early 1990s. *Hamilton County Historical Society.*

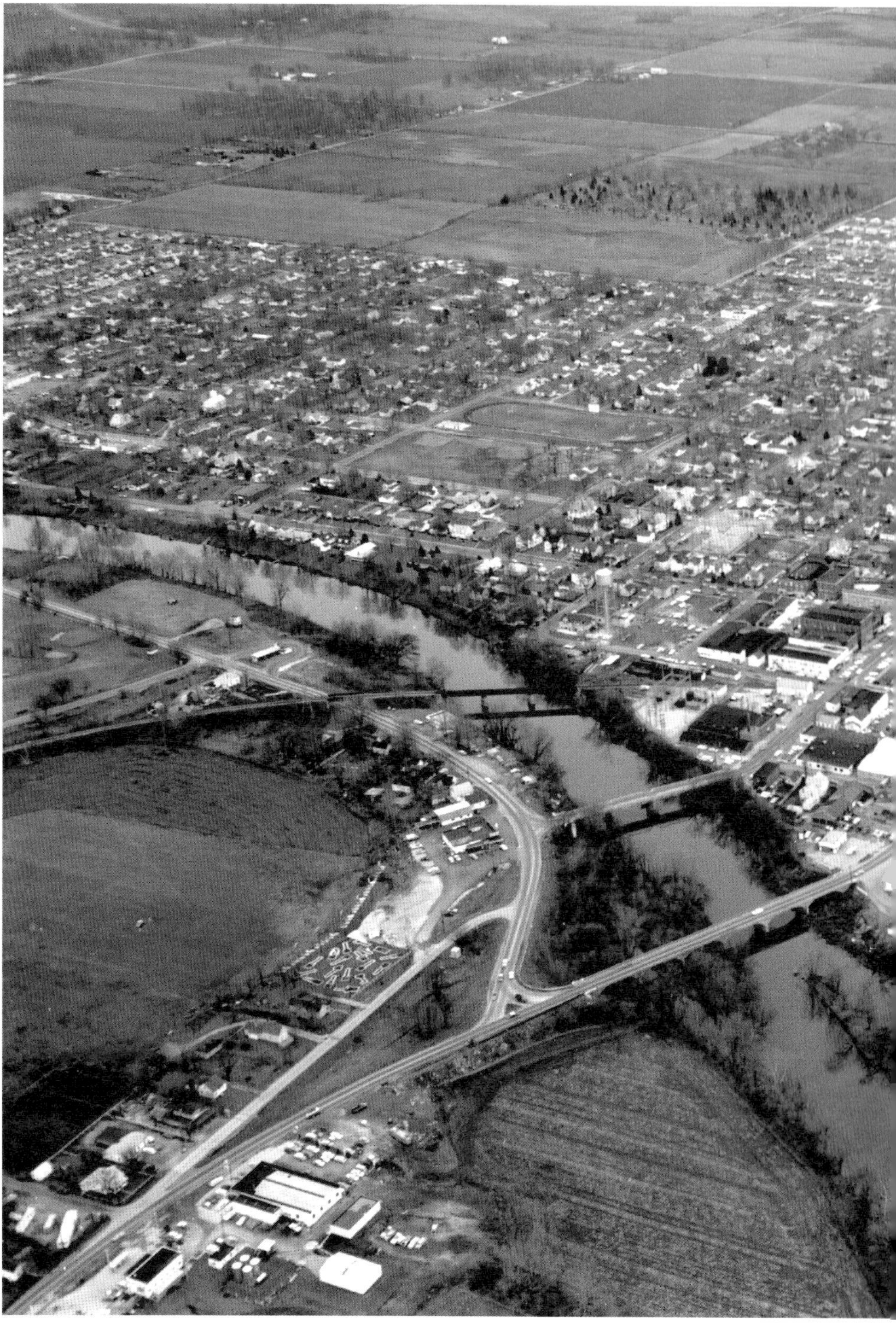

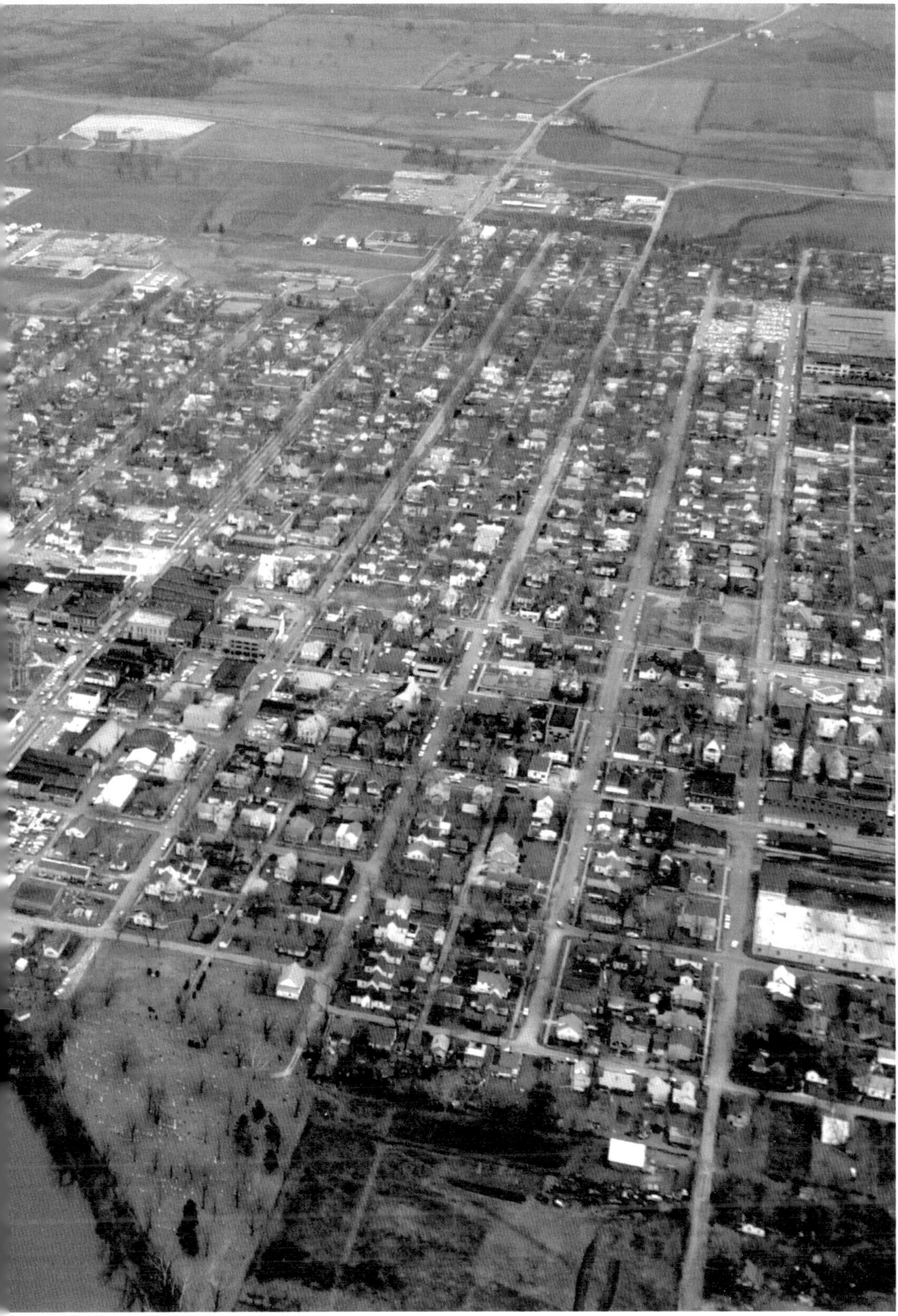

The Hamilton County Historical Society is another county-wide organization based in Noblesville. Founded in 1963, the society is dedicated to the preservation, collection and interpretation of Hamilton County history. After the construction of the county jail on Cumberland Road, the society restored the old sheriff's residence and jail on the courthouse square in downtown Noblesville. That building now houses the society's museum.

The Noblesville Preservation Alliance (NPA), organized in 1987, works to preserve Noblesville's historic architecture and neighborhoods. Several historic structures have been saved from the wrecking ball thanks to the intervention of the NPA, but perhaps its most memorable achievement came in 1988 when the group was instrumental in saving the William Houston Craig House by moving it across Conner Street and restoring it.

By the year 2000, Noblesville's population stood at 28,590—almost six times the number of residents with which it had begun the century. No longer the largest city in Hamilton County (its southern neighbors, Carmel and Fishers, had both overtaken it), it nevertheless remained the county seat and continued to grow at an incredible rate.

4
TAKING CARE OF BUSINESS

It would be an impossible task to attempt to list all the businesses that have called Noblesville home, but there are several that stand out due to their longevity and/or their impact upon the community.

The oldest company in Noblesville—and incidentally the oldest transportation company in the country—dates to 1847, when Wesley Hare, the son of German immigrants, opened a carriage and wagon shop, the Hamilton County Wagon Works, in a log building just off the courthouse square. Hare produced many types of wagons, buggies and carriages, all made by hand.

In 1856, Hare formed a partnership with J.G. (John George) Heylmann, and the name of the business was changed to Hare & Heylmann.

About twenty years later, Heylmann left, and Hare's son, E.M. (Elbert), joined the organization, which then became known as W. Hare & Son. E.M. eventually took over from his father and moved operations into a four-story brick building on the southwest corner of 10th and Conner Streets, where he began selling horseless carriages alongside the company's buggies. By 1912, W. Hare & Son was selling more automobiles than buggies. Although the company initially handled several different car makes, after 1921, it exclusively sold Chevrolets.

During World War II, when Chevrolet stopped production of automobiles in support of the war effort, Jack Hare, the fourth-generation owner, bought up as many cars as he could and put them into storage, ensuring that the company would be able to continue to sell cars after

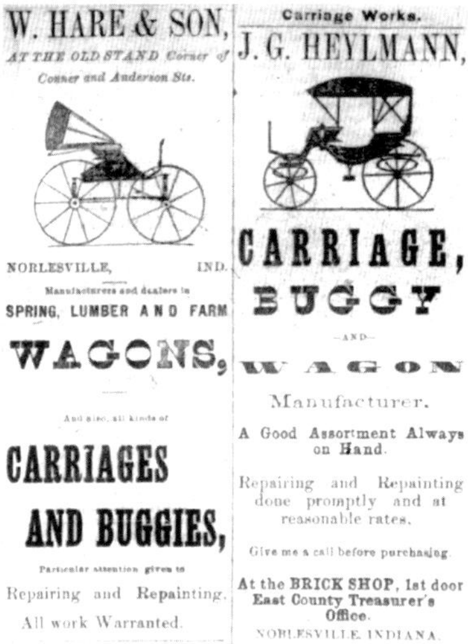

After Hare and Heylmann dissolved their partnership in 1877, ads in the local newspapers for each business could be found side by side. Hamilton County Democrat, *Friday, 28 June 1878, p. 8.*

hostilities ended. He then went off to war himself, where he earned a medal flying a dangerous supply route over the Himalayas. While he was away, his loyal employees managed to keep the business afloat by selling used tires, lube jobs and tune-ups.

Commonly known as Hare Chevrolet today, the company has relocated twice since the war—first to 10th Street in 1957 and then to the current location on State Road 37 in 1999. In 2017, after six generations of family ownership, Hare Chevrolet was sold to Asbury Automotive Group, an automotive retailer with dealerships nationwide.

When Hare and Heylmann dissolved their partnership in 1877, J.G. Heylmann simply moved across Conner Street and began to manufacture wagons, carriages and buggies in his own factory. His sons, George and Fred, joined him in the venture, which became known as J.G. Heylmann & Sons.

Born in Prussia, Heylmann arrived in America in 1852 at the age of eighteen. He settled first in Ohio, where he learned the wagon and carriage trade, then moved to Noblesville in 1855. Like Wesley Hare, Heylmann developed a reputation for building fine handmade wagons and buggies. Also, like Hare, his company later sold automobiles.

Heylmann was a prominent member of Noblesville's business community for nearly sixty years. At the time of his death, he owned quite a bit of land, and was a stockholder in the Wainwright Trust Company and a director in the Citizens State Bank.

Citizens State Bank—or as it was originally known, Citizens' Bank—was located on the southeast corner of 9th and Conner Streets, and was Hamilton County's first bank. Founded in 1871 as a private institution by William M. Locke and his son-in-law, George H. Bonebrake, it was reorganized six years later and granted a state charter. Around 1888, it became Citizens State Bank, reflecting the change in status.

Locke was the bank's first president, Bonebrake the first cashier and William E. Dunn, only seventeen at the time, was hired as the first teller. Bonebrake

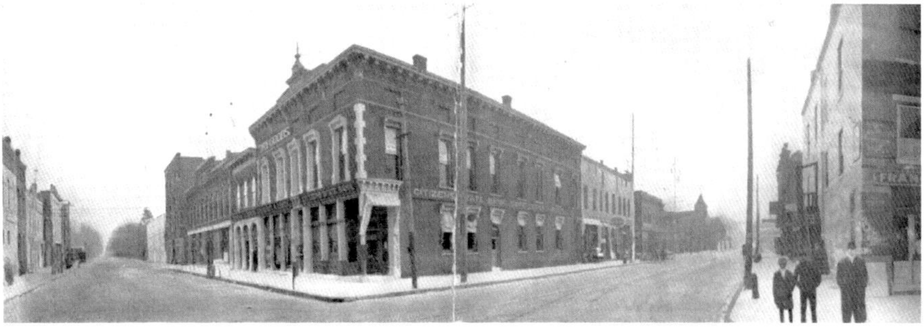

Citizens State Bank on the corner of Catherine (now 9th) and Conner Streets. Note the change in name, which appeared on the building about 1888, reflecting the acquisition of a state bank charter in 1877. *Hamilton County Historical Society.*

eventually moved to the West Coast, where he became a prominent figure in early Los Angeles, while Locke left Citizens' Bank in 1883 to establish another privately owned Noblesville bank, the Commercial Bank. When poor investments forced the Commercial Bank to close after only a year, Locke also moved out of state. Dunn, the only one of the three to remain in Noblesville, worked his way up the ladder and eventually became Citizens State Bank's president. He served in that capacity for thirty-eight years.

Citizens State Bank closed its doors, and that of its branch in Arcadia, in 1933, but in the meantime, other banks had opened in Noblesville.

The First National Bank received a charter from the U.S. government in 1893. In 1909, it moved into a handsome new Bedford stone building on the northeast corner of 9th and Logan Streets. First National occupied that building, considered the finest of its kind in central Indiana, until 1926, when it became caught up in the Steinbrenner Rubber Company check kiting scandal and was forced to close.

Two years after First National folded, its magnificent home was purchased by the American National Bank, another local bank which had been established in 1910. American National went on to serve the Noblesville community for over seventy-five years.

For much of that same period, a second bank, the Wainwright Bank and Trust Company, also operated in the city. Located on the southwest corner of 10th and Conner Streets, Wainwright was originally established in 1901 as a trust company. It became a state-chartered bank in 1951.

The banking business throughout Indiana changed drastically in 1985 when cross-county banking became legal. The following year, American National was bought by Ameritrust National Bank, and Wainwright was acquired by Huntington Bank. In 1992, Ameritrust merged with Society, and in 1996, Society became KeyBank.

Two local banks, MetroBank and Community Bank, were organized after the law was changed—MetroBank in 1988 and Community in 1991—but they, too, eventually disappeared. MetroBank became First Indiana Bank in 2003, which in turn became BMO Harris Bank in 2011. Community, the last locally owned bank, became First Merchants Bank in 2015.

Forty-two years before the First National Bank building was erected, the corner on which it sat was the original location of another memorable Noblesville business, the Craycraft Dry Goods Company, which opened in 1867.

Daniel Craycraft came to Noblesville as a photographer and ultimately became one of the town's most prominent and prosperous businessmen. He held interests in several different enterprises, but his most successful venture was his dry goods store. The store moved to its permanent location on Conner Street next to Citizens' Bank some time before 1883 and proved so profitable that when the bank closed, the dry goods company took over that building in order to expand its dress department.

After Daniel's death in 1902, his son, George, headed the business, along with a former Craycraft's clerk, Eugene Osbon. The store operated as Craycraft & Osbon until 1910, when Osbon left and George's brother, Albert, joined the company. Over the next several decades, the Craycraft Dry Goods Company supplied Noblesville with items such as ready-to-wear, rugs, carpets, millinery, men's shirts and pajamas. It also sold Victor Talking Machines in the store's balcony and even provided soundproof rooms where customers could listen to records in private. Craycraft's closed in 1962, just short of celebrating one hundred years of business.

In 1887, the discovery of an immense reservoir of natural gas sparked an economic boom for Noblesville. In the years that followed, several new factories opened in town, all eager to take advantage of the cheap, available fuel. Among these were the Noblesville Foundry and Machine Company, and the National Carbon Works.

The first, and largest, factory established in the wake of the gas discovery, however, was the Strawboard. Organized in 1889 by James L. Evans, Leonard Wild and some Kokomo businessmen, the plant was taken over by the American Strawboard Company a year later, before it was even finished. Occupying over two hundred acres next to the White River at the west end of Chestnut Street, the Strawboard was, according to a January 18, 1893 *Indianapolis News* article, the second-largest paper mill in the world at that

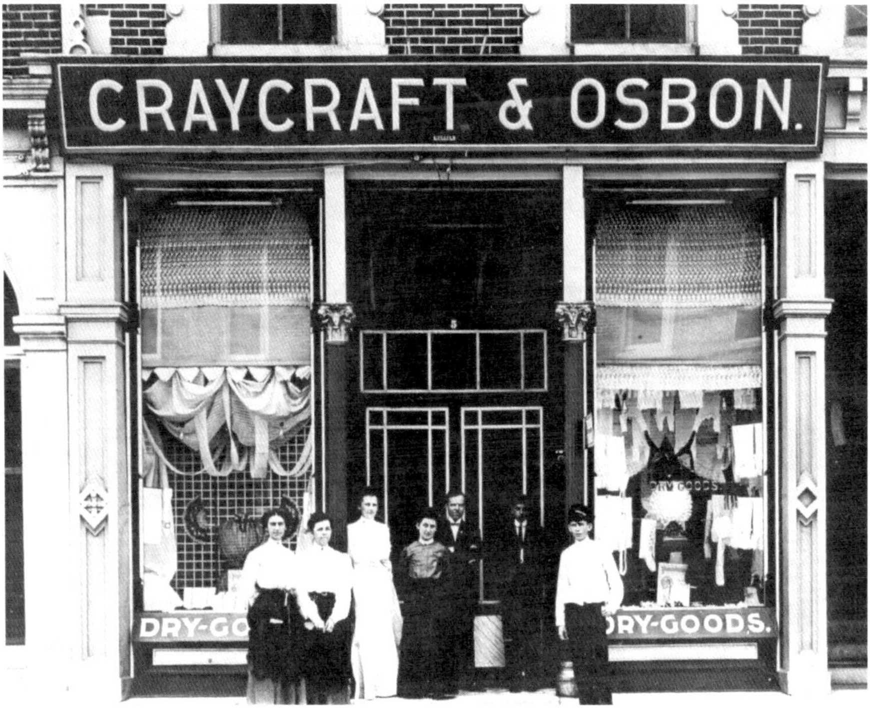

Craycraft & Osbon Dry Goods Store in the early 1900s. *Hamilton East Public Library, Joe Roberts Collection.*

time. During its early years, it was powered by the plant's own gas wells, and the straw needed to produce the strawboard or pasteboard was supplied by local farmers. Later, after the gas supply was exhausted, coal was used as fuel, and most of the straw was brought in from outside the state.

In 1923, the Ball Brothers Company bought the Strawboard to produce cardboard boxes for its glass canning jars. Ball, in turn, sold the plant to the Container Corporation of America in 1954. The factory closed in 1964.

Another important business to come out of the gas boom was the Noblesville Milling Company—the latest, and largest, of a long line of Noblesville flour or gristmills, going all the way back to the first horse-drawn mill constructed by the Horseshoe Prairie settlers.

The roots of the Noblesville Milling Company can be traced to a mill built by James L. Evans on the southeast corner of 8th and Clinton Streets in 1856. Just a few days before the mill was to have opened, it was destroyed by arson. Evans quickly rebuilt and ran the business until selling it in 1861. During the next few years, the mill's ownership changed many times, but by

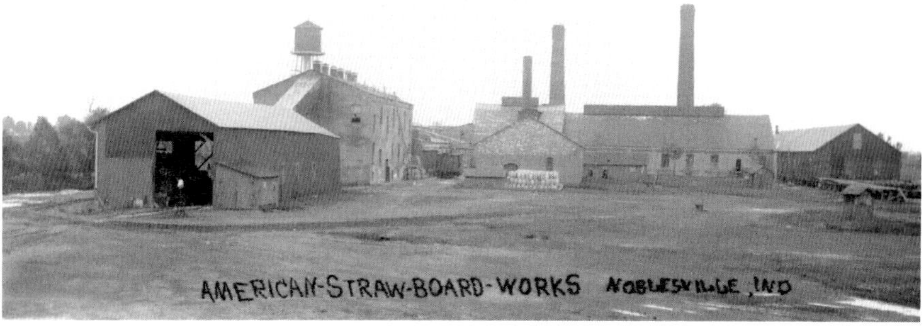

American Strawboard Company located on the southwest side of the city between Chestnut Street and the White River. *Hamilton County Historical Society*.

1868, it was back in Evans's hands. In 1875, Evans partnered with Levi Sohl, and the name of the venture was changed to Evans & Sohl.

The Evans & Sohl mill was sold sometime around 1890 to the Nordyke and Marmon Company, one of the country's most prominent manufacturers of milling machinery. Under Nordyke and Marmon, the business became known as the Noblesville Milling Company, and a new facility, the Model Mill, was constructed at the corner of 8th and Mulberry Streets to provide a place to test and showcase Nordyke and Marmon's latest equipment.

Addison Nordyke departed in 1904, leaving Daniel Marmon in charge of the company until his death in 1909. Afterward, Daniel's sons, Howard and Walter, took over. By 1913, the mill was producing 1,200 barrels of flour—sold around the country primarily under the brands Diadem and Kismet—a day.

Howard Marmon's fascination with automobiles (he created the "Marmon Wasp" race car, which won the first Indianapolis 500 Mile Race) ultimately led Nordyke and Marmon away from milling, and in 1926, the company's milling interests were sold to Allis-Chalmers. The Noblesville Milling Company continued to operate until the early 1940s, when the plant was sold to the Acme-Evans Company. Papers were filed for a legal dissolution of the Noblesville Milling Company in 1944.

The Noblesville Milling Company wasn't the only flour mill in Noblesville during this period. A smaller mill, located on the northwest corner of 6th and Conner Streets, was founded in 1871 by T. and D. Carey. It passed through several hands before ending up as the property of the

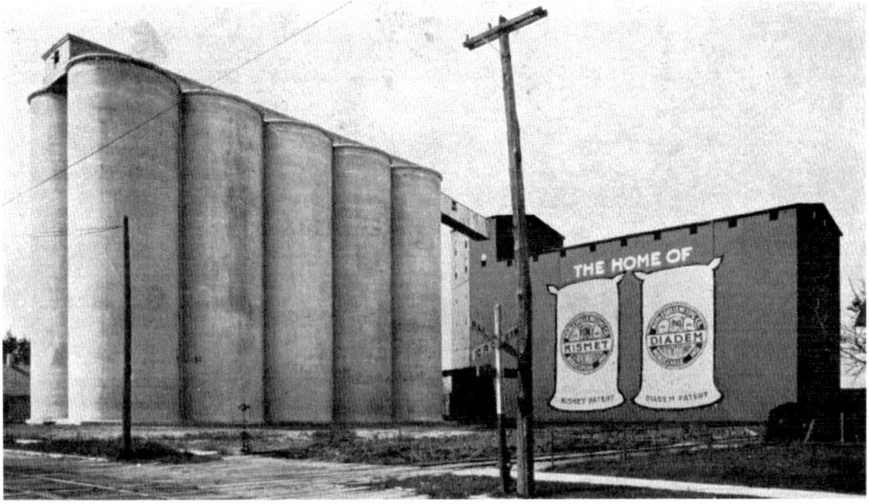

Noblesville Milling Company grain storage facilities at 8th and Vine Streets. The square elevators were built in 1899 and the concrete round silos in 1912. Note advertisement of Diadem and Kismet flours. *Hamilton County Historical Society.*

Smock/Caca family in 1901. As the City Mills, it produced wheat flour and cornmeal for many years before switching to grinding feed for livestock and poultry. The mill closed in 1975.

Gran'Pa's candy store was a favorite destination for many a child growing up in Noblesville during the first half of the twentieth century. The original Gran'Pa was George Hawkins, a Civil War veteran who sold his homemade sweets at various events around the county and at a confectionery and restaurant on the north side of the courthouse square.

Hawkins taught his son-in-law, Will Mabee, the business, and Mabee eventually took it over, operating out of a small store he built on the southeast corner of 10th and Harrison Streets in 1923. Mabee sold forty-nine kinds of homemade candy there, including his own version of Crackerjack, "Gran'Pa's Wonderful Popcorn Candy."

The family business was later run by Mabee's nephew, George Cullen, and George's wife, Lora Jane. Although Gran'pa's closed in 1976, the building still exists.

During the last half of the twentieth century, Noblesville's largest industry was Firestone Industrial Products, another company with a complicated history, one which began when the Burdick Tire & Rubber Company, a Delaware-based corporation, moved its Chicago plant to Noblesville in

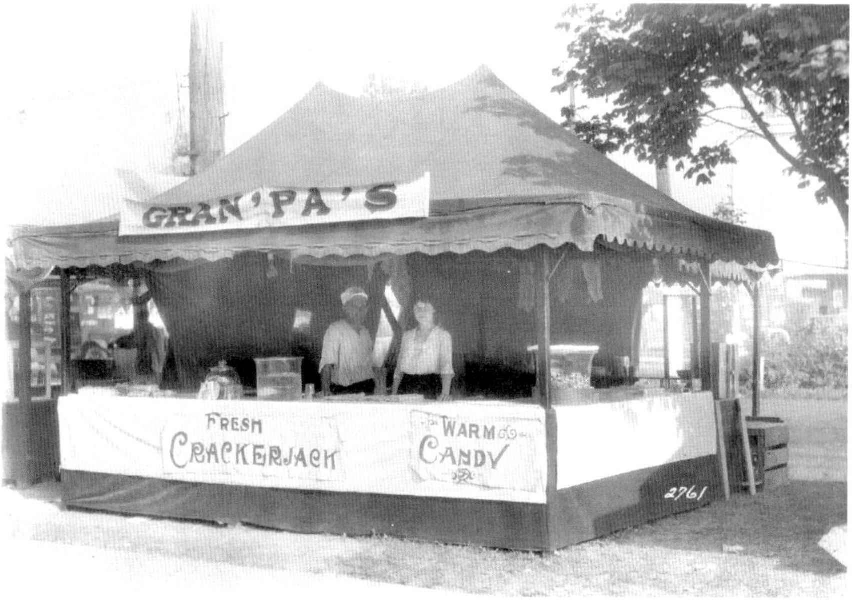

Gran'Pa's open stand used at county fairs. *Jane Cullen Gawthrop.*

1918. Burdick temporarily operated out of the old Heylmann building in downtown Noblesville while a new factory was constructed in the area of 16th and Division Streets. The three-story plant was completed in 1920.

Four years later, Burdick declared bankruptcy. The following year, the company was bought by Burdick's former president, Henry G. Steinbrenner, but the Steinbrenner Rubber Company didn't last long, either. Steinbrenner had written fraudulent checks to cover the purchase, and in the resulting scandal, Noblesville's First National Bank and the Huntington County State Bank of Huntington, Indiana, were forced to close, and Steinbrenner committed suicide.

In 1928, William H. Schacht bought the plant at a receiver's sale. The Schacht Rubber Company produced rubber novelties and games at the factory until becoming a subsidiary of the Firestone Tire and Rubber Company in 1936. At that time, the plant became the Firestone Industrial Products Company.

Over the next seventy-three years, Firestone Industrial Products played a major role in the lives of all Noblesville residents, even those who didn't have a family member working there. The company actively supported various community organizations such as the Boys Club, but as Noblesville's main employer, each time its labor force went on strike, the effects were felt by the entire city.

In 1988, Firestone Tire and Rubber Company was acquired by the Bridgestone Corporation of Japan. After the sale, the local Firestone plant continued to operate as Bridgestone/Firestone, but demand for the air springs it manufactured for trucks and buses began to dwindle, and in 2009, the factory closed.

Several years before McDonald's came to town, Noblesville was home to its own fast food restaurant, Clancy's Hamburgers. The restaurant chain was founded in Noblesville in 1965 by Carl Fogelsong, who took the restaurant's name from an old movie with a Keystone Cop named Clancy. Fogelsong felt "Clancy the Cop" represented the cheerful, community service–oriented American values he wanted associated with his business.

Besides offering such menu items as shakes, tenderloins, Clancy's Toppers (a double-decker hamburger) and the best french fries in town, the restaurant boasted a thirty-five-seat dining room and the first double drive-thru in the Midwest.

At its peak, there were thirty-one Clancy's spread across four states. Two of those were located in Noblesville—the original Clancy's on 10th Street and a second on State Road 32, across from Noblesville Square Shopping Center.

In 2004, the 10th Street Clancy's was torn down to make a parking lot for Noblesville's city hall. The other Clancy's was turned into Michaelangelo's Italian Bistro, another restaurant owned by Clancy's Inc. For several years,

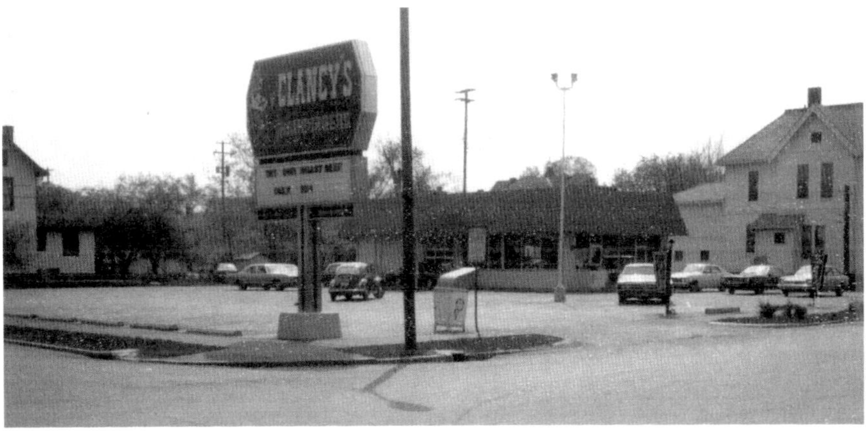

Clancy's restaurant at the southeast corner of 10th Street and Maple Avenue, 1965. *Hamilton East Public Library, Irv Heath Collection.*

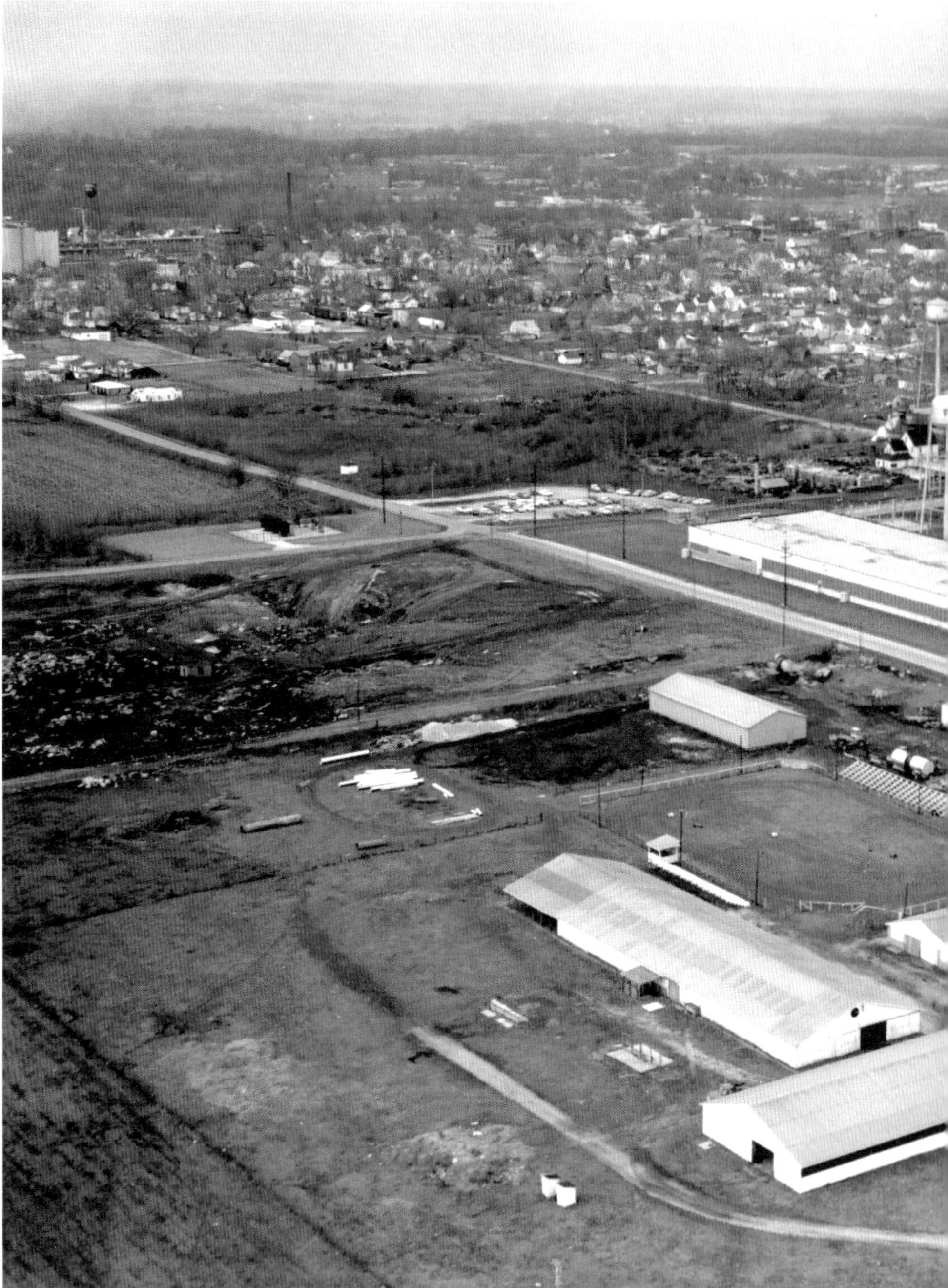

Late 1960s aerial of Firestone Industrial Products shows Plant 1 (*upper right*) and Plant 2 (*center*). 4-H Fairgrounds shown beneath Plant 2. Plant 1 was demolished in 2014, leaving

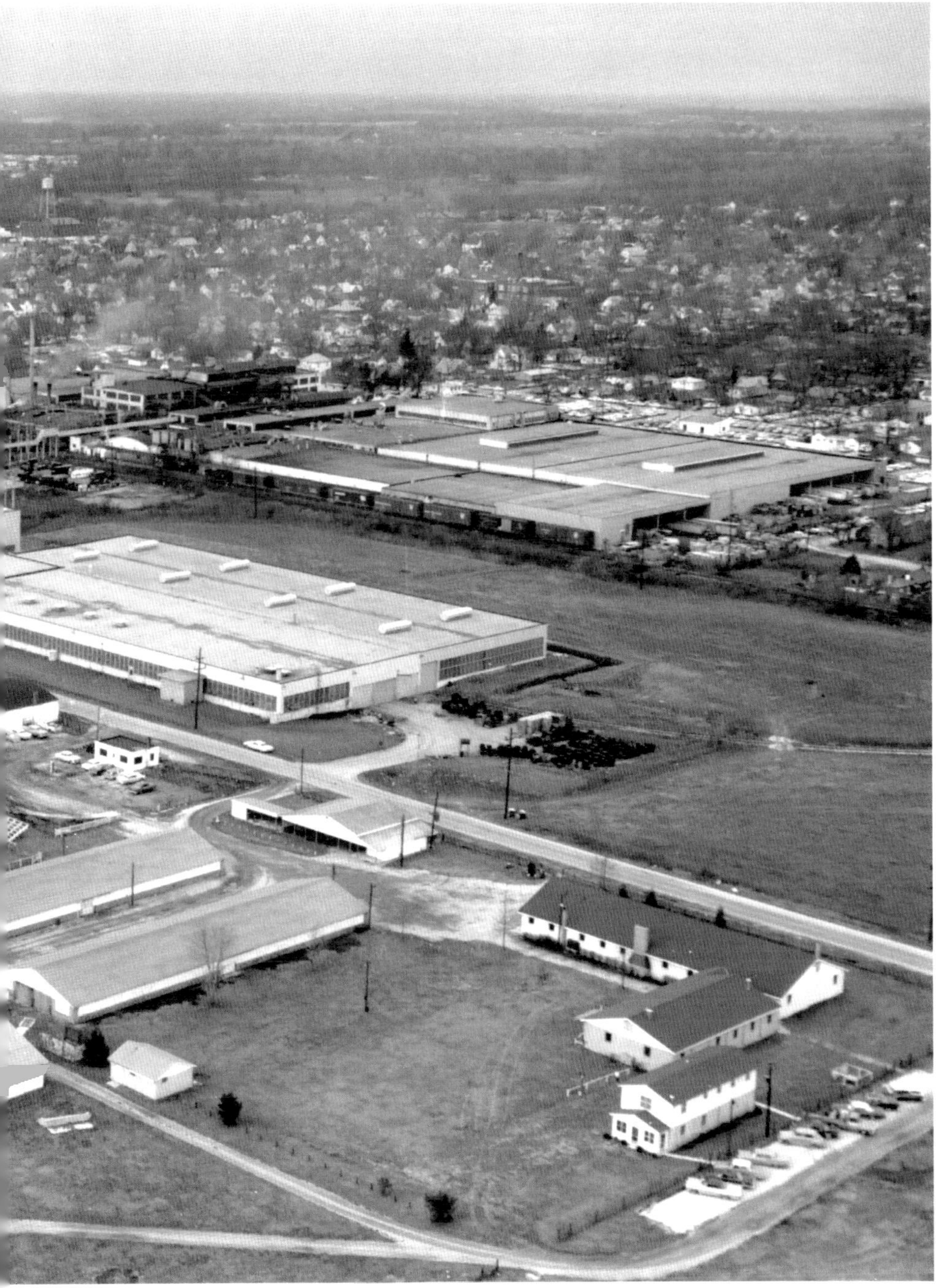

what is now known as "The Slab." Plant 2 opened on Pleasant Street in 1964 and closed in 1989. The building now houses several small businesses. *Hamilton County Historical Society.*

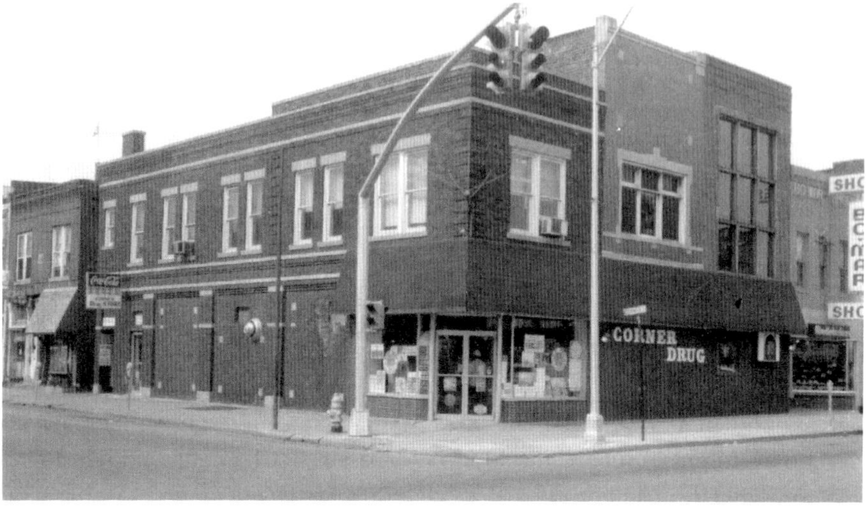

Corner Drug underwent several renovations since its establishment in 1850. The original building was replaced in 1915. This photo shows the store in the 1960s. It now houses A Corner Cottage. *Hamilton East Public Library, Irv Heath Collection.*

the company also operated a Grindstone Charley's restaurant next to Riverview Hospital, but it closed in 2005. The Grindstone Public House, a new restaurant combining elements of both Grindstone Charley's and Clancy's, opened in downtown Noblesville in 2018.

Another local restaurant chain also got its start in Noblesville. In 1964, Harry Reasner opened the first Jim Dandy on Conner Street across from the Noblesville Plaza. The restaurant was originally a drive-in, and for many years, "cruising the J.D." was a favorite pastime of local teens. In 1982, however, it was remodeled and enlarged, and curb service was eliminated. Today, the Jim Dandy continues to play an active role in the community, serving up its namesake "Jim Dandy" double-decker hamburgers and other tasty treats.

No list of Noblesville's businesses would be complete without a mention of the Corner Drug, the last of a long line of drugstores to occupy the southwest corner of 9th and Conner Streets. Although the tradition managed to endure through at least two buildings and a span of about 145 years, it came to an end when the Corner Drug closed its doors in 1995.

Two other businesses, still in operation, can claim a similar history. Syd's Bar, on the northeast corner of 8th and Logan Streets, has been around for over seventy years, but—with a short break for Hamilton County's dry years,

1909 to 1933—the building housing Syd's has been home to a tavern ever since it was erected in 1889. A few doors east of Syd's, Kirk's Hardware, established in 1956, has a lengthy history of its own. It's the latest in a long line of hardware stores that have occupied that space since Thomas and George Griffin opened Griffin Bros. Hardware in the building in 1889.

In fact, Noblesville has been home to a number of notable long-lived local businesses. Some of these are just a fond memory today—Kenley's two supermarkets, Beanie's Cafeteria, the McMahon Food Company, the Blue Ribbon and Hoosier Dairies, Levinson's and Zeckel's clothing stores and Dorman's Paint and Wallpaper store, to name a few.

There are, however, a surprising number of local establishments fifty years or older that are still in business. Among them are the legal firm of Church Church Hittle and Antrim (established 1880); Gatewood's Vegetable Farm and Greenhouses (1922); Harger Farms (around 1940); the Uptown Cafe, currently known as the Sunrise Cafe @Uptown (1945); Smith's Jewelers (1946); Arbuckle's Railroad Place and Mallery Realtors (1948); Scott Plumbing, Heating and Cooling, and the Noblesville Veterinary Clinic (1953); Field Rubber Products (1955); Beaver Materials (1959); and Bolden's Dry Cleaners (1960). In addition, scrap metal recycling company Lusco Corporation grew out of a junkyard established by Louis Smith in 1917.

In years past, farming would also have been a prominent part of Noblesville's economic picture. However, as the city enters the twenty-first century, more and more of the surrounding farms have given way to subdivisions, and agriculture is no longer as widely practiced in the area as it once was.

5

READING, 'RITING, 'RITHMETIC... AND ROOTING FOR THE BLACK AND GOLD

The history of education in Noblesville can be traced back to the Horseshoe Prairie settlement's first school, which opened in a small cabin during the summer of 1820. The teacher was Sarah Finch, the daughter of John Finch, and all the pupils were young Finch children.

According to an April 2, 1896 *Indianapolis News* article by Augustus Finch Shirts, the first male teacher was an Englishman named Barren who established a school in a cabin about a half mile south of Horseshoe Prairie. This Barren was something of a mystery at the time and remains so to this day. Nothing is known of his background beyond the fact he was well educated. Curiously, Shirts fails to even mention him in his book, *A History of the Formation, Settlement and Development of Hamilton County*.

Curtis Mallory, a native of New York State who settled on Horseshoe Prairie during the summer of 1820, was another early teacher. In 1829, after moving off the prairie to a spot near Stony Creek, Mallory set up a school in his home and not only taught, but also boarded two of the sons of prominent Indianapolis attorney Calvin Fletcher. The boys were only four and five when they were sent off to Mallory's school, but they got along well with the "old Gentleman." (Mallory later began spelling his name "Mallery" after eastern relatives made an insulting remark about his decision to live in the backwoods of Indiana.)

The first school in the town of Noblesville was a log cabin located on the corner of 8th Street and Maple Avenue. Robert L. Hannaman was the first teacher. This schoolhouse was followed by a second log cabin on the corner of 10th and Clinton Streets, which was, in turn, followed first by a frame structure on 6th Street, then by a brick building on the southwest corner of 11th and Logan Streets.

The earliest schools were subscription schools, where teachers were paid by students' parents. While Indiana's 1816 state constitution had made provisions for a state-wide system of public schools, no time frame was specified for the creation of the schools, and most communities were slow to act. No serious progress was made toward the establishment of a common or public school in Noblesville until the county seminary was organized around thirty years later. (A seminary in those days was simply an institution of higher learning. There was no religious association.)

When educator and minister Francis Whitefield Emmons laid out his addition to Noblesville in 1838, he reserved a lot for a county seminary on the west side of Anderson (10th) Street between Hannibal and Division. Emmons offered the land to the county on the condition that within a year the lot would be enclosed with "a good post and rail or board fence" and within three years, the county would erect a two-story brick building worth at least $1,200 "in which the youth of both sexes shall receive instruction in the arts and sciences usually taught in academies and high schools."

Emmons's conditions weren't met, however, and it wasn't until 1845 that steps were actually taken toward obtaining land for a county seminary. The piece of ground the county commissioners chose was in Emmons's addition, but sat across the street from the lot Emmons had designated, in the block bounded by Hannibal Street on the north, Anderson (10th) Street on the west, Division Street on the south and 11th Street on the east. Plans for a two-story brick building were drawn up, and in 1846, bids for its construction were solicited in the *Indiana State Sentinel*. William Bauchert, who made the winning bid, set to work on the project, but progress was slow and the building wasn't ready for classes until 1852.

In 1869, the school trustees decided a new schoolhouse was in order, and bonds were issued to finance its construction. Three years later, the school known originally as the Noblesville Seminary, and later as Second Ward, welcomed its first students. Throughout the years it was open, this two-story brick structure (plus a basement) housed all grades, from the first through high school, at various times and in various combinations, depending upon the school system's needs.

Two more ward schools were built in the years following the construction of Second Ward in 1872. First Ward opened in 1889 in a grove of trees bounded by Monument Street on the north, 10th Street on the west, Harrison

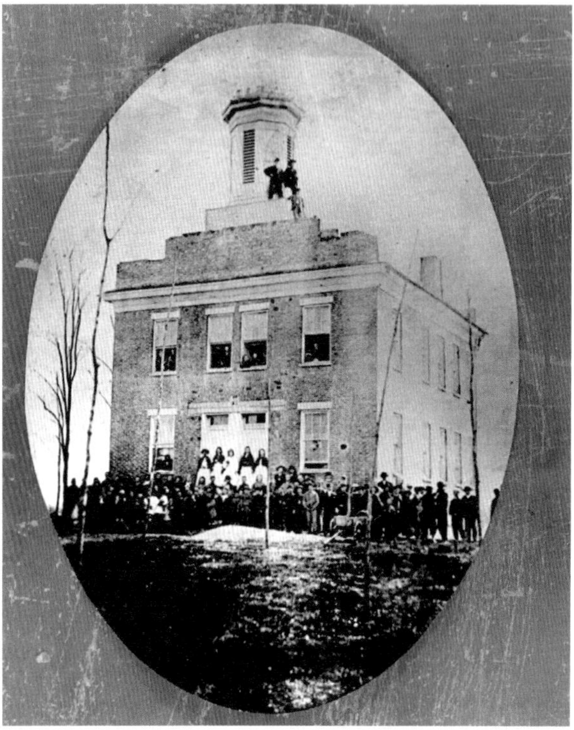

The old Seminary School pictured here was torn down to build a new building known as Second Ward. *Hamilton East Public Library, Joe Roberts Collection.*

Street on the south and 12th Street on the east. Three years later, students on the south side of town began attending Third Ward on the northwest corner of 10th Street and Christian Avenue. Like Second Ward, both schools were two-story brick structures with basements, but they differed in that classes were always confined to grades below the high school level.

Those weren't the only schools in the Noblesville area during the nineteenth century, however.

Integration didn't take place in Noblesville's schools until 1890, so throughout most of this period, local African American children were educated separately from their white counterparts. Although information on Noblesville's "colored" schools is scanty, some definitely did exist. There is evidence a small school was conducted north of town during the 1850s or 1860s, and the November 9, 1870 *Hamilton County Register* reported that a frame schoolhouse was being constructed on the southeast side of town "for the special benefit of the colored folks."

During the last half of the nineteenth century and extending into the first half of the twentieth century, rural students in the Noblesville area attended one of several township schools scattered throughout the nearby countryside.

NOBLESVILLE'S TOWNSHIP SCHOOLS

Compiling a complete list of the Noblesville Township schools is difficult, as over the years, one building would sometimes be replaced by another in a different location. A partial list of schools, based on the most recent names and locations, follows:

- School #1, Providence (1908–1923), located on 211th Street, between Little Chicago and Mill Creek Roads.
- School #2, Little Chicago (1889–1941), located on State Road 38, a little east of Little Chicago Road.
- School #3, Hazel Dell (1892–1935), located at 169th Street and Hazel Dell Road.
- School #4, Gray (1891–1921), located at 146th Street and Gray Road. (Although in Noblesville Township, it also served Washington and Delaware Townships. In 1921, it became part of the Washington Township school system.)
- School #5, Federal Hill (1917–1960), located on the southwest corner of Logan Street and Lakeview Drive in Noblesville.
- School #7, Stringtown (1890–1925), located on Stringtown Pike (Hague Road), about halfway between 196th and 206th Streets.
- School #8, Baton Rouge (1893–1930), located at 206th Street and Cumberland Road.
- School #9, Refuge (?–1941) located at 196th Street and Promise Road.
- School #10, Rose Bud (1901–1927), located at the junction of State Roads 38 and 32, east of Noblesville.
- School #11, Wheeler (1887–1951), located on Greenfield Avenue/State Road 238 at Howe Road.
- School #12, Spannuth (1878–1908), located on the Noblesville/Delaware Township line. It served both townships.

By the 1940s, nearly all the township schools were gone. Most of the buildings were eventually either torn down or converted into private residences. Only two township schools, Federal Hill and Wheeler, remained after the Noblesville school system's consolidation in 1947. Both were kept open and operated as grade schools for a few years—Wheeler until 1951, and Federal Hill until 1961. For several years after closing as a grade school, Federal Hill housed the Hamilton County Opportunity School, a facility for students with special needs.

In 1900, Noblesville opened a new high school on the northeast corner of 14th and Conner Streets. Described by the *Hamilton County Ledger* as "one of the most convenient and modern High School buildings in the State," the stone and brick structure included recitation rooms, a laboratory, an assembly room and a library.

What the new high school was missing, however, was a gymnasium. That omission was corrected twenty-three years later when a second building was erected east of the original structure, thanks to the efforts of the local Kiwanis Club and a generous donation from prominent Chicago attorney S.O. Levinson and his brother, Harry, founder of the Harry Levinson clothing stores. In addition to a gym, the new building held classrooms, a trophy room and a basement cafeteria. Travel between the school's two sections was made easier by a walkway connecting the upper floors.

It would be over fifty years before Noblesville's next school was built. When Conner Elementary opened at 17th and Conner Streets in 1952, it was noticeably different from the other schools in town. Conner was the first single-story Noblesville school in over one hundred years and the first elementary school to have a cafeteria.

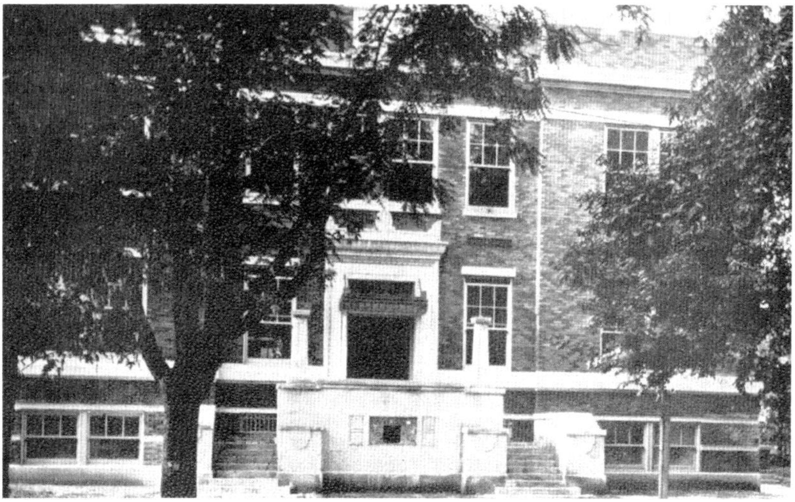

The Noblesville High School gym on Conner Street, built in 1923. *Hamilton County Historical Society*.

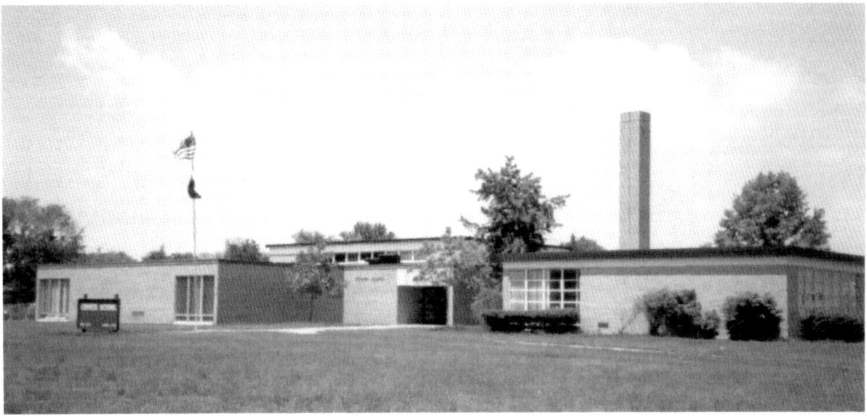

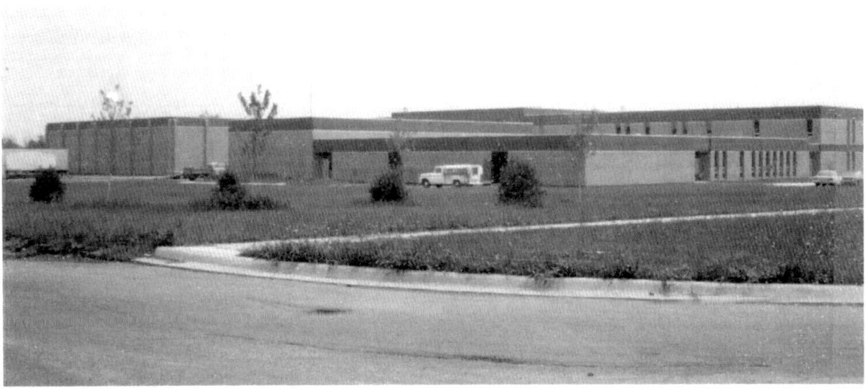

Top: Conner School's last year, 1989. *Nancy A. Massey*.

Bottom: South Elementary became Stony Creek Elementary when parents and teachers campaigned for the change of the school name. *Hamilton East Public Library, Irv Heath Collection*.

Two years later, ground was broken for a new $1.1 million Noblesville High School in a field just north of Conner Elementary, between Clinton and Harrison Streets. The finishing touches were still being added to the new 17th Street high school when classes began in the fall of 1955.

Following the opening of the new high school, students in grades seven and eight moved into the old Conner Street high school, which then became the Noblesville Junior High.

The 1960s saw the construction of even more schools. In 1961, Forest Hill Elementary opened on Lakeview Drive, just west of Forest Park, and took in the students from the recently closed Federal Hill school. Five years later, North Elementary opened at 10th and Monument Streets, just north of First

Ward, which it replaced. In 1968, the other two ward schools, Second and Third Ward, closed, and their students were sent to the new Stony Creek Elementary on Greenfield Avenue.

The year 1968 also marked the opening of a new Noblesville Junior High School. Located at the intersection of 16th Street and Field Drive, the building was notable for its multilevel "cafetorium," a combination cafeteria and auditorium, and for the first swimming pool in the Noblesville school system.

By the 1990s, the 17th Street high school, once considered spacious, was no longer able to keep up with the city's skyrocketing population. It was replaced in 1996 by the present-day Noblesville High School, a $65 million facility on the southwest corner of Field Drive and Cumberland Road. Indiana senator Richard Lugar delivered the keynote address at the building's dedication.

The opening of the Cumberland Road high school prompted a reorganization of the lower grades. The newly vacated 17th Street high school became the Noblesville Middle School (grades seven and eight), and the former junior high on Field Drive became the Noblesville Intermediate School (grades five and six). In 2007, the Noblesville Intermediate School moved to a new facility on Hague Road, just north of 196th Street, and the Field Drive building became Noblesville High School's freshman campus. A few years later, the Intermediate School became Noblesville West Middle School, and the Noblesville Middle School on 17th Street was renamed Noblesville East Middle School. In 2014, renovations to Noblesville High School allowed the freshmen to return to the Cumberland Road building. The Noblesville East Middle School then moved into the Field Drive facility left empty by the freshmen.

Currently, there are ten schools in Noblesville's public school system. In addition to the high school and two middle schools, there are seven grade schools. North Elementary and Stony Creek Elementary have been joined by Hinkle Creek Elementary, which opened in 1980 and is located on South Harbor Drive in the South Harbor subdivision; Hazel Dell Elementary, which opened in 1989 and is located on State Road 32 (Westfield Road) near Hazel Dell Road; White River Elementary, which opened in 1999 and is located on Cumberland Road, between 191st Street and Field Drive; Noble Crossing Elementary, which opened in 2007 and is located on Noble Crossing Parkway, near 156th Street and Hazel Dell Road; and Promise Road Elementary, which opened in 2012 and is located on Promise Road, south of Greenfield Avenue.

Noblesville also is home to three parochial schools.

From 1948 to 1974, Our Lady of Grace Catholic Church operated a grade school in a small brick building on 11th Street next to the church. After the church moved to its present location on 191st Street in 1991, the school was reopened with expanded classes. It now accepts students from preschool through eighth grade.

Since 2004, Catholic students have been able to continue their education at St. Theodore Guerin Catholic High School, one of the top Catholic high schools in the country. Guerin's Golden Eagles also participate in a full range of athletic programs. The school is located on Gray Road, just north of 146th Street.

A third parochial school, Legacy Christian School, opened in the former Forest Hill school building in 2011. Legacy Christian's classes range from preschool to the high school level.

In 2014, a landmark in the history of education in Noblesville was reached when Ivy Tech Community College established its Hamilton County campus in the old 17th Street high school. A $30 million renovation was completed in 2016, adapting the building to the needs of students seeking a postsecondary education. Also located in the facility is the Excel Center, a public school offering classes geared toward adults interested in obtaining a high school diploma, job certification and/or college credits.

Throughout their long history, Noblesville's schools have undergone many changes. Buildings have been renovated, student populations have been shifted between schools and courses once considered important, such as penmanship and agriculture, have given way to others like mass media and computer sciences. One thing that hasn't changed in the last one hundred years, however, is the popularity of the city's high school athletic teams.

Originally called the Black and Gold, Noblesville High School's athletes have been the Millers since 1925. That's when school board president C.B. Jenkins, who also happened to be the manager of the Noblesville Milling Company, told a gathering of students and faculty that his company would buy the school new athletic uniforms if the NHS teams' nickname was changed to the Millers. It was an easy decision given the important role the milling industry had played throughout Noblesville's history.

Track, tennis, golf, basketball and football were early NHS sports, with the latter two the most popular. Prior to the construction of the first high school gym in 1923, basketball games were played on outdoor courts next to the Conner Street high school in good weather and in whatever indoor facilities were available when the weather was bad. Since 1923, however, Miller basketball has always had a home in the high school.

Early football games were played at the Horse Show Grounds. After 1923 they moved to the rented Joseph Field, which would later become the site of Conner Elementary. In 1941, plans were drawn up for a new athletic field, to be owned by the school system and located east of First Ward in the area called the Commons, but World War II delayed its construction. When the new facility was finally dedicated in 1945, it was named Memorial Field to honor NHS students, living and dead, who served during the war. Memorial Field was home to both the football, and track and field teams until 1969, when a new athletic field opened on the east side of the 17th Street high school. The new facility was originally christened Swanson Field in honor of Noblesville school superintendent Dale V. Swanson, but the name was changed to Hare Chevrolet Field in 2006 in recognition of the sponsorship of Hare Chevrolet. In 2018, it became Beaver Materials Field.

Today, the high school has several sports venues in addition to Beaver Materials Field. The school gymnasium, known as "The Mill," is not only home to Millers' basketball, but also to dance, volleyball and wrestling. Swimming and diving competitions are held in the school's natatorium. Varsity baseball is played at Donald J. Dunker Field on Westfield Road, freshman baseball at Logan Field in Forest Park and softball at the NHS Softball Complex next to the high school. Gymnastics meets are held in the Noblesville East Middle School gymnasium. Cross country is run at

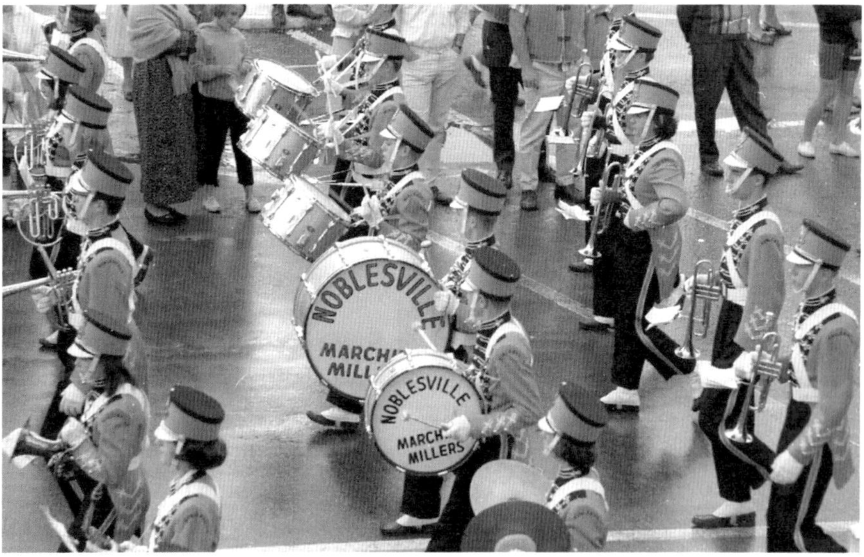

NHS marching band in the mid-1960s. *Hamilton County Historical Society*.

the Chinquapin Ridge Cross Country Course and soccer is played at the White River Elementary Soccer Complex, both of which are located on Cumberland Road near White River Elementary.

Over the years, Noblesville High School has produced some outstanding athletes, such as Tom Coverdale, Indiana's 1998 "Mr. Basketball." It has also won state championships in several sports—boys track and field (1913), girls golf (1986 and 1987), girls basketball (1987), girls soccer (1991), boys golf (1998 and 1999), varsity baseball (2014) and competition cheerleading (2016 and 2017)—and the school band, the Marching Millers, placed first at the 1952, 2017 and 2018 Indiana State Fair Band Competitions.

One other aspect of the Noblesville schools that hasn't changed in over one hundred years is the support of the Noblesville High School Alumni Association. Since 1876, this organization, open to all NHS graduates, has celebrated the history of the Noblesville schools while paving the way to the future by providing scholarships to promising NHS students.

6

KEEPING THE FAITH

Today, churches representing many different denominations can be found in Noblesville, but that wasn't always the case.

There was no dedicated house of worship at the Horseshoe Prairie settlement. When Curtis Mallory organized the first Sunday school in 1820, it was held in the same building in which Sarah Finch taught her school, and the first sermon, delivered that same year by a "hard-shell" (conservative) Baptist preacher, took place in John Finch's home.

Baptist services continued to be held at irregular intervals in various homes until about 1827, when a log church was constructed on the northwest corner of Catherine (9th) and Emmaus (Cherry) Streets. Reverend Nathaniel Richmond, a missionary from Madison County, preached there once a month.

Meanwhile, in 1834, two newcomers to the county, John Jones and Chauncey Butler, the father of Butler University founder Ovid Butler, began preaching a new doctrine known as the Restoration or Stone-Campbell Movement in the old frame county courthouse. Their church, the Church of Christ, would later be known as the First Christian Church.

In September 1835, Noblesville's Baptist congregation merged with Jones and Butler's group, and the Baptist Church ceased to exist in Noblesville at that time. The Baptists' property and records were transferred to the Church of Christ, and the newly united congregation began holding services in the building formerly used by the Baptists.

Despite some squabbling, church membership increased, and by 1839, the old log church had been replaced by a new, larger frame church on the same site.

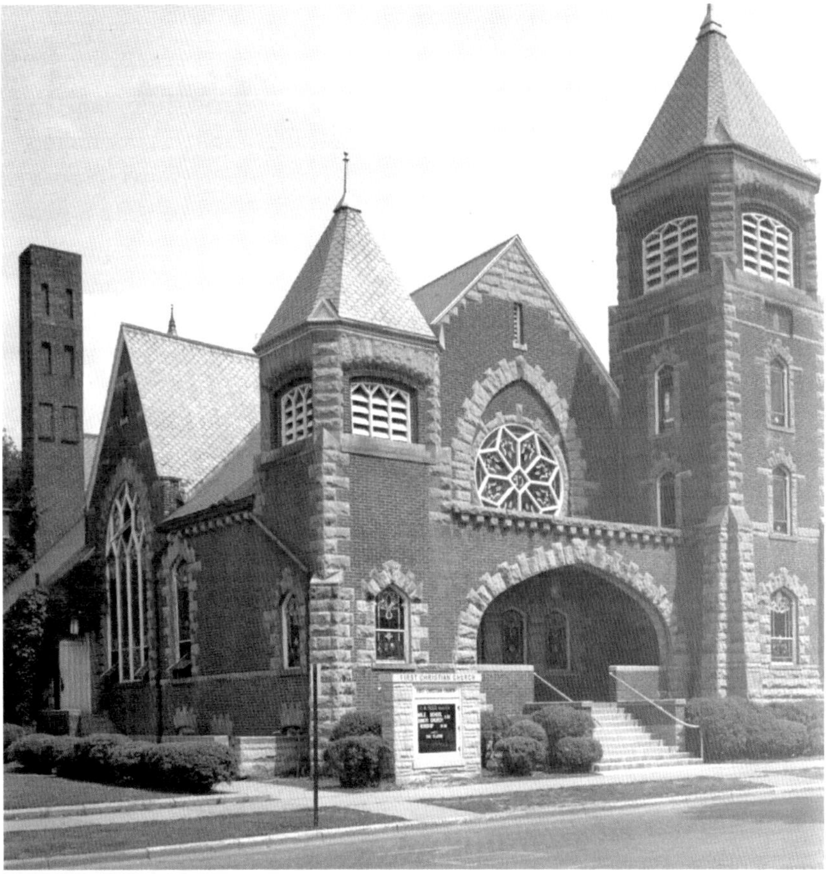

First Christian Church on Catherine (now 9th) Street. *Hamilton County Historical Society.*

In 1853, about fifty church members left to form their own congregation. Two years later, that group purchased a lot on the corner of Catherine (9th) and Wiltshire (Maple Avenue) and built a third church, a brick building called the Christian Chapel. William Stoops, a member of the congregation who ran a gristmill on Stony Creek about a mile and a half away, offered to pay for a bell for the new church, provided it was loud enough he could hear it at his home. He could, he did and the bell was used for years.

The two factions reunited in 1868, but since church records between 1852 and 1926 have disappeared, many other details from that period, such as exactly when the Church of Christ became the First Christian Church, are unknown. The new name was definitely in use by the time the next church was dedicated in 1898. The new church, a Victorian Gothic building of brick and limestone, was constructed on the same site as the Christian Chapel.

After ninety-one years, the 1898 church was replaced by the current building at Herriman Boulevard and Greenfield Avenue. The move to the new Herriman Boulevard church in 1989 was a festive occasion, marked by a parade of antique cars, decorated trucks, tractors and people on foot, accompanied by a police escort and a band playing "When the Saints Go Marching In."

The old 1898 church was then renovated and turned into office space, and is now known as the Adler Building.

Noblesville's Methodists can trace their history back nearly as far as the Baptists. Like the Baptists, they were initially ministered to by traveling preachers. Methodist circuit rider James Scott conducted the first services in the Noblesville area in 1822 and 1823.

The first Methodist—or, as it was officially known then, Methodist Episcopal—church was built in 1836 on the northwest corner of Anderson (10th) and Clinton Streets. This meetinghouse, believed to have been constructed of logs, was replaced by a brick church around three years later.

In 1852, church trustees decided a new church was in order. Failing to obtain the property they had in mind, they simply built on the existing lot. The third Methodist Episcopal church was dedicated in 1853.

Yet another brick church was built on the same site in 1891, thanks in large part to the efforts of the church's Ladies Aid Society. Through their various charitable activities, the women managed to collect more than $5,000 for the building fund. They also carpeted the entire church.

The 1891 church, which came to be known as the First Methodist Church, was replaced by the current church on Monument Street in 1963. At the time of the move, the new church's sanctuary had yet to be constructed, so services were conducted in the basement's Fellowship Hall for a few years. The first service in the new sanctuary was held on Christmas Eve 1967. The following year, the Methodists merged with the Evangelical United Brethren Church, changing the church's official name to the First United Methodist Church.

Noblesville's Presbyterian Church was formally organized by Reverend William H. Rogers in 1848 as part of the New School Presbytery of Indianapolis. It was the successor to the first Presbyterian church in the county, the Stony Creek Church, which had been located a few miles east of Noblesville. The congregation's first meetinghouse, a white frame Greek Revival–style building, was erected around 1850 on the east side of Catherine (9th) Street, a half block south of Conner Street.

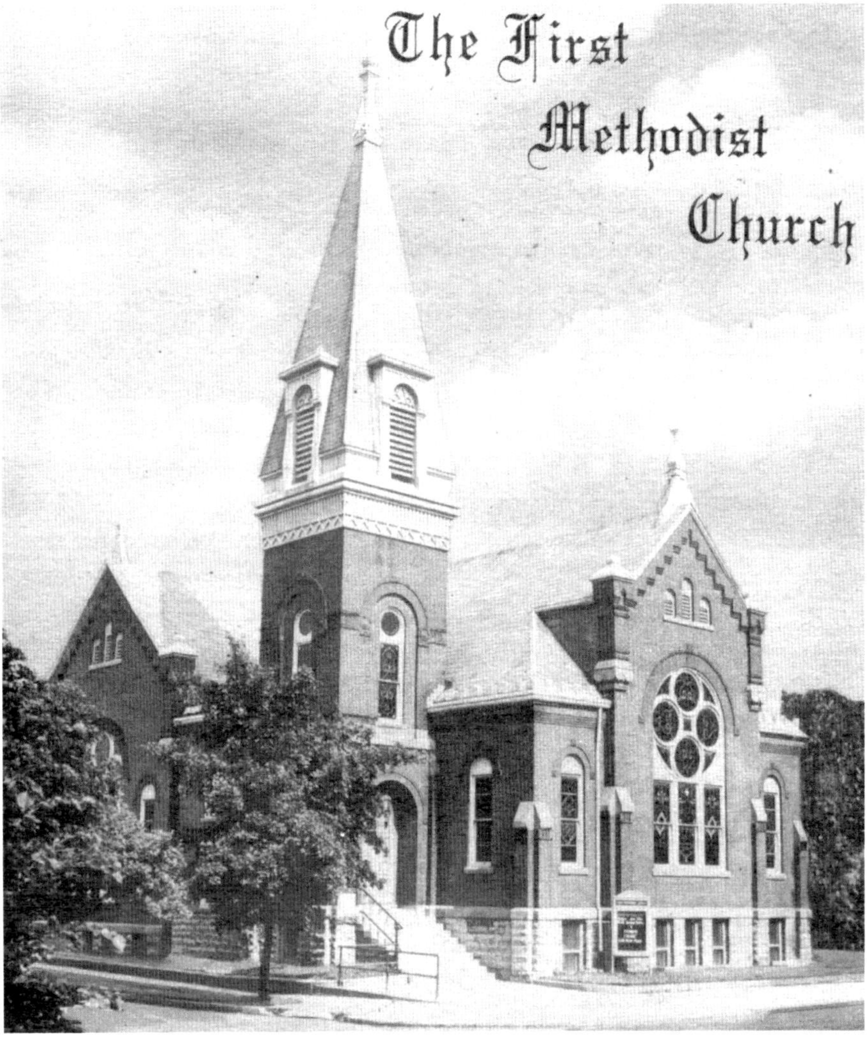

First Methodist Episcopal Church on 10th Street, 1891. *First United Methodist Church.*

After Reverend Rogers's departure in 1854, the church went through some rough times. During most of that period, there was no regular minister, and few sermons were preached. Records show that a resolution to sell the church bell to pay for painting the church and its fence passed in 1862, and in 1865, the church itself was put up for sale, but apparently there were no takers. The church reorganized in 1867 and has been a fixture in Noblesville ever since.

The current First Presbyterian Church was constructed on the southeast corner of 12th and Conner Streets in 1893. The old white frame church was then sold to the Church of the Brethren, who moved it to 12th and Grant. In 1945, the building was sold once again and became the first Our Lady of Grace Catholic Church.

The 1893 Presbyterian Church so impressed church trustee William H. Craig that he commissioned the same architect to design a home for him on the lot to the east. The three-story brick Craig House eventually became the property of the Presbyterians, who referred to it as the East House. It was used for classrooms and meeting space until being sold in 1988 to make room for the church's expansion.

After an absence of nearly twenty years, the Baptists returned to Noblesville when Reverend Jesse Young organized the First Baptist Church in the public schoolhouse in 1853. The church, sometimes referred to as the African Baptist or Colored Baptist Church, held regular meetings until Reverend Young left in 1859. Then, like the Presbyterian Church, it underwent a dormant period until Reverend Young returned in 1865 and reorganized it.

In 1875, the congregation moved into a one-story frame building at the corner of Harrison (5th) and Emmaus (Cherry) Streets, on the eastern edge of Riverside Cemetery. It remained there for 130 years.

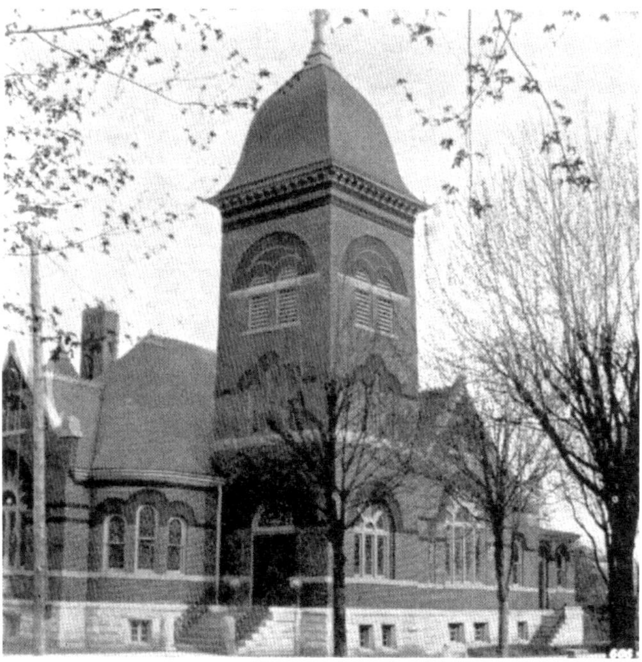

First Presbyterian Church on the corner of 12th and Conner Streets, 1893. *Hamilton County Historical Society.*

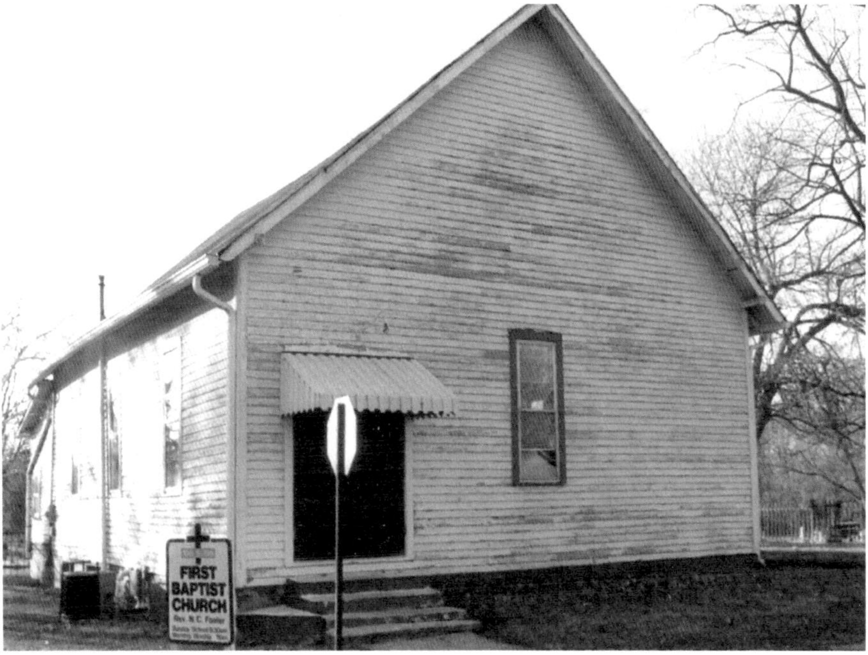

First Baptist Church on the corner of Harrison (5th) and Emmaus (Cherry) Streets, 1875. *Hamilton County Historical Society.*

The First Baptist Church had some prominent pastors, such as Civil War veteran and former slave Barney Stone and civil rights activist Ernest Butler, but over time, its congregation gradually dwindled and eventually disbanded. The last service took place in 2005. Today, the building is the Hamilton County Art Center, the home of the Hamilton County Artists' Association.

Bethel African Methodist Episcopal (AME) Church also has a long history. It was founded in 1862 by an Indianapolis preacher named Indicutt at a log schoolhouse on the Pleasant Evans farm, three and a half miles northwest of Noblesville.

The congregation moved to Noblesville in 1868. Purchasing a lot at 14th and Division Streets, the members built a one-story frame church, which they occupied from 1874 to 1914. On Easter Sunday 1914, they moved into the former Wesleyan Methodist Church on the northwest corner of 5th and Walnut Streets.

The congregation obtained land for a new church on Sheridan Road (State Road 38) in 2003, but the building never materialized. Instead, the church members moved into the Worship Center of Hamilton County in

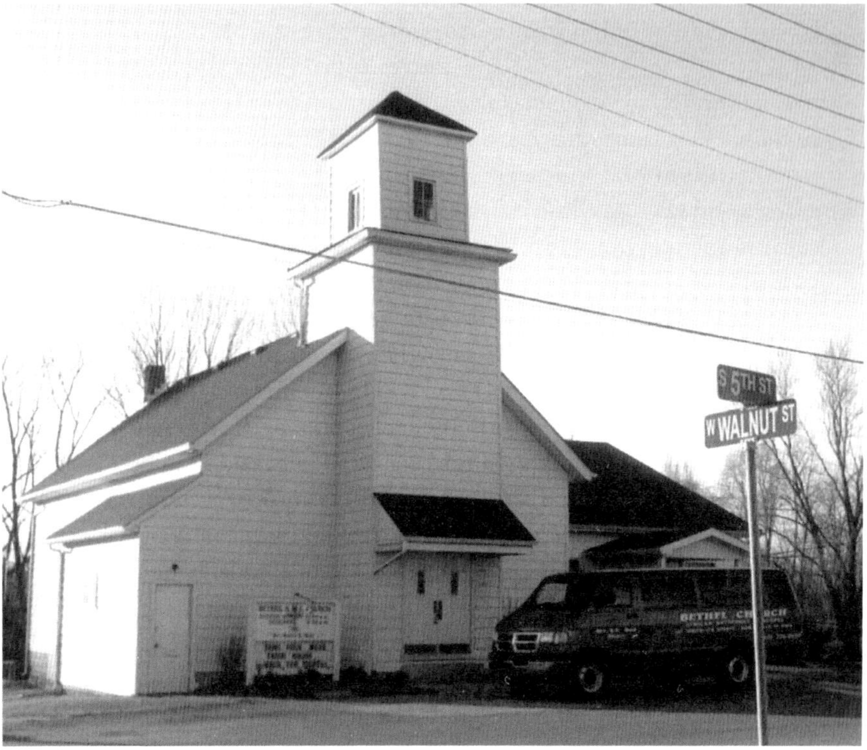

African Methodist Episcopal Church on the corner of 5th and Walnut Streets. *Hamilton County Historical Society.*

2011. After two years of sharing space at that location, they finally moved into a new building of their own in 2013. Their current home is on Little Chicago Road, just north of Westfield Road (State Road 32).

Many of Hamilton County's earliest settlers were Quakers or Friends, most of whom lived in the country and worshiped in rural churches. When the first Friends moved into town, they initially attended other Noblesville churches rather than travel the distance to their home churches. (The nearest Friends Church was six miles away.)

By the late 1880s, however, enough Friends resided in Noblesville to consider organizing a meeting, and in 1890, Amos Sanders, a minister on the faculty of Union High School in Westfield, began to hold cottage meetings every Sabbath. Funds collected at those services were enough to rent a hall in the Fishers Building on the northeast corner of the town square.

The Fishers Building was sold early in 1892, but plans were already in place for the construction of a Friends church on the southwest corner of

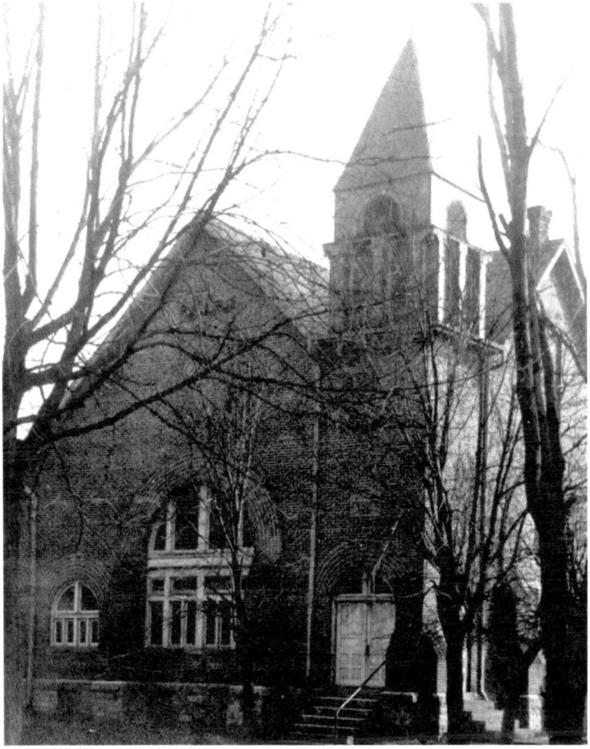

First Friends Church (1892) with its tower. The tower was later removed permanently due to water leakage. *Hamilton East Public Library.*

11th and Division Streets. While the congregation waited for the church to be finished, services were held on the third floor of the courthouse. The new brick church's dedication ceremony that fall was so well attended, a tent had to be set up for an overflow meeting across the street on the Second Ward school grounds.

The Friends continue to worship in the Division Street church today, making it, along with the First Presbyterian, the oldest Noblesville churches still in use.

Like the Friends, Catholics have long had a presence in the Noblesville area but haven't always had a church. As far back as 1836, a Shelbyville priest came on horseback to conduct Mass. Later, priests came from Peru, Frankfurt and Lebanon.

During the gas boom years of 1899 to 1904, Noblesville actually had a parish named St. Vincent de Paul, but when the gas ran out, forcing the local glass factory to shut down, the parish also closed. For the next forty years, Noblesville's Catholics had to travel to Indianapolis or Cicero to hear Mass.

In 1944, the Montfort Fathers, a religious community from New York, established a permanent parish in Noblesville, Our Lady of Grace. The following year, they purchased the frame church originally used by the Presbyterians and moved it to 11th Street.

As the county's Catholic population increased, the Our Lady of Grace congregation split twice, once in 1955 when Our Lady of Mount Carmel was formed in Carmel and again in 1980, when St. Louis de Montfort was established in Fishers. Noblesville's own growth resulted in the construction of a new Our Lady of Grace Church on 10th Street in 1974, but by the late 1980s, it was determined even larger facilities would be necessary in the future. The current Our Lady of Grace Church at 191st Street and State Road 37 was dedicated in 1991.

A handful of Jewish families have called Noblesville home since the middle of the nineteenth century despite the fact the closest synagogue was in Indianapolis. Although some family members married out of the faith and/or converted to Christianity, others retained their Jewish heritage. Several have played prominent roles in Noblesville's social, economic and political development. The Levinsons, Josephs, Haases and Zeckels operated successful clothing stores on the courthouse square at various times. Three generations of the Dorman family ran Dorman's Paint and Wallpaper store before it closed. The Smith family's Lusco Corporation, which has also seen three generations of owners, is still in business.

The Lutherans are comparatively new to Noblesville. Christ Lutheran Church, at 186th Street and State Road 37, is the oldest Lutheran church in the city, having been established in 1931. However, Bethel Lutheran Church, which moved to Noblesville (206th Street and Cumberland Road) in 1998, is one of the oldest congregations of any denomination in the county. It originated in Cicero in 1856.

Other current Noblesville churches established fifty or more years ago include: Calvary Baptist (organized 1910), the First Church of God (1930), the First Church of the Nazarene (1932), Green Valley Church of Christ (1949) and St. Michael's Episcopal (1954.) In addition, Lakeview Wesleyan has a complicated history that's difficult to track, but is believed to date back to 1895.

The Seventh-day Adventists and the Christian Science Society also were present in Noblesville for decades, but they are not currently represented in the city.

Noblesville's churches, particularly the Methodist, Christian, Presbyterian and Friends, have a long history of cooperation. During the last two centuries, it wasn't unusual for their congregations to join together to hold union services in response to various events.

Perhaps the largest such gathering was a revival staged by nationally known evangelist Bob Jones in January 1915. A temporary tabernacle, designed to seat nearly three thousand, was constructed at the old fairgrounds, across 10th Street from First Ward School. During the month-long event, services at twelve of Noblesville's churches were cancelled to allow parishioners to attend the meetings at Jones's tabernacle instead.

Noblesville's church congregations also share common ground—both figuratively and literally—in the city's two main cemeteries, Riverside (the "Old Cemetery") and Crownland (the "New Cemetery.")

As its name suggests, Riverside is located on the east bank of the White River in downtown Noblesville, between Maple Avenue and Cherry Street. The Hamilton County Art Center (the former First Baptist Church) is on the cemetery's eastern edge, and Noblesville's Veterans Memorial, dedicated in 2008, lies on the north side.

It's not clear exactly when Riverside was established. A large stone engraved with "1824" sits near the south entrance, but it was placed there in 1941 and merely represents the date believed to have been the first year the cemetery was in use. The stone itself was taken from the old Levinson home when it was razed.

In earlier years, an even larger stone, brought from the farm of Judge William Garver across the river, served as a speaker's stand. Many a

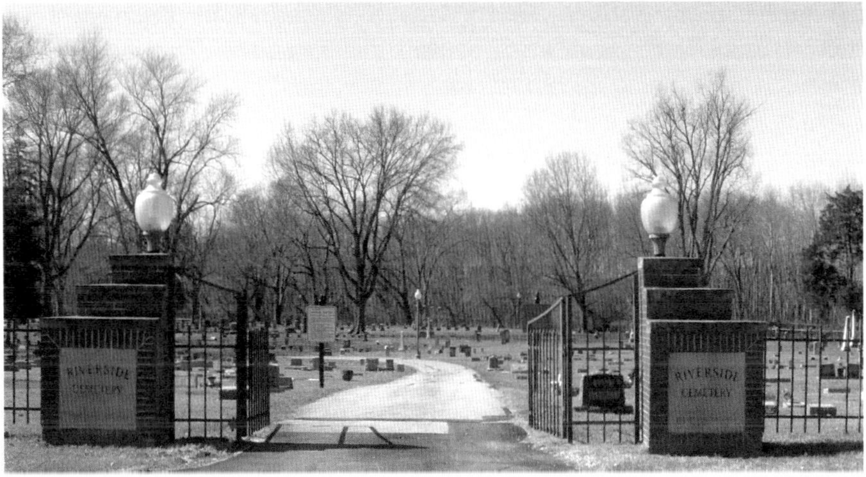

North entrance to Riverside Cemetery. *Nancy A. Massey.*

Decoration (Memorial) Day speech was delivered from Garver's stone before it was replaced by the cement platform near the center of the cemetery.

Riverside is the final resting place of many of Noblesville's earliest settlers. Among the prominent names found there are Indiana Adjutant General William Winship Conner and his son, John C. Conner, a two-term U.S. congressman from Texas; Reverend Barney Stone, pastor of the First Baptist Church; and Judge William Garver. Many American veterans also are buried there—the earliest from the War of 1812—as is one Canadian solder, John W. Cowie.

Riverside's location next to the White River made it vulnerable to flooding—it was devastated by the Great Flood of 1913—and is undoubtedly one of the reasons Crownland Cemetery on Monument Street eventually became Noblesville's main burial ground.

The oldest part of Crownland lies east of James Drive. For over one hundred years, an iron fence guarded those graves, but the only portions of the historic fence remaining are the main gate and a short section along the west side. Today, Crownland is unenclosed and stretches from 19th Street to 16th Street.

The cemetery's first burial was that of three year-old Clark Cottingham in November 1867. His grave is located near the main Monument Street entrance.

A large number of Noblesville's most prominent citizens have been buried in Crownland. Pioneers William and Elizabeth Conner (moved from Riverside), U.S. Congressman James L. Evans, businessman Leonard Wild, Milwaukee madam Helen "Dirty Helen" Worley Cromell, stunt driver Earl "Lucky" Teter, race car driver Bryan Clauson, and Fascist writer and spiritualist William Dudley Pelley are just a few.

Additionally, there are two mausoleums. The Longley mausoleum contains the remains of Indiana's first state fire marshal, William E. Longley, and other members of his family, including his son-in-law, Noblesville mayor Emmet Fertig. The Levinson mausoleum holds Harry Levinson, founder of the Indianapolis clothing stores; his wife, Nettie; and their son, famous fashion designer Norman Norell.

Three war memorials are located in the original graveyard. The oldest and largest of these is the Civil War monument, an octagonal marble pillar over twenty feet tall located at the south end of the cemetery. Dedicated in an 1868 ceremony attended by Indiana governor Conrad Baker, it contains the names of all Hamilton County soldiers who fought in the "Rebellion of 1861." A short distance to the north, next to a Civil War–era cannon

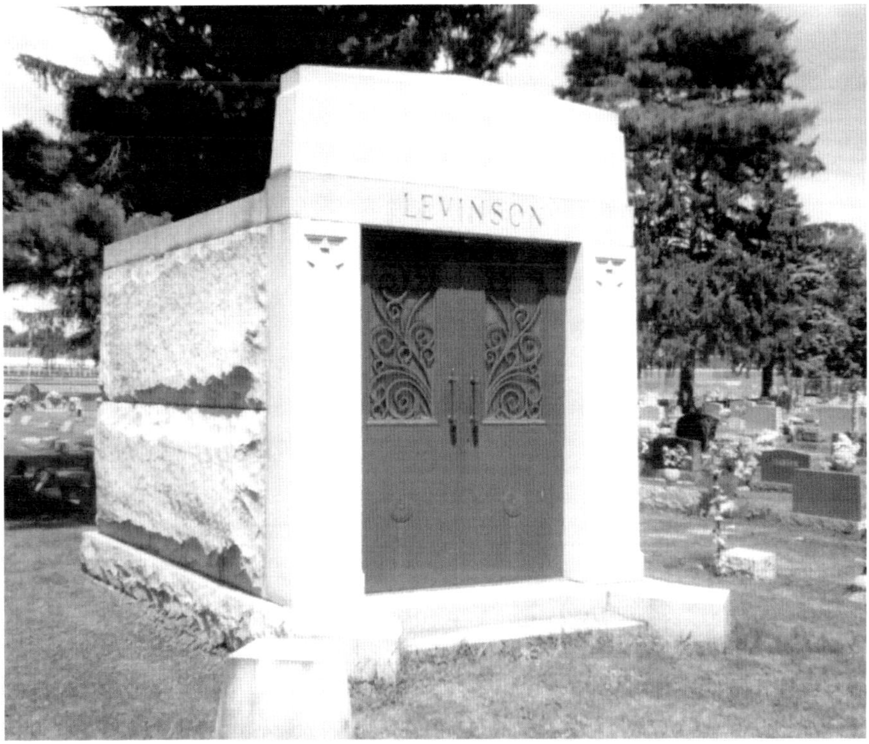

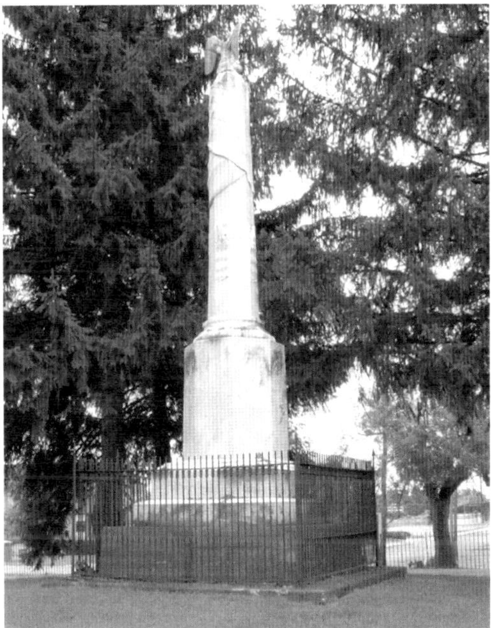

Above: Levinson mausoleum constructed shortly after the death of Harry M. Levinson in 1930. *Nancy A. Massey*.

Left: The Civil War monument at Crownland Cemetery. *Nancy A. Massey*.

and the graves of Civil War soldiers, is a smaller memorial to that war's unknown dead erected in 1900 by the Women's Relief Corps, an auxiliary of the Grand Army of the Republic. A third monument honoring Gold Star veterans who served in World War II, Korea and Vietnam lies on the east edge of the cemetery in the section where veterans of wars since the Civil War are buried.

An area dedicated to infants, Babyland, is located on the north side of the older part of the cemetery.

In addition to Riverside and Crownland, there are several smaller cemeteries in Noblesville Township.

NOBLESVILLE'S OTHER CEMETERIES

Bradley Cemetery, on a small hill next to the loading dock of a business at 15232 Stony Creek Way.

Caylor Family Cemetery, on the east side of Stony Lane, about 300 feet south of State Road 38.

Gascho-Trissal Cemetery, one block east of 17th and Clinton.

Gray Cemetery, north of Gray Friends Church on the northeast corner of 146th Street and Gray Road.

Hurlock Cemetery, on the south side of 166th Street at Stony Ridge Drive. (It's also been called Stony Creek Cemetery, but shouldn't be confused with the cemetery of the same name in Wayne Township.)

Tharp-Mott (Thorpe) Cemetery, on the west side of Little Chicago Road, just south of Sand Brook Drive.

Weaver Cemetery, on the east side of Cherry Tree Road, at the third curve south of 160th Street.

Zimmer Cemetery, on the north side of 206th Street, a little east of Overdorf Road.

Additionally, Metsker Cemetery, now destroyed, is believed to have been north of State Road 32, near where Sly Run branches off Cicero Creek.

7

SPREADING THE NEWS

Over the years, Noblesville's residents have been able to keep up on events going on around them through a variety of sources. The earliest of these—apart from the proverbial grapevine—was their local newspaper.

The first such publication, aptly titled *The Newspaper*, appeared on January 12, 1837. It cost readers two cents a week, or one dollar per year in advance. Among the items included in the initial issue were part of an address to Congress by the president of the United States, public notices, advertisements for local businesses, a list of letters to be picked up at the "Post Office at Noblesville, Ia." ("Ia." was the accepted abbreviation for Indiana at that time) and a poem, "The Buccaneer to His Crew."

The man behind *The Newspaper* was Lucius Hannibal Emmons, one of three brothers from Vermont who made Noblesville their home for several years. All three men played an active role in the town's development. The oldest brother, Francis Whitefield Emmons, was a minister, writer and educator who laid out Noblesville's second addition and launched plans for the county seminary. Another brother, William Augustus Emmons, was a saddler and merchant who platted Noblesville's first and third additions, and served as an associate judge of the Hamilton County court. Lucius Emmons himself served as a probate judge in addition to his publishing duties.

When *The Newspaper* proved unprofitable, Lucius Emmons suspended operations with the March 22, 1838 issue and left town. During his absence, an attempt was made by another man to revive the publication, but it didn't last.

Emmons returned to Noblesville in 1842 and tried again with *The Little Western*, which was published weekly from June 4, 1842, through January 25, 1845. Sometime around the latter date, Emmons moved to Washington, D.C., where he'd been appointed to a clerical position.

Five years later, while returning to Noblesville, Emmons contracted cholera. Although he managed to make it home, he died soon after his arrival and set off a serious epidemic that killed a number of the town's residents.

Noblesville saw many more newspapers come and go over the years. Some went under so quickly little is known about them aside from their names. Most were weeklies affiliated with a political party. In fact, at times during the nineteenth and early twentieth centuries, as much space—or more—was devoted to the platform of the party controlling the newspaper as was given to the events of the day. When two newspapers of opposing parties operated in town at the same time, sniping at each other in print was a common practice, and attendance figures reported for local events could vary widely, depending upon which party the event favored and which paper published the story.

Noblesville's two longest-running newspapers have both gone through several name variations but are generally known as the *Ledger* and the *Times*. The *Ledger* was a Republican paper. The *Times* originally supported the Democratic Party, but today is independent.

The *Ledger* was created when William Bodenhamer and Oscar Miles purchased the *Hamilton County Register* and merged it with the *Commercial*. The first issue went to print on September 8, 1871. In 1881, after several changes in ownership, the *Ledger* was sold to the owners of the *Republican* and became the *Republican-Ledger*. Another set of owners shortened the name back to the *Ledger* in August 1887, and a month later turned it into the *Daily Ledger*. The following year, the weekly version became the *Hamilton County Ledger*.

In 1914, both the weekly and daily papers were sold to the Enterprise Publishing Company, owned by brothers Charles S. and E.E. (Edward Everett) Neal. The Neals merged their newspaper, the *Enterprise*, with the *Ledger*; changed the name of their publishing company to the Noblesville Daily Ledger Inc.; and stopped publication of the *Hamilton County Ledger*.

The Neal family ran the *Noblesville Daily Ledger* for seventy-one years. Charles initially served as publisher, while E.E. was the editor. When E.E. retired in the mid-1940s, he sold out to Charles, who eventually passed the business on to his son, Ralph. Ralph published the *Ledger* from 1959 to 1965, then Ralph's sons James (Jim) and John, took over.

NOBLESVILLE'S NEWSPAPERS

The Newspaper (1837–1838)
Intelligencer (1839, Whig)
Magician and the *Hamilton Gazette* (both 1840)
The Little Western (1842–1845, Democrat)
Plain Dealer (1849, Independent)
News (late 1840s or early 1850s. It may have also been called the *True Whig*. It was sold in 1854 and renamed *Hoosier Patriot*. In 1862, it became the *White River Clipper* and the *Hamilton County Register* in 1869.)
Hoosier Patriot (1854-1862, Republican)
White River Clipper (1862-1868)
Reconstructionist (1866, radical Republican)
Hamilton County Register (1869-1871)
Commercial (Established in 1870. It merged with the *Hamilton County Register* in 1871 to become the *Ledger*.)
Ledger (1871–2009, Republican)
Independent (Founded in 1874. It became the *Democrat* in 1876, reverted back to the *Independent* in 1877 and became the *Democrat* again in 1888. It operated under that name until ceasing publication in July 1901. The following December, it was resurrected as the *Hamilton County Democrat* and continued until 1904. In 1905, new owners changed its party affiliation to Republican and renamed it the *Enterprise*.)
Hamilton County Democrat (1901–1904)
Republican (1880 to 1881, when it merged with the *Ledger*)
Republican-Ledger (1881–1887)
Standard (1884, Republican)
Tribune (1895 to 1897, Republican)
Times (1904–present, originally Democrat, now Independent)
Enterprise (1905, Republican. It merged with the *Ledger* in 1914.)
Free Lance (1906, Independent)
Noblesville Topics (1974–1981)
Noblesville Telegraph (1981–1987)
Noblesville Image (1999–2001)
Current in Noblesville (2009–present)
Hamilton County Reporter (2013–present)

In addition to their work with the newspaper, Jim and John Neal were both politically active. John was a member of the Noblesville Common Council for twelve years and served as mayor of Noblesville twice. Jim was secretary of the Indiana Republican Party for eleven years and acted as a delegate to the Republican National Convention three times.

Jim Neal may be best remembered, however, for a 1965 *Ledger* column that criticized Judge Edward F. New Jr.'s plans to crack down on traffic offenders. The judge responded to the column by having Neal arrested for contempt of court. The resulting case, which raised the issue of freedom of the press and made national news, dragged on for three years and reached the Indiana Supreme Court before the charge was finally dismissed.

In 1985, the Neals sold the *Ledger* to a group headed by LeRoy Stauffer. The following year, Stauffer bought the *Topics* weekly papers and merged them with the *Ledger* to form the Topics Suburban Newspapers Inc. In 1993, that company was purchased by Central Newspapers Inc., the parent company of the *Indianapolis Star* and *Indianapolis News*. Three years later, the *Ledger* was moved from its longtime home in downtown Noblesville to a new building in Fishers.

When Gannett, the country's largest newspaper chain, bought Central Newspapers Inc. in 2000, it was the beginning of the end for the *Ledger*. In 2002, the paper, then known as the *Daily Ledger*, was cut back to twice a week and renamed the *Noblesville Ledger*. In 2009, it became the *Noblesville Star* and was delivered weekly with the *Indianapolis Star*. Two years later, the *Noblesville Star* was absorbed into the *Indianapolis Star*'s Local Living section and ceased to exist—a sad end for a newspaper that had served Noblesville for 140 years.

The *Ledger*'s Democratic counterpart, the *Times*, actually began in Atlanta, Indiana, as the *Atlanta Herald*. In 1904, the owner, W.H. Roney, moved the weekly publication to Noblesville and renamed it the *Times*. Another paper, the *Free Lance*, was published in the *Times* office for a few months in 1906 and may have been a daily edition of the *Times*.

In 1907, the latest of several owners changed the paper's name to the *Hamilton County Times*. Eventually, its frequency was increased to three times a week. Later, another set of owners cut it back to a weekly again.

Daily M. Hudler bought the newspaper in 1917, and it remained in the hands of the Hudler family for the next eighty-two years. During their ownership, the *Times* was published as a weekly, except for a short period from 1922 to 1923 when it again appeared three times a week.

Renamed the *Noblesville Morning Times* in the early 1920s, the newspaper was run by Daily Hudler until his death in 1946, although he nearly sold it

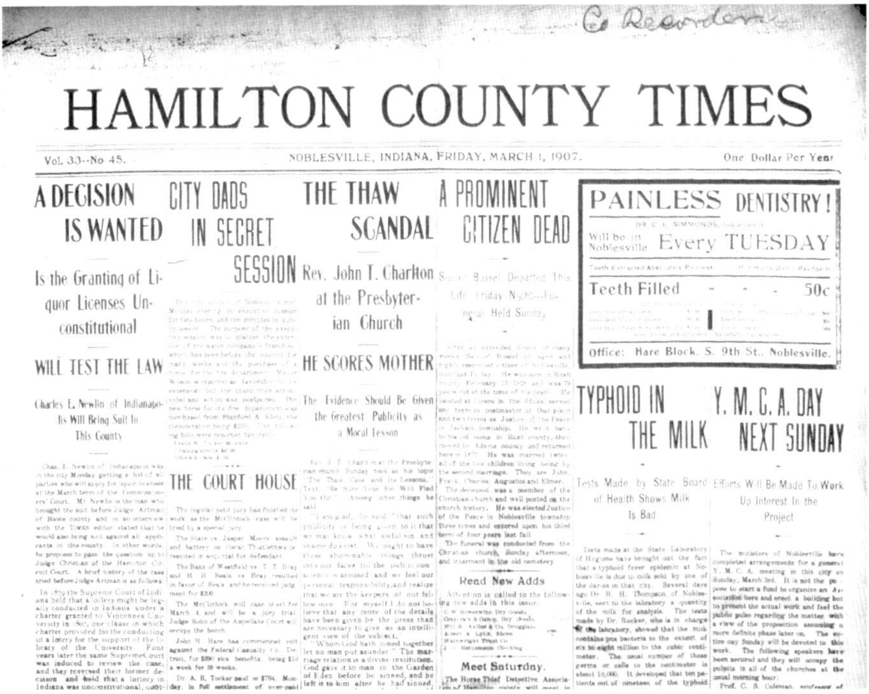

HAMILTON COUNTY TIMES

Vol. 33--No 45. NOBLESVILLE, INDIANA, FRIDAY, MARCH 1, 1907. One Dollar Per Year

A DECISION IS WANTED

Is the Granting of Liquor Licenses Unconstitutional

WILL TEST THE LAW

Charles E. Newlin of Indianapolis Will Bring Suit In This County

CITY DADS IN SECRET SESSION

THE COURT HOUSE

THE THAW SCANDAL

Rev. John T. Charlton at the Presbyterian Church

HE SCORES MOTHER

The Evidence Should Be Given the Greatest Publicity as a Moral Lesson

A PROMINENT CITIZEN DEAD

Read New Adds

Meet Saturday.

PAINLESS DENTISTRY!

Will be in Noblesville Every TUESDAY

Teeth Filled - - - 50c

Office: Hare Block, S. 9th St., Noblesville.

TYPHOID IN THE MILK

Tests Made by State Board of Health Shows Milk Is Bad

Y. M. C. A. DAY NEXT SUNDAY

Efforts Will Be Made To Work Up Interest In the Project

Hamilton County Times masthead. *Hamilton East Public Library, microfilm,* Hamilton County Times, *Friday, March 1, 1907, p. 1.*

in 1941. When the would-be buyer attempted to pay with $10,000 in cash, Hudler became suspicious and called off the sale. It was soon revealed that the "Mr. Henderson" who'd wanted to purchase the business was actually William Dudley Pelley, leader of the Fascist Silver Shirts. (Pelley later settled in Noblesville and established his own printing firm, the Fellowship Press Inc., in the old box factory on the south edge of town.)

Daily's son, L. Reid Hudler, became the *Times*'s publisher and the president of the family printing business, Hudler Press Inc., after his father's death. Under Reid Hudler, the newspaper became the *Noblesville Times* in 1966. When Hudler died in 1973, his widow, Martha, took over and continued family control of the paper until 1999.

After Martha Hudler sold the *Times* in 1999, former Noblesville mayor Mary Sue Rowland and her husband, Ted, kept it alive for about four years, then sold it to Schurz Communications of South Bend in 2003. Schurz turned the *Times* into a daily publication, the *Noblesville Daily Times*, to fill the void created by the loss of the *Ledger*. By 2008, however, economic concerns had forced the company to attempt to sell the paper. Failing to find a buyer, the *Times* ceased publication at the end of August.

The newspaper returned to circulation in October after being purchased by the Paper of Montgomery County (known today as Sagamore News Media). Currently, the print edition of the *Times*, as it's now officially known, is published every day except Tuesday and Sunday. An electronic edition has been available since 2008.

In 2013, the *Times* was joined by another newspaper, the *Hamilton County Reporter*. The *Reporter*, which covers the entire county, but is based in Noblesville, appears in print weekly and offers a daily edition online.

Two additional local periodicals are the *Hamilton County Business Magazine* and *Current in Noblesville*. The *Hamilton County Business Magazine*, founded in 2008, is a bimonthly publication focusing primarily on the area's business community. *Current in Noblesville*, a free, tabloid-style paper, has been published weekly since 2009. Both are available online.

Noblesville residents acquired another means of communication around 1883 when the Central Union Telephone Company brought telephone service to town. Central Union was a part of the Bell System, which at that time had a monopoly and behaved that way. The company's high rates, lack of reliability and arrogant attitude left many customers grumbling.

One of those customers, Eugene L. Brown, the druggist at the Corner Drug store, became so fed up with Bell's outrageous fees, he decided to take action. As soon as the patent on Bell's telephones expired in 1893, Brown organized some of the city's prominent citizens into the Noblesville Telephone Company and engaged a Kokomo man, P.C. Burns, to supply the telephones. Burns had been manufacturing phones in St. Louis before Bell's exclusive claim to those apparatuses was upheld by the Supreme Court, and he had no qualms about striking back at the company that had put him out of business.

The only real problem the Noblesville men faced was the switchboard. Bell still owned the patents to that part of the equipment and would for some time to come. Brown found a way around the hurdle, however, by constructing a simple switchboard similar to the one used by the local telegraph company.

Believed by some to have been the first independent telephone company in the country, the Noblesville Telephone Company served the town for about five years before being sold to the Central Union Telephone Company for a tidy sum. Central Union then granted a franchise for a Noblesville telephone exchange to the New Long Distance Telephone Company. The franchised

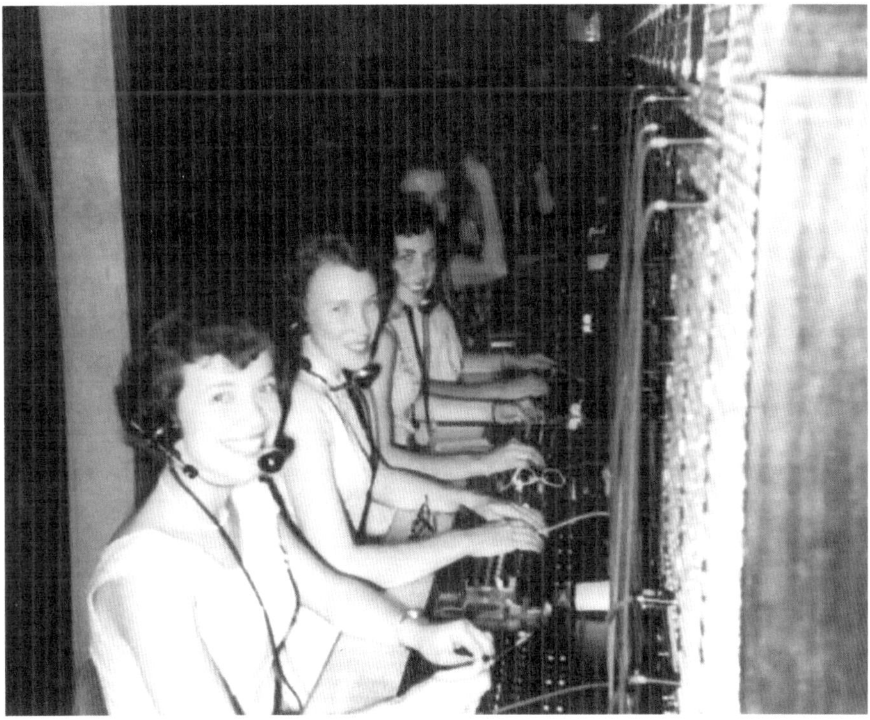

Telephone operators at switchboard. *Hamilton County Historical Society.*

company, the Home Telephone Company, began operations in 1899 and continued to serve Noblesville until the early 1950s.

In 1953, Noblesville's telephone company, known once again as the Noblesville Telephone Company, was acquired by Indiana Bell. It became an official Indiana Bell exchange on January 1, 1954.

Another milestone in local phone service was reached at 2:01 a.m. on August 17, 1958, when Noblesville became the third Indiana city to convert from a manual switchboard to direct distance dialing. The company offices were moved into a brand-new building on the southeast corner of 9th and Cherry Streets, and Noblesville was assigned the "Prospect" exchange. Residents quickly adapted to adding the Prospect-3 (773) prefix to all in-town calls.

In the latter part of the twentieth century and early twenty-first century, even more ways of keeping up with the neighborhood news arrived in the form of local radio and television stations.

WHYT-AM (1110), a daytime only radio station, signed on in 1973. Located north of Noblesville on State Road 19, it broadcast a mix of

Christian and popular music throughout the 1970s. In 1979, new owners altered the format and changed the call letters to WFBM. Two years later, they moved operations to Logan Street in downtown Noblesville. The format was changed yet again in 1987 when the station became WYIC and moved west of town to South Harbor Drive. Financial troubles took WYIC off the air in 1991.

Another station, WSQM-FM (90.9) or Catholic Radio Indy, operated out of the WHMB television studio on Greenfield Avenue when it signed on in 2011 but has since moved to Marion County.

In 1971, WHYT-AM's president, Dr. Wendell Hansen, established WURD-TV, one of the earliest religious television stations in the country. An independent station, WURD transmitted as UHF Channel 40 for only a few months. Its license and Greenfield Avenue studio were then acquired by Reverend Lester Sumrall and his LeSEA Broadcasting Corporation. The station, now known as WHMB, has been broadcasting Christian and family-oriented programs, as well as local sporting events, since 1972.

Noblesville acquired another television station in 1990 when Hamilton County Television, Channel 19 on the local cable outlet, began airing programs from a studio on 8th Street. Although the name was changed to Hoosier Cities Television for a few years during the 1990s, it eventually reverted back to Hamilton County Television or, more commonly, HCTV.

In 2002, under new ownership, the station was renamed HomeTown Television, but continued to broadcast community-oriented programming such as church services, public meetings and local sports from a studio in the Stony Creek Industrial Park near 146th Street and State Road 37. Four years later, operations were moved to South 9th Street in downtown Noblesville.

Channel 19 went off the air in 2011, but the type of local programming it once carried is currently available on the internet through the web-based Hamilton County Television, which broadcasts from its location on 10th Street.

8
PLANES, TRAINS AND AUTOMOBILES

When William Conner and Josiah F. Polk laid out the town of Noblesville on the west fork of the White River in 1823, it was hoped the river would play a key role in the region's transportation system, providing an easier means of moving people and goods than was available overland.

That didn't happen.

In 1831, the stranding of the steamboat *General Robert Hanna* on a sandbar south of Indianapolis forced central Indiana residents to admit that extensive travel on the White River was not in their future. The river contained too many obstructions and was too shallow for anything larger than a flatboat. Even flatboats could only make it so far upriver.

As it was, White River was as much an obstacle as it was an asset during Noblesville's earliest days. Before the first bridges were built, travelers' options for getting across the river were fairly limited. They could use small watercraft, brave the fords or take the ferry—when it was running.

There were three fords in the Noblesville area. The most prominent was located at what is today the west end of Plum Street. This ford later became known as the Strawboard Ford due to its proximity to the strawboard factory. Another shallow spot where crossing was possible was in the vicinity of 160st Street, near the site of Horseshoe Lodge on Horseshoe Prairie. A third ford, Potter's Ford, named for the family who owned the land, would eventually become the location of Potter's Bridge.

When the river was high, a ferry was available. According to Augustus Finch Shirts in his book *A History of the Formation, Settlement and Development of Hamilton County, Indiana*, William Carlin was granted a license to operate a ferry across the White River at Noblesville in 1846. Carlin built a flatboat large enough to accommodate a wagon and four horses, and rigged up a system of ropes and pulleys by which the boat could be pulled across the water. The ferry's tolls ranged from five cents for foot passengers, who were taken across in an old canoe, to thirty-five cents for a wagon and a team of four horses. Public messengers were transported for free.

It wasn't until the late 1850s that Noblesville's first bridge across the White River was erected at the west end of Logan Street. This wooden structure was replaced in 1867 by a covered bridge usually referred to as the "wagon bridge" to distinguish it from the city's railroad bridges. Logan Street's wagon bridge remained the only means of crossing the river in downtown Noblesville until the Conner Street bridge opened in 1930. At that time, the Logan Street bridge closed. In 1933, however, an iron bridge was constructed to replace the wagon bridge, and vehicles were once again able to cross the river at Logan Street. The iron Logan Street bridge was replaced in 1986.

In addition to the Conner and Logan Street bridges, three other bridges currently span the White River in Noblesville Township. The most northern of these, the 206th Street bridge, opened in 1988 to the relief of people living in Clare and Riverwood. For several years, the residents of those two small communities had been forced to go out of their way to cross the river because the bridge that had previously connected them, an eighty-year-old iron structure at 211th Street, closed in 1977 due to safety concerns. Similarly, the Cumberland Road bridge, which opened on Noblesville's northern outskirts in 1971, replaced nearby Potter's Bridge after Potter's Bridge was declared unsafe for vehicles. A third bridge was constructed at Field Drive in 2003 in response to Noblesville's population growth.

The most celebrated bridge in Noblesville is undeniably Potter's Bridge. This historic Howe Truss structure is the only remaining covered bridge in Hamilton County. Located about two miles north of downtown on 10th Street (Allisonville Road), it was built by Josiah Durfee & Company and was completed in 1871. The bridge was nearly dismantled in 1936 when State Road 13 was rerouted away from it, but a vehement protest by area farmers saved it. The rebuilt bridge was rededicated two years later and continued to be open to vehicles until 1971. Listed in the National Register of Historic Places in 1991, today it's the centerpiece of Potter's Bridge Park and foot traffic is still allowed across it.

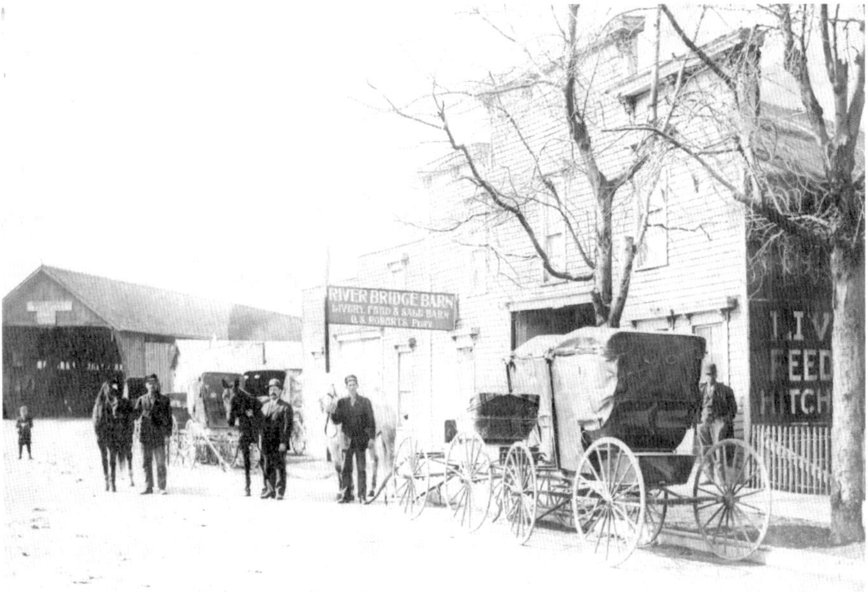

The old wagon bridge at Logan Street originally had a pedestrian walkway on both sides of the bridge until the flood of 1913 washed out the walkway on the upstream side. The livery pictured was torn down in 1928 to make way for the National Guard Armory. *Westfield Washington Historical Society, Roberts Collection.*

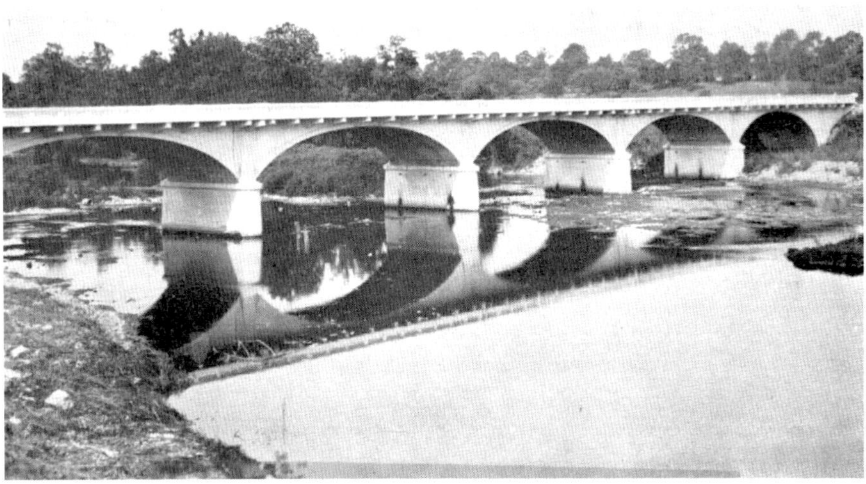

When the Conner Street bridge first opened, it also was known as the Bridge to Forest Park because it made it more convenient to reach the park. *Hamilton East Public Library, Forest Park Historical Postcards.*

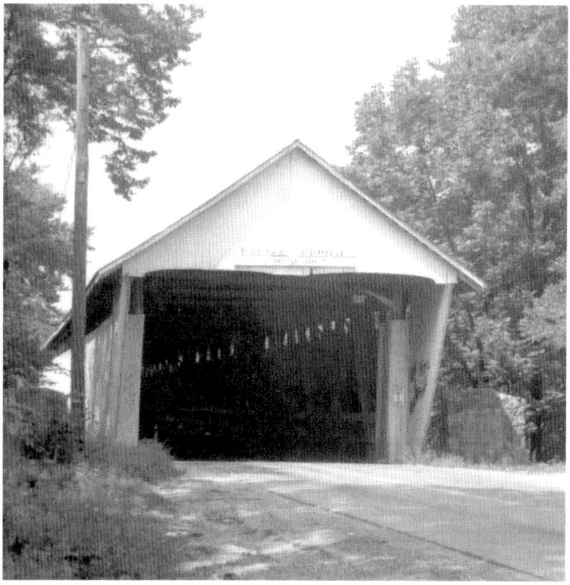

Potter's Bridge is the only surviving covered bridge in Hamilton County. *Hamilton County Historical Society.*

The old iron bridge over Stony Creek on State Road 238 (Greenfield Avenue) didn't fare as well. Constructed in 1915 to replace an earlier covered bridge, it was one of the few Baltimore Truss bridges left in Indiana. Although listed in the National Architecture and Engineering Record and in line to be added to the National Register of Historic Places, it was in such bad shape it was closed to traffic in 1981. Six years later, after its historic status was revoked, the bridge was torn down and replaced.

Additionally, there were once three railroad bridges across the White River. The Midland Railroad crossed at the west end of Vine Street, the Nickel Plate Railroad bridge angled to the northwest across the river from Clinton Street and the interurban bridge was located near what is today Field Drive. Only the Nickel Plate bridge still exists.

In 1836, hopes of large-scale water travel through the county were revived when the state legislature, spurred on by the success of New York's Erie Canal, passed the Mammoth Internal Improvement Act. The act provided for several major transportation projects, one of which was the construction of a system of canals throughout Indiana.

The Central Canal was planned to pass through the middle of the state, connecting the Wabash and Erie Canal in northern Indiana to the Ohio River. The canal's route would have taken it through Noblesville, running parallel to and a little east of the White River, but the state had overreached itself and was unable to pay for the project. Work halted in 1839 with only

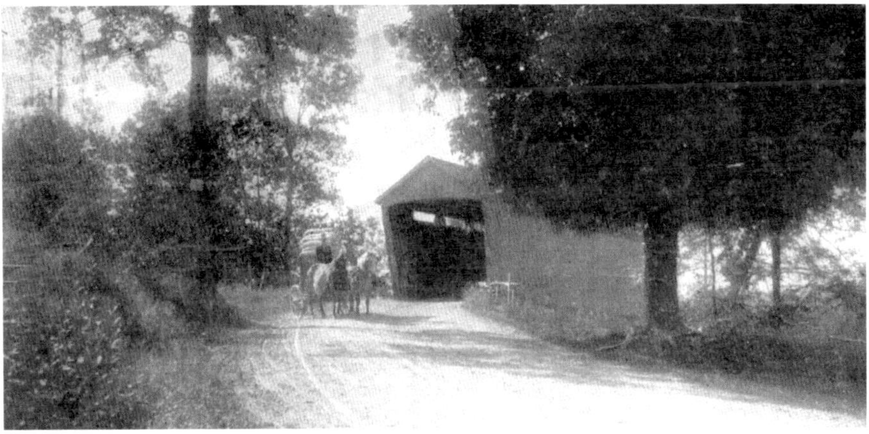

This covered Stony/Stoney Creek Bridge washed out in the spring flood of 1927. An iron bridge replaced it. *Hamilton County Historical Society.*

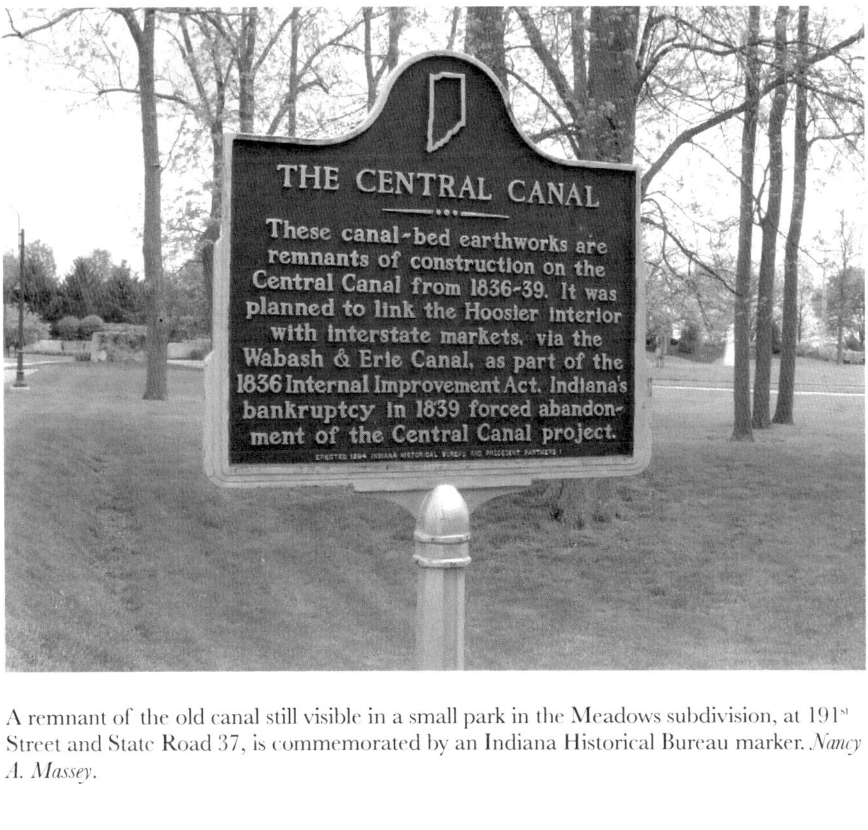

A remnant of the old canal still visible in a small park in the Meadows subdivision, at 191st Street and State Road 37, is commemorated by an Indiana Historical Bureau marker. *Nancy A. Massey.*

a small portion of the canal in Indianapolis finished. The State of Indiana, and many of its citizens who'd invested in the canals, were driven into bankruptcy, and Noblesville was left with an empty ditch.

With the White River proving largely unnavigable and the canal project shelved, Indiana's need to develop a good road system took on added importance.

The state's earliest roads were simple Indian paths like the Conner Trail, which brought the original settlers to Horseshoe Prairie. Narrow and meandering, they weren't made for wagons. The tracks the settlers carved out of the wilderness for themselves weren't much better. Moreover, those roads generally followed the easiest route possible and often had to be altered later when it was discovered they crossed private land.

After the acquisition of the New Purchase, the state legislature began planning many new roads through the area. At first, these state roads differed little from neighborhood roads. The only distinction was the number of marks blazed in the trees along the way—three for a state road, one for a neighborhood track. In later years, however, there were clear differences in size. Generally, state roads were sixty feet wide, while those maintained by the county board varied according to their importance. Cartways for individuals' use were only eighteen feet wide, township roads measured from twenty-four to thirty feet across and county roads were from thirty-three to forty feet in width.

Noblesville's proximity to Indianapolis, its status as a county seat and the fact that it was one of the oldest communities in the region ensured it a prominent place in the state's transportation network. Eventually, six different state roads passed through the city. State Road 238, also known as Greenfield Pike or Greenfield Avenue, was one of the earliest, angling southeast from Noblesville to Greenfield. State Roads 32 and 38, from Anderson and Pendleton, respectively, merge east of downtown Noblesville to become Conner Street, then separate again west of the White River, with State Road 38 heading to Sheridan and State Road 32 to Westfield. State Road 19 begins in Noblesville and travels north to the county line and beyond. State Road 37, originally the Noblesville bypass, is now the main north–south artery through Noblesville.

The sixth state highway, today's Allisonville Road (10th Street in downtown Noblesville), was designated State Road 13 during the early years of the twentieth century, but after that highway was re-routed to the east, it became first State Road 37, then 37A when the State Road 37 bypass was constructed, then simply Allisonville Road.

In addition to being served by the state roads, Noblesville's growth in recent years has expanded the city's boundaries so far east they now touch a federal highway, I-69.

Today, drivers can travel freely throughout Hamilton County, but from the 1860s to around 1890, the county's gravel roads were all turnpikes, owned and maintained by private companies that collected tolls from travelers. A company might own an entire road or just a section of it. Six tollgates were operated in the Noblesville area—one at Federal Hill on the Westfield road, one at the edge of Brown's Woods (today's Forest Park) on the road to Cicero, one just west of Stony Creek on the Greenfield Pike and three additional ones on the Strawtown Pike, the Clarksville Pike and the Indianapolis Pike.

In the early 1890s, these toll roads were all bought by the county and turned into free public highways. The last toll road in Hamilton County was Greenfield Pike, southeast of Noblesville. The old Greenfield Pike tollhouse, like many others in the county, was eventually turned into a private residence.

During that same period, Noblesville's city streets underwent a major change when Mayor James. W. Smith had them bricked. Not everyone was pleased with the improvement, however. Some residents were unhappy that so many of their beloved locust trees had to be destroyed when the streets were widened as part of the process. Today, sections of the old brick streets still exist on Logan and Clinton Streets between 10th and 16th Streets.

Another important event for local motorists was the installation of Noblesville's first "Stop and Go" signals, in 1924. Leslie Haines, who'd erected one of the first traffic signals in the country in nearby Carmel, was contracted to provide similar devices for Noblesville. The new lights were placed at 10th and Logan, 10th and Conner and 10th and Christian Avenue, and Mayor Horace Greely "Pop" Brown warned drivers they'd better obey them or face arrest.

Perhaps the most important development in Noblesville's transportation history was the arrival of the Peru and Indianapolis Railroad, the second railroad in the state and the first in Hamilton County.

When the first train chugged into Noblesville on March 11, 1851, it was met by hundreds of cheering, handkerchief-waving spectators. A daylong celebration followed, during which former Indiana governor David Wallace delivered an address at the courthouse, a brass band provided music and the ladies of the Presbyterian Church supplied dinner for the masses attending the festivities.

Like the Central Canal, the Peru and Indianapolis Railroad was intended to link the Wabash and Erie Canal in Peru with the state capital. Running up

8th Street in downtown Noblesville, the railroad became such a fixture that the street, which had originally been named Polk Street, came to be called Railroad Street in the years before the city's north–south thoroughfares were given numbers.

The railway experienced several changes in name and ownership. In 1887, it was bought by the Lake Erie and Western Railroad; in 1923, it became part of the New York, Chicago and St. Louis Railroad (nicknamed the "Nickel Plate" for its high standards); and in 1964, it was sold to the Norfolk and Western.

For eighty-one years, the railroad, generally called the Nickel Plate these days, carried presidents and common folk alike to Noblesville. Even after passenger service stopped in 1932, it continued to haul freight for many more years.

A new era was entered in 1995 when the Indianapolis to Tipton portion of the line was sold to the Hamilton County Port Authority (the cities of Noblesville and Fishers). Three years later, Hamilton County joined the two cities, and the name was changed to the Hoosier Heritage Port Authority. Various excursions, including the popular Indiana State Fair Train, were run on the line by Indiana Transportation Museum volunteers until 2015.

Noblesville's second railroad, the Anderson, Lebanon and St. Louis, arrived in 1877. Like the Nickel Plate, it also underwent several incarnations, becoming the Cleveland, Indiana and St. Louis Railway in 1882, the Midland

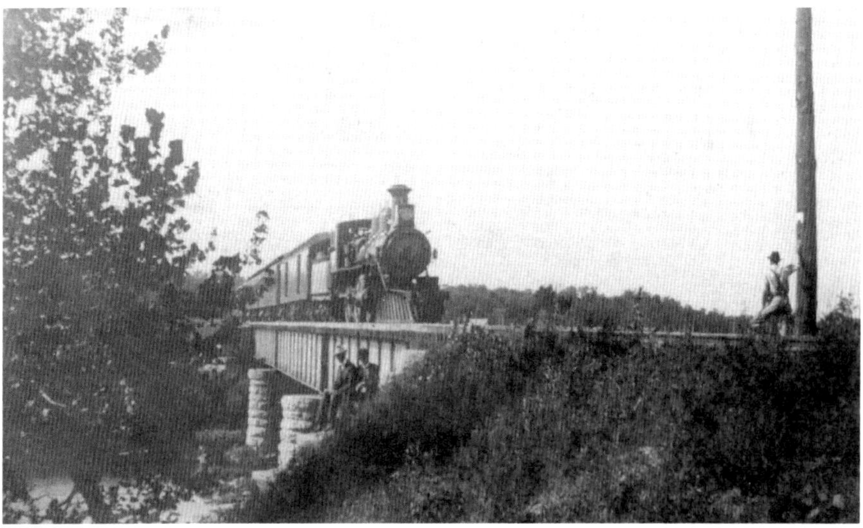

Lake Erie and Western Railroad bridge. *Hamilton East Public Library, Joe Roberts Collection.*

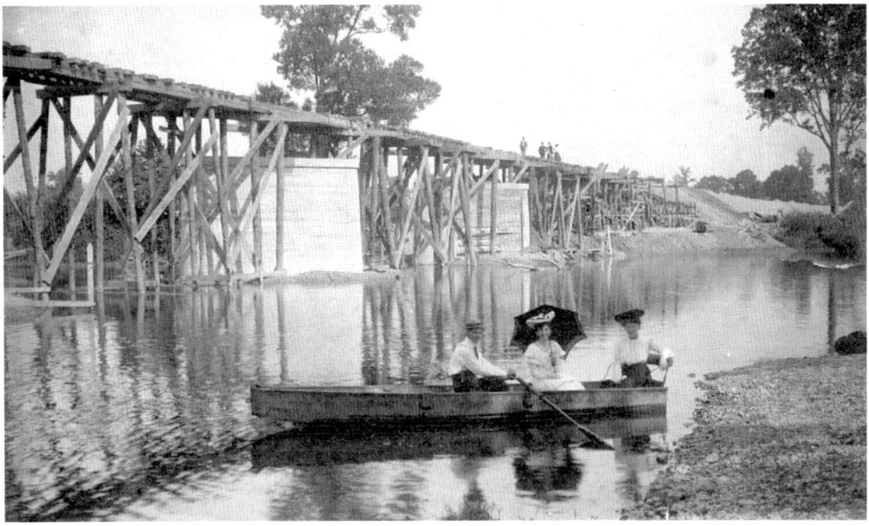

The construction of the interurban bridge over the White River. *Sid Davis.*

Railway in 1885, the Chicago and South Eastern Railway in 1891 and the Central Indiana Railway in 1903. It's best known as the Midland, however.

The Midland ran east and west through the county and followed Vine Street in Noblesville. Never as successful as the Nickel Plate, it had a reputation for rough rides and was notoriously slow—so slow in fact, passengers were said to be able to get off and hunt game or gather wildflowers while the train was in motion. It acquired the nickname "The Blackberry Route," because the conductor was known to make stops to allow riders to pick blackberries off the thick bushes that lined the tracks.

The Midland's tracks were abandoned in 1986 and ultimately removed. Today, the old Midland Railroad corridor is the Midland Trace Trail.

Noblesville's third railroad was quite different from the other two. Unlike the steam-powered Nickel Plate and Midland Railroads, the interurban ran on electricity. It was essentially a line of big, fast streetcars linking small towns and large cities all over the state—hence the term *interurban*.

The first interurban passenger car arrived in Noblesville on October 31, 1903, and was greeted by a large crowd of curious onlookers as it came up the tracks on 9th Street and stopped at the courthouse square. (The station, located on the southwest corner of 9th and Clinton Streets, wasn't constructed until 1906.)

The interurbans were an incredibly convenient means of travel. Cars ran every hour, from early in the morning until after midnight, and not only

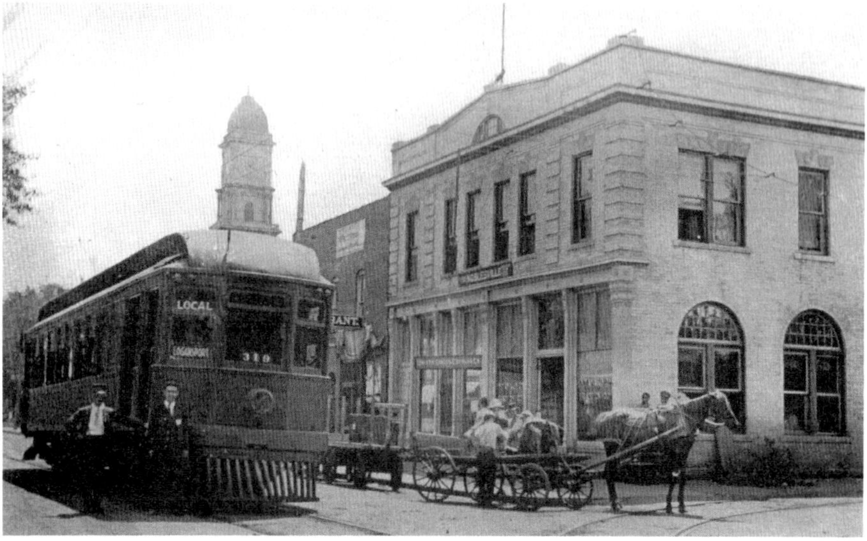

Union Traction Company Interurban Station. *Hamilton County Historical Society.*

could they be boarded at the stations, but local cars would also make stops out in the country for the convenience of farmers.

The interurban tracks came north from Indianapolis, entering Hamilton County at Home Place and continuing to Carmel. From there, they angled northeast to Noblesville, and from Noblesville, they ran north to Cicero, Arcadia and Atlanta, shadowing the Nickel Plate tracks to the Tipton County line.

In 1930, the company that owned the line, the Indiana Union Traction Company, became part of the Indiana Railroad System. By then, however, automobiles were taking over as the preferred form of travel, and the interurbans' days were numbered. The last interurban came through Noblesville on September 11, 1938.

Noblesville acquired yet another means of transportation on August 20, 1944, when Monte Jessup, a local road and bridge contractor, opened a ninety-two-acre private airport southeast of the city near the Firestone plant.

To launch the new facility, the State Civil Air Patrol and the Indiana State Guard conducted a mock invasion in which the Civil Air Patrol, playing the role of the enemy, attempted to take over the Firestone factory by dropping red fire bombs, yellow gas bombs and flour demolition bombs from their planes. The State Guard countered by attacking the "enemy" planes with aerial torpedoes representing antiaircraft fire. The guard, cheered

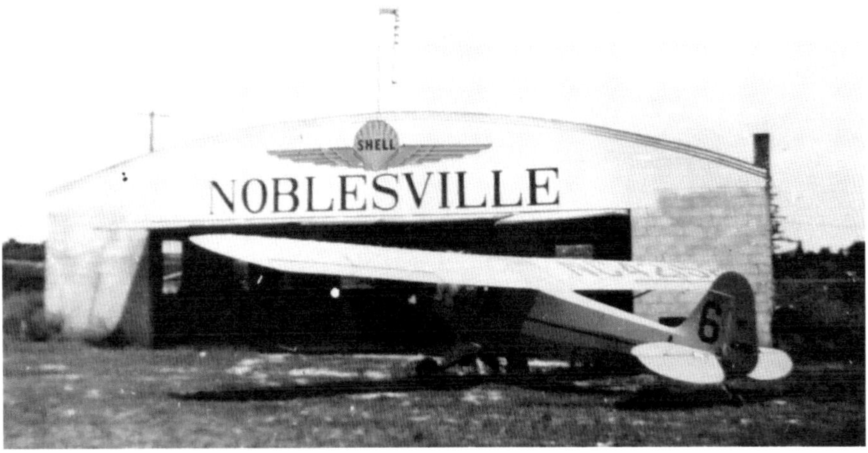

Noblesville Airport hangar now houses the Hamilton County Hazardous Waste Center. *Hamilton East Public Library, Joe Roberts Collection.*

on by several thousand spectators, ultimately captured their opponents' headquarters and won the day.

In 1947, new owners, the Noblesville Flying Service Inc., took over the airport. The company continued to offer civilian and G.I. flying instruction, sightseeing and passenger rides, as well as charter service, and completed the construction of a new hangar. The airport failed to generate enough business to be profitable, however, and it closed two years later. Jessup, who still owned the property, sold the buildings and three acres of land to the Hamilton County Highway Department. Today, the Hamilton County 4-H Fairgrounds sits on part of the old airport, and the Hamilton County Household Hazardous Waste Center occupies the old hangar.

In 1952, a new airstrip was established in a field east of State Road 37 and north of 166th Street. It served small aircraft in the area until 1984, when the landowners decided they wanted to farm the field instead. By then the airstrip was owned by Noblesville High School teachers Don Roberts and Larry Jacobi and was known as the Roberts-Jacobi Landing Strip.

The following year, Roberts and Jacobi acquired eighty acres about two miles from their old facility and laid out a new airport with a grass runway. Located on Promise Road, just north of 146th Street, the Noblesville Airport has been in operation ever since. The airport is open to the public and is home to the Noblesville chapter of the Experimental Aircraft Association (EAA).

9

LOCAL LANDMARKS

Throughout Noblesville's nearly two-hundred-year history there have been several structures, past and present, that have become well-known local landmarks.

Perhaps the most conspicuous of these is the Hamilton County courthouse, located on the square in downtown Noblesville. It's the fourth building to serve the county as a courthouse.

The first courthouse was a one-and-a-half-story log cabin built in 1826 at the intersection of 10th and Clinton Streets. After four years, the county commissioners ordered the construction of a replacement, a one-and-a-half-story frame building, which was to be located on the southwest corner of Logan and Anderson (10th) Streets. Before the building was finished, however, it was decided the public square was a more appropriate site, and construction was moved there. This frame courthouse was occupied from 1831 to 1837.

In 1837, the frame courthouse was replaced by a two-story brick structure with a cupola and a steeple. The county's business was transacted in that courthouse for nearly forty years, but by 1875, it was in sad shape. When one of the walls gave way during an important murder trial and the judge in the case refused to hold court there again, a proposal to replace the aging structure was put before the county's voters. Surprisingly, the proposal was voted down.

The negative vote slowed the movement to get rid of the courthouse, but didn't stop it, and in 1877, the commissioners went ahead with plans for a

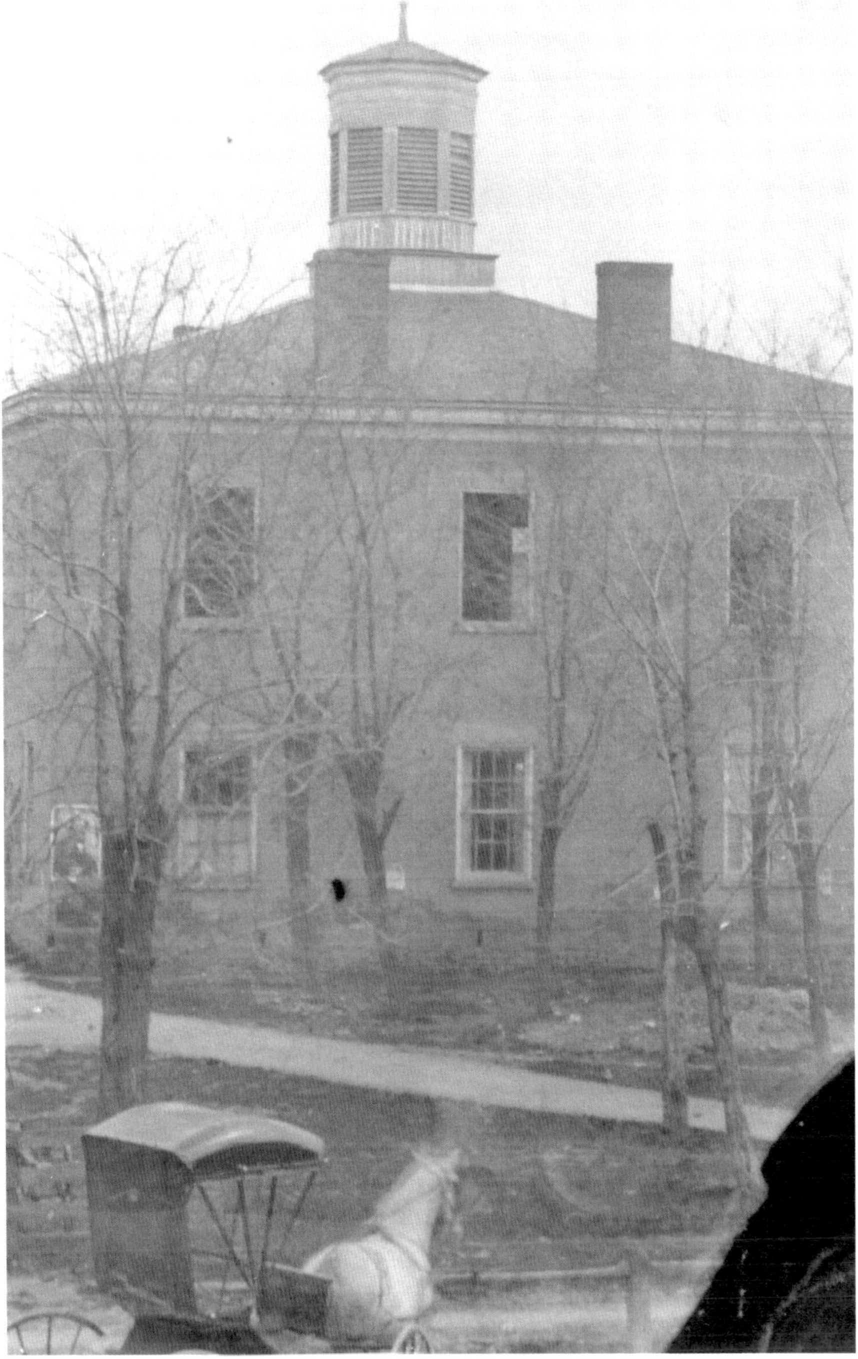

The 1837 brick courthouse. *Hamilton County Historical Society.*

new center of county government. On April 20, 1878, the cornerstone of the new courthouse was laid by members of the Masonic order—despite a protest from a group of citizens who objected to the participation of a secret society at the ceremony. Completed in 1879, the three-story courthouse has been the scene of some memorable trials, including the 1925 murder trial of Indiana Ku Klux Klan Grand Dragon D.C. Stephenson.

The entire courthouse square was placed in the National Register of Historic Places in 1978. However, after one hundred years, the old 1879 courthouse proved incapable of handling the county's escalating population. Rather than demolish the historic building, a decision was made to erect a second facility across the street. To clear the way for the new government center, all buildings west of the old courthouse between Conner and Logan Streets were torn down.

Dedicated in 1992, the 200,000-square-foot Hamilton County Government and Judicial Center currently contains most county government offices and the county court system. A tunnel connects it to the old 1879 courthouse, which, after undergoing a major renovation in 1994, has continued to house some county offices.

Next to the 1879 courthouse sits the Old Sheriff's Residence and Jail—the county's third jail. The first jail, a log building, was completed at the north edge of Riverside Cemetery in 1825. It was moved to the northwest corner of the town square a year later after the original site was judged unsuitable. In 1853, the log jail was replaced by a brick structure. This was the first jail to include a residence for the jailer.

The third jail, the Old Sheriff's Residence and Jail, opened in 1876. The county commissioners originally intended to place it on the northwest corner of the square like its predecessors, but switched to the southwest corner after businessmen on the south side of the square objected to the view they would have. The south end of the building, which is constructed of brick, was designed as living quarters for the sheriff and his family. (The sheriff's wife used to be responsible for feeding the inmates.) Prisoners were housed in the limestone cell block at the rear.

Although there's no truth to the rumor John Dillinger was once incarcerated in the jail, it has seen other notorious inmates. Robert and Willadene Wotring, a couple wanted by the FBI for check fraud, were held there in 1953. In 1950, long before he became the leader of the infamous Manson family, a teenaged Charles Manson was locked up there for car theft during an escape from the Indiana Boys School. D.C. Stephenson was housed at the jail during his trial, as well as during his subsequent appeals.

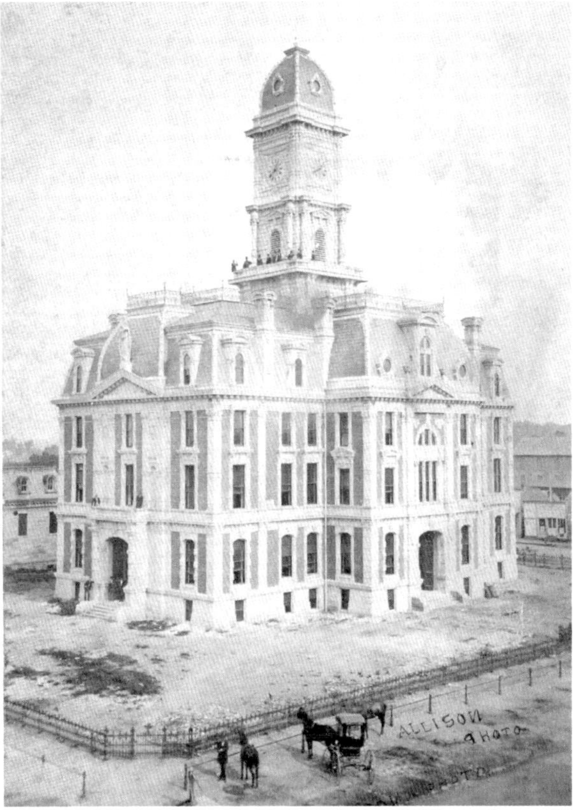

Left: The 1879 courthouse. *Hamilton County Historical Society*.

Below: Sheriff's residence, old jail and 1879 courthouse. *Hamilton County Historical Society*.

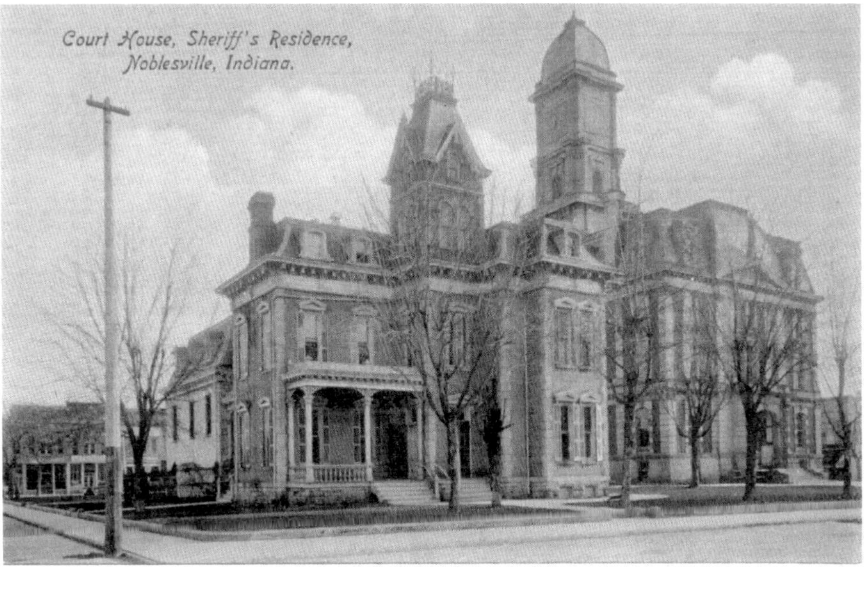

The 1876 jail served the county for about one hundred years before being replaced by a new building on Cumberland Road in 1977. That jail was in turn replaced in 1993 by another building at the same location. Since that time, the jail has become part of a larger complex that includes facilities for juvenile and female offenders, a community corrections center and the offices of the Hamilton County Sheriff's Department.

In 1979, the Old Sheriff's Residence and Jail was leased by the Hamilton County Historical Society. The building currently houses the society's Hamilton County Museum of History.

Noblesville's present city hall is just one of several in which the city's affairs have been conducted.

In 1870, the city hall shared space with the *Hamilton County Register* and other businesses in a building on the southeast corner of 9th and Logan Streets. From 1906 to 1955, Noblesville's municipal offices, including the fire department, were located on Maple Avenue between 8th and 9th Streets. That city hall was replaced in 1955 by a newer building erected on the same

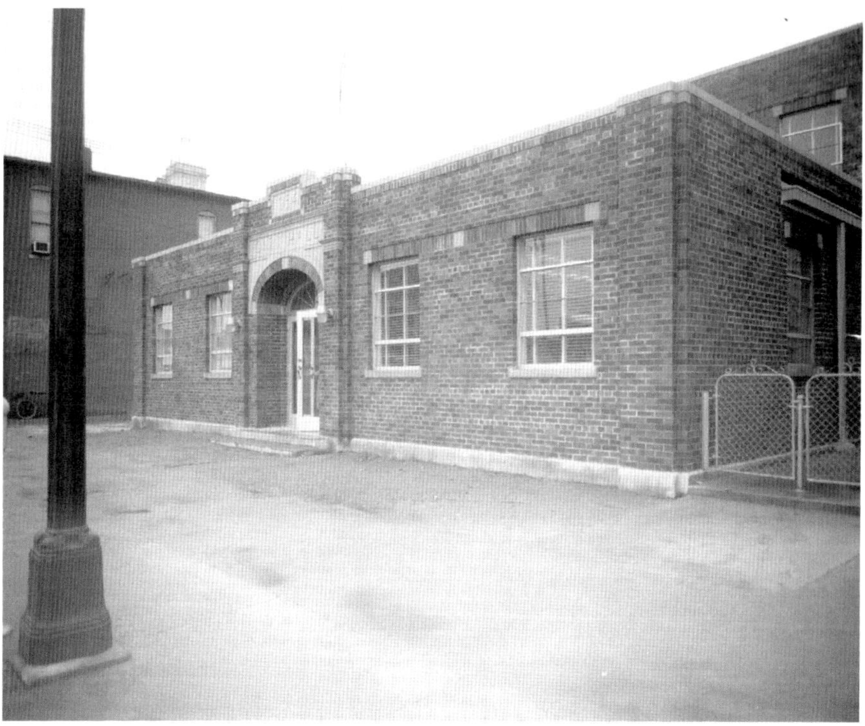

The 1955 city hall on 8th Street. *Hamilton County Historical Society.*

site and adjacent ground. The new 1955 city hall was an L-shaped structure with two main entrances—one on 8th Street and another on Maple Avenue, which was used for the fire department.

In 1987, the city renovated the former Carnegie library on the southeast corner of 10th and Conner Streets, and turned it into yet another city hall. As the population grew, however, more space was needed. In 2005, the nearby Hare and Axline homes and the Axline carriage house were relocated, and the Fertig home and the original Clancy's restaurant were demolished in order to make room for an entirely new building and parking area. The new city hall opened in November 2006 and was dedicated the following January. Designed to echo the architectural features of the Carnegie library it replaced, Noblesville's city hall now stretches from Conner Street to Maple Avenue.

The old Carnegie library, which became the 1987 city hall, also had a long history, dating back to 1856 when the first of a series of subscription libraries was established in Noblesville. When the Conner Street high school was dedicated in 1900, one of its rooms was reserved for use as a public library, and books from some of the town's early subscription libraries were combined with those of the school library to form the collection. This room served as Noblesville's public library or "reading room" until a group of women led by librarian Lulu Miesse launched a campaign to acquire a grant from philanthropist Andrew Carnegie for the construction of a new library building. They were successful, and Noblesville's Carnegie library opened in 1913.

Parnassus

Lulu Miesse was the driving force behind the Noblesville Public Library becoming one of the first libraries in the country to have a bookmobile. The retrofitted Dodge Brothers Commercial Car was dubbed "Parnassus" after the Christopher Morley novel *Parnassus on Wheels*, a tale about a traveling bookstore. From 1920 to 1922, Parnassus brought library services not only to rural Noblesville patrons but also to those in Wayne, White River and Fall Creek townships. Service was dropped from the townships in 1922, but the library's "book wagon" continued to travel around Noblesville until 1932.

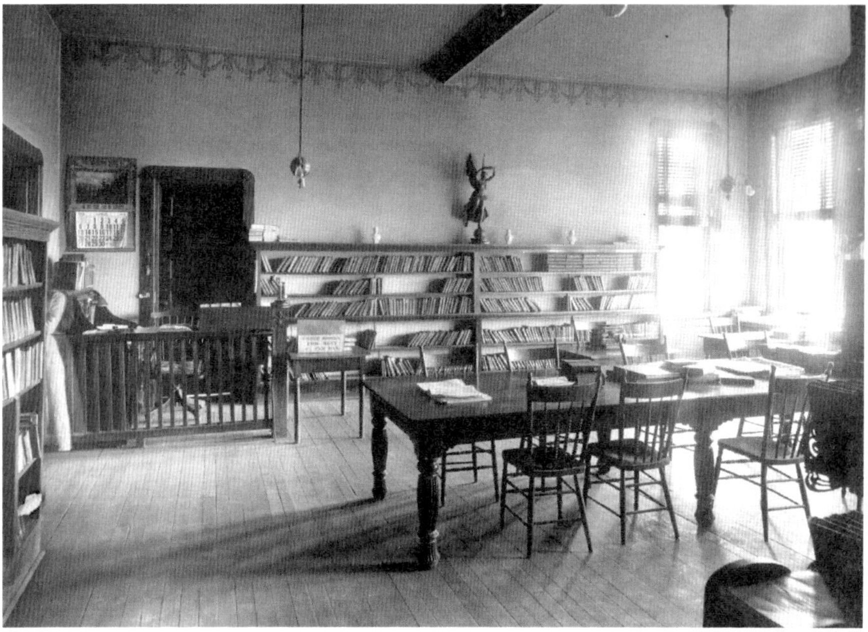

The "new" high school on Conner Street in 1900 included a "splendid large" room built especially for the public library called the Reading Room. *Hamilton East Public Library.*

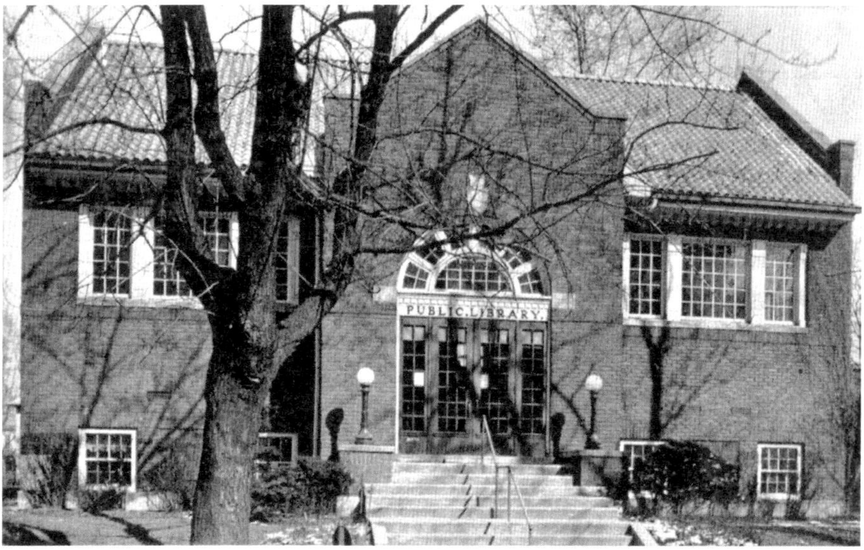

The Carnegie library was built for future growth to hold 10,000 volumes on its shelves. At the time of its dedication, the Noblesville Public Library had 4,500 books. It had an assembly room with a 225-seat capacity where literary groups and other organizations could hold meetings. *Hamilton East Public Library.*

Since 1986, Noblesville's public library has been located on Cumberland Road near the Hamilton County Jail. In 1993, when a new branch was constructed in Fishers, the two libraries became known collectively as the Noblesville-Southeastern Public Library. Ten years later, the name was changed to the Hamilton East Public Library.

Noblesville's post office has moved several times since being established in 1824. During the city's early years, it was located in various buildings around the courthouse square. The first building specifically constructed as a post office opened on Logan Street between 9th and 10th Streets in 1906. The post office remained there until 1932, when it moved into new quarters on the southwest corner of 9th Street and Maple Avenue. In 1989, the 1932 post office was replaced by the current building on Pleasant Street across from the Hamilton County Fairgrounds. The old 1932 post office was then remodeled to become the Noblesville Public Safety Building.

A block south of the Public Safety Building, on the northwest corner of 9th and Hannibal Streets, sits another city landmark, the Masonic Temple.

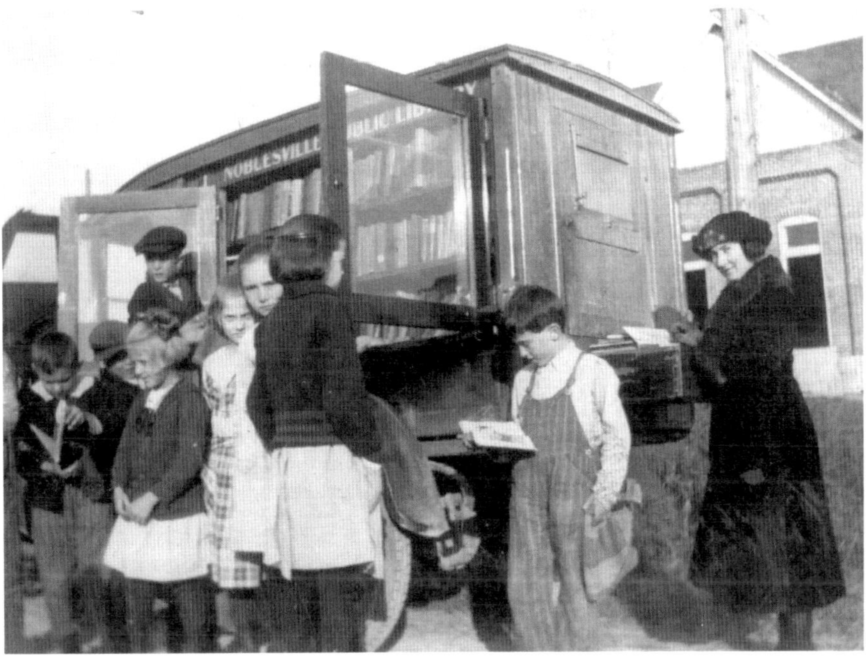

During its twelve years on the road, Parnassus went door to door throughout four townships. Miss Miesse is on the far right at a Noblesville township school stop. *Hamilton East Public Library*.

The temple is the first permanent home of Noblesville Masonic Lodge No. 57. Prior to the temple's construction, the Masons met in several different places around the square, including the old city hall building on the southeast corner of 9th and Logan Streets. (The Masonic square and compass symbol is still visible on the building.) The laying of the Masonic Temple's cornerstone in 1914 was an event celebrated by the entire city, with Masons from all over central Indiana in attendance. Dedicated the following year, the Masonic Temple has served both the Masons and the community ever since.

Riverview Hospital's history can be traced back to the privately owned Harrell Hospital and Sanatorium, located on 9th Street, half a block north of the courthouse square. The hospital was founded in 1909 by Drs. Samuel and Madison Harrell, although Dr. Samuel Harrell bought out his brother shortly after the opening. Designed to accommodate fifty patients, the hospital was considered quite impressive in its time. It boasted an electric elevator and Turkish baths, and each of its large, well-ventilated rooms came equipped with three electric buttons: one to call the head nurse, one to control the lights and one to operate a fan.

Dr. Harrell sold the hospital to the county in 1913. As the Hamilton County Hospital, the facility continued to treat patients at the 9th Street location for almost forty years. Eventually, more space was needed, however, and in 1951, the hospital moved into a new eighty-six-bed building west of town on Federal Hill. The following year, it was renamed Riverview Hospital, partly to highlight its wonderful view of the White River and partly to correct the erroneous impression held by some that, as a government institution, treatment was free.

In the years since then, the original Riverview Hospital has more than doubled in size through many renovations and additions. Now part of a growing network that includes off-site medical care facilities, the hospital was officially renamed Riverview Health in 2014 to acknowledge that expansion.

On the southeast corner of 10th and Harrison Streets, directly across from Dr. Samuel Harrell's former home, sits the small building which used to be Gran'Pa's candy store. Although vacant since the store's closing in 1976, it remains a fondly remembered landmark for several generations of Noblesville children.

Noblesville boasts several other listings in the National Register of Historic Places in addition to the courthouse square.

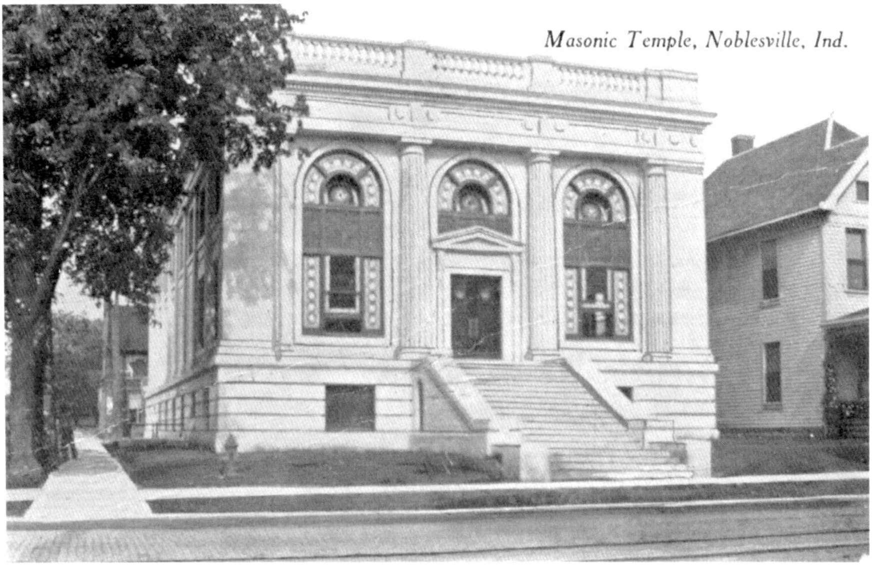

Masonic Temple designed by architect Don Graham, a Noblesville native. *Hamilton County Historical Society*.

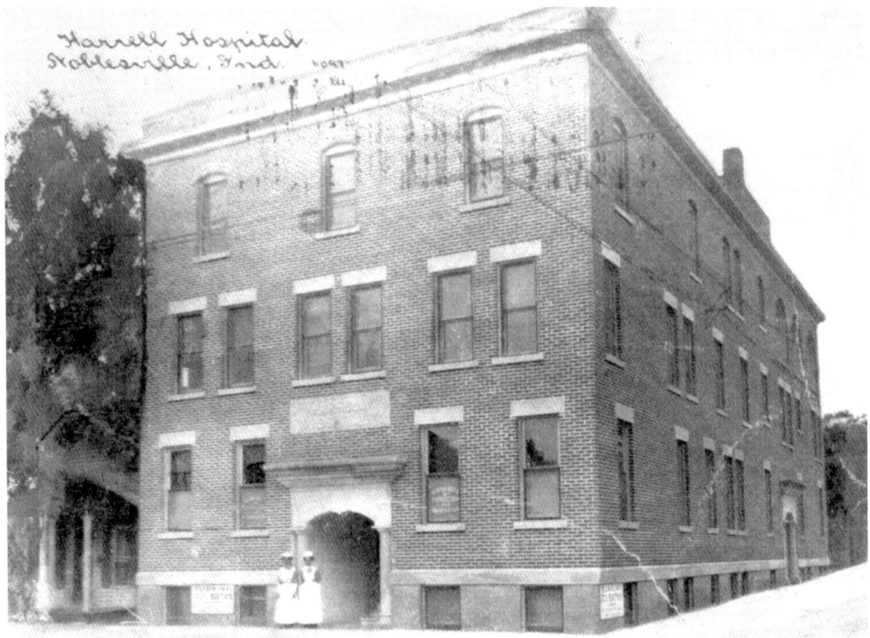

The Harrell Hospital and Sanatorium located on 9th Street. *Sherry Faust*.

Noblesville Landmarks in the National Register of Historic Places

Hamilton County Courthouse Square (added in 1978)
Judge Earl S. Stone House (1978)
Dr. Samuel Harrell House (1984)
Nickel Plate Road Steam Locomotive No. 587 (1984)
Daniel Craycraft House (1989)
William Houston Craig House (1990)
Noblesville Commercial Historic District (1991)
Potter's Bridge (1991)
Holliday Hydroelectric Powerhouse and Dam (1995)
Conner Street Historic District (1999)
Cole-Evans House (2000)
Catherine Street Historic District (2001)
Model Mill (2001)
South 9th Street Historic District (2001)
Robert L. Wilson House (2008)

The Noblesville Milling Company's Model Mill was built to show off and test the company's cutting-edge equipment. The oldest part of the 8th Street structure was originally a planing mill erected in the early 1870s. When the Nordyke and Marmon Company organized the Noblesville Milling Company around 1890, it established the Model Mill just south of the planing mill. Eventually, the milling company absorbed the planing mill, creating a factory that stretched from Division Street to Mulberry Street.

Following the Noblesville Milling Company's dissolution in the 1940s, the building was successively occupied by the Doughnut Corporation of America, McMahon Foods and the Indiana Seed Company. Today, after an extensive remodeling, the historic old Model Mill houses multiple businesses.

The Holliday Hydroelectric Powerhouse and Dam, commonly known as Holliday Station, is believed to be the only original electrical generating plant left in Indiana. The French Chateauesque powerhouse and concrete dam were constructed on the White River at the south edge of Riverwood in 1922 by Alexander R. Holliday and Samuel B. Mott. During its years

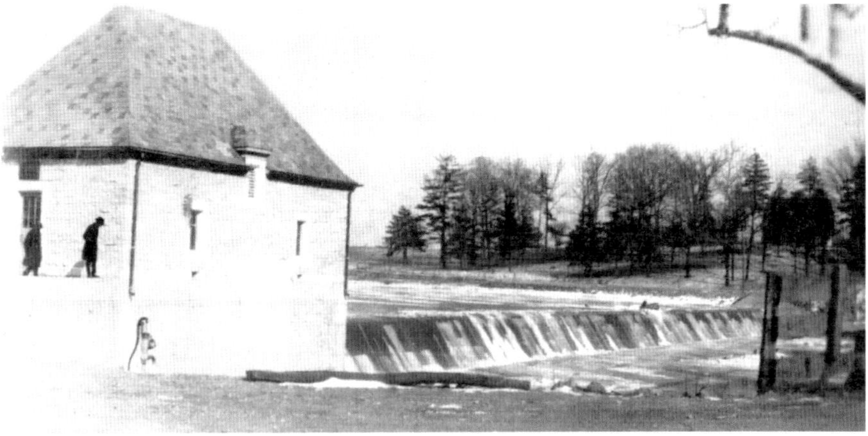

Holliday Station Powerhouse and Dam at Riverwood. Far side of the dam is Clare. *Hamilton East Public Library, Jane Crook Collection.*

of operation, the plant generated enough power to serve six hundred Noblesville homes. Closed since 1965, it was replaced by a modern facility across the street, but still contains the old generators and control board.

Of the residences listed in the National Register of Historic Places, three are currently private homes: the 1892 Daniel Craycraft House at 1095 Conner Street, the 1898 Dr. Samuel Harrell House on the southwest corner of 10th and Harrison Streets and the Cole-Evans House, which was built around 1840 and is located on the northeast corner of 10th and Monument Streets.

The other three residences have been repurposed. The Judge Earl S. Stone House, which dates from around 1849 and is located on the southwest corner of 8th Street and Maple Avenue, is home to the Nickel Plate Arts campus. The Robert L. Wilson House, constructed in the late 1860s at 273 South 8th Street, is currently owned by a business that hosts catered events there. The 1893 William Houston Craig House, 1250 Conner Street, is occupied by several businesses. The Craig House originally stood next to the Presbyterian church, but was moved across the street in 1988 when the church's planned expansion threatened it with demolition. During the massive undertaking, busy Conner Street was shut down for an entire day.

A residence not on the list, but no less imposing, is the William Rooker house, also known as Golden Manor. The 1910 mansion sits on a hill south of downtown Noblesville, near the mouth of Stony Creek and the Nickel

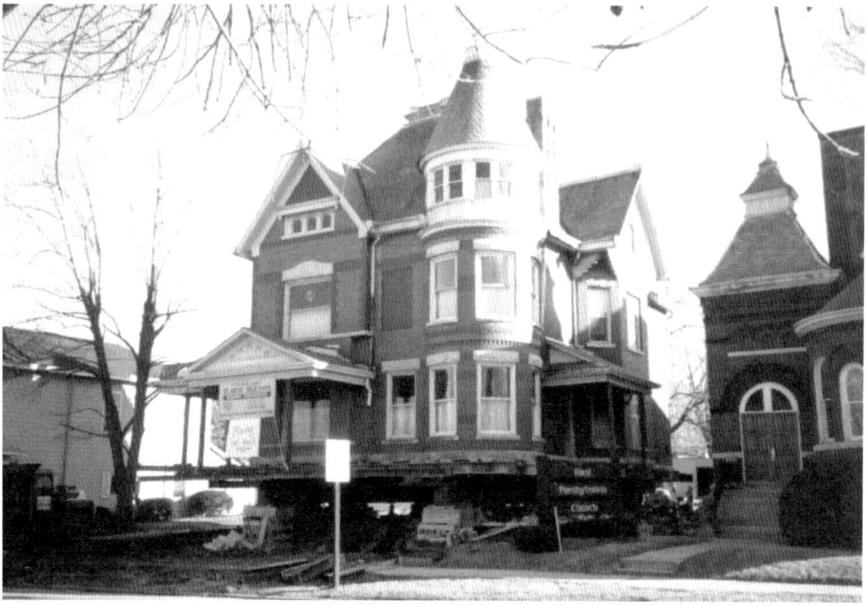

Moving day for the Craig House. *Sherry Faust.*

Plate railroad overpass on Allisonville Road. It's been a nursing home and a restaurant, but currently houses the Third Phase Christian Center.

Some Noblesville landmarks have disappeared without a trace.

When the Old Sheriff's Residence and Jail was built on the courthouse square in 1876, the Hamilton County Recorder's office, which had previously occupied that site, was demolished. The small brick structure, the oldest public building in the county at that time, was erected in 1832 because the frame courthouse wasn't considered a safe place to store the county's records. In the years following 1838, the building was used alternately as the recorder's office and for private business until being razed in 1875.

One of Noblesville's most memorable landmarks was the Wild Opera House, located on the west side of 9th Street between Conner Street and Maple Avenue. The impressive brick theater was erected in 1895 by Noblesville businessman Leonard Wild to replace a similar establishment that had burned down four years earlier. During the early 1900s, the opera house was the city's main venue for stage performances as well as graduations and political events. When motion pictures arrived, they were shown there, too, until 1939. In later years, the building was occupied by apartments and even a warehouse. Demolished in 1959, the site is now a parking lot.

Pioneer John Conner's early death prevented him from enjoying the home he planned on the west edge of Horseshoe Prairie, but his son, William Winship Conner, finished the project. The craftsmen hired by William Winship Conner created a magnificent structure with black walnut paneling, thirteen-inch brick walls and large glass windows shipped in from Cincinnati. The home fell into disrepair in later years and was torn down in the mid-1960s.

Another elegant local residence, the Swain mansion, was built on Federal Hill in the early 1850s by Judge William Garver. Around 1876, it came into the possession of Noblesville farmer/merchant Ezra Swain, and it remained in the Swain family until Ezra's son, Charles Morton Swain, sold the land to the county in 1944. The mansion was razed to make way for the new Hamilton County (Riverview) Hospital.

After Riverview's construction, the old Harrell Hospital building was used as apartments and office space for several years, but was eventually demolished. The site is now a parking lot.

The Noblesville Milling Company's concrete silos and wooden grain elevators, long a Noblesville landmark at 8th and Vine Streets, were torn down in 2015, despite protests from preservationists.

The County Home/County Farm, which provided a refuge for Hamilton County's poor for 137 years, also is gone. Located on Cumberland Road, just

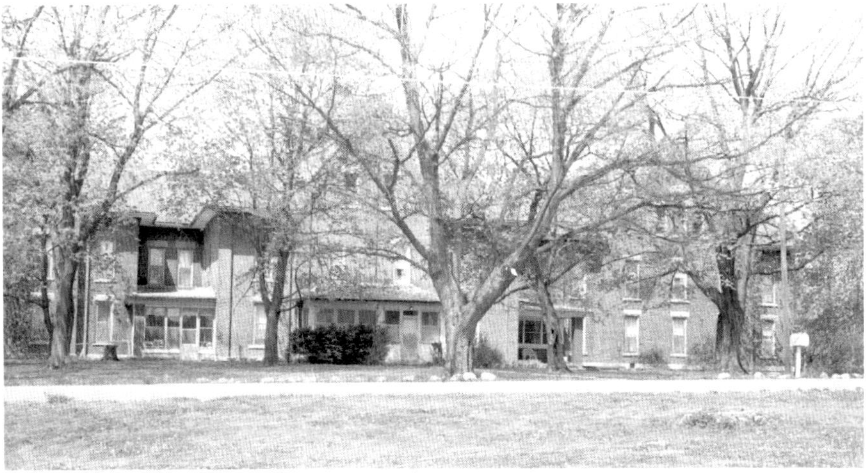

The County Home on County Home Road (now Cumberland Road) closed in 1983. It had more than sixty rooms to house the residents who operated the surrounding county farm. Noblesville High School now sits on that land. *Hamilton East Public Library, Ken Wright Collection.*

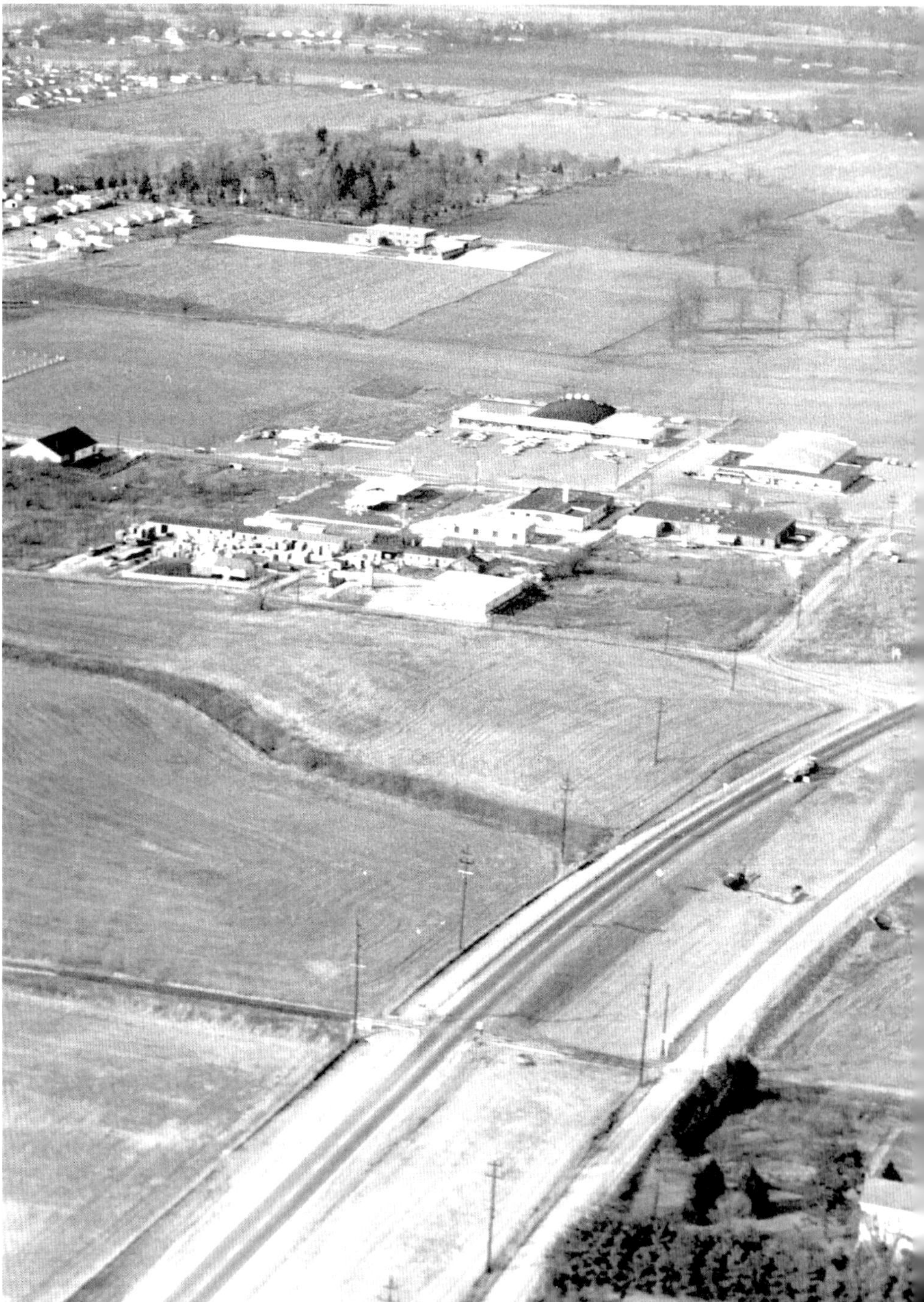

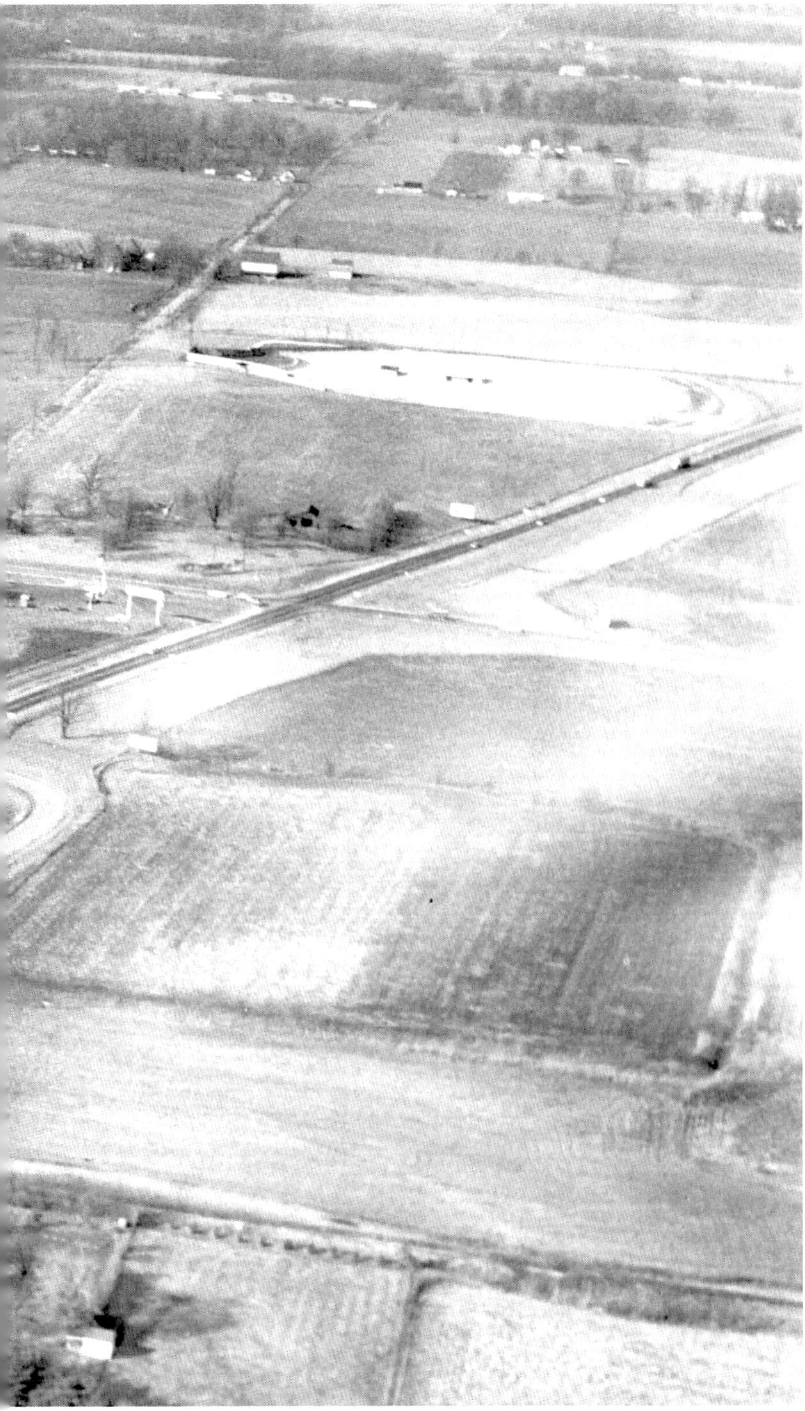

Aerial photo of the east side of Noblesville. Note State Road 37 (*bottom right*), Rainbo Skating Rink (*middle left*), County Home (*top right*), Noblesville Drive-In (*center right*) and Noblesville Plaza Shopping Center (*center left*). *Hamilton County Historical Society*.

north of Monument Street, it began in 1846 with a log cabin. In the 1850s, the cabin was succeeded by a brick building to which various additions and improvements were made over the years. At one time, those living in the County Home worked the farm, raising cattle, hogs and various crops, but during the institution's final years, the residents were too old for such labor, so the farmland was leased to others.

A 1982 inspection of the County Home by the state fire marshal revealed multiple violations, which led to the home being closed the following year and the fifteen remaining residents being transferred to other facilities. In 1985, the vacant building burned down in what is believed to have been a case of arson.

10

PROTECTING, SERVING AND POLITICKING

The first major event in the formation of Noblesville's municipal government took place on January 19, 1850, when the Indiana state legislature passed an act approving Noblesville's incorporation as a town. Under the terms of this legislation, qualified voters were to meet on the first Monday of the following March to elect a mayor and other officers for the "Corporation of Noblesville." For some reason, the voting didn't take place, however, and an amendment had to be passed in January 1851, which loosened the time requirements for holding the election.

When voters finally went to the polls on March 29, 1851, the outcome was 54 to 2 in favor of incorporation. David Moss was elected as Noblesville's first mayor, and William Bauchert, Jacob B. Loehr, Jesse Lutz, Josiah M. Mallery and John D. Stephenson were chosen to serve on the town board. Other officers elected at that time were John L. Cox, treasurer; Emery Powell, marshal; and Joseph A. Messick, street commissioner. John P. Patterson was chosen as secretary, but soon resigned because he felt his business interests wouldn't allow him time to adequately perform the duties of the office. Eddy R. Cole was appointed to replace him.

Joseph Carlin was elected mayor a year later. In 1853, Carlin was succeeded by D.C. Chipman, but Chipman held the office for less than two months, because on May 21, 1853, the town board passed a resolution to incorporate Noblesville in accordance with an act the state legislature had passed the previous June. That act redefined the powers and structure of incorporated towns. As a result, Noblesville's elections were changed to the first Monday in May of each year, and the position of mayor was eliminated. In place of a mayor, the town's five board members, now termed the Board of Trustees, were to run the municipal government.

Thirty-four years later, on May 4, 1887, Noblesville's status changed again when residents voted overwhelmingly (311 to 77) to incorporate as a city. The transformation from town to city meant the office of mayor was reintroduced, and Edgar C. Wilson became the first mayor elected by Noblesville's citizens since 1853.

Noblesville also acquired a new official seal at that time. The old town seal, received on June 12, 1853, had consisted of the words "Seal of the Corporation of Noblesville, Indiana," and a sheaf of wheat. The new design displayed the date of Noblesville's incorporation as a city, May 6, 1887, and a natural gas wellhead scene, reflecting Noblesville's prominent role in the gas boom taking place at that time. The 1887 seal is still in use today.

Over the years, only five Democrats have held the office of mayor: David Moss, John L. Dulin, Gordon Olvey, Charles Meredith and Robert V.

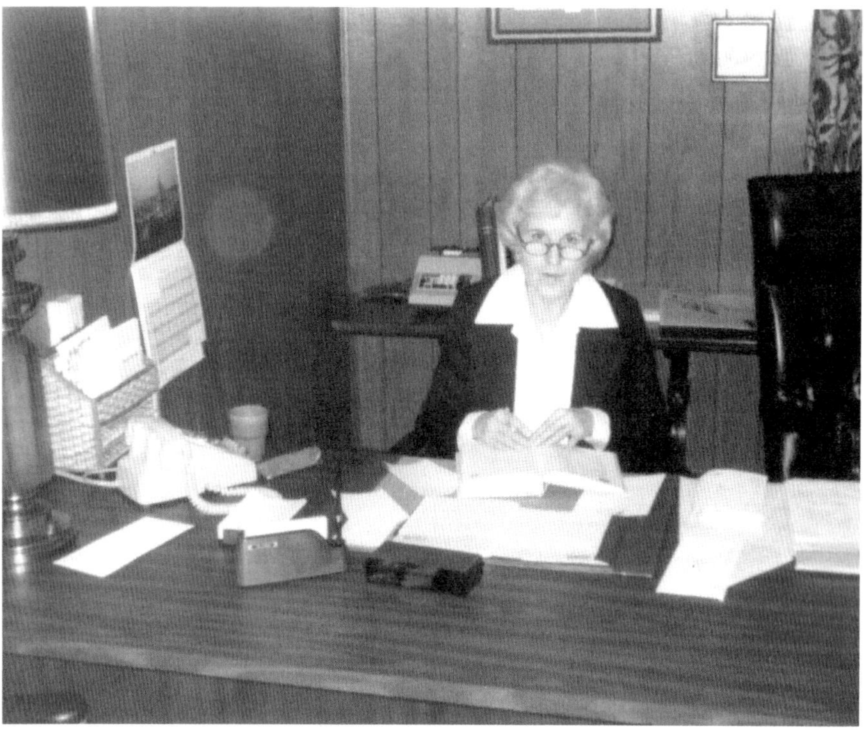

Mayor Pat Logan serving her first day in city hall on 8th Street. *Hamilton East Public Library, P. Logan Collection.*

Noblesville's Mayors

1851–1852	David Moss
1852–1853	Joseph Carlin
1853	Dewitt C. Chipman
1853–1887	(Board of Trustees)
1887–1889	Edgar C. Wilson
1889–1890	John F. Neal
1891–1894	James W. Smith
1895–1899	Edgar C. Wilson
1900–1902	Albert R. Baker
1903–1904	George Snyder
1905–1906	John L. Dulin
1907–1909	Edgar C. Wilson
1910–1917	Dr. Edgar C. Loehr
1918–1921	Daniel B. "Jack" McCoun
1922–1925	Horace G. "Pop" Brown
1926–1929	Julius X. Joseph
1930–1934	William E. Gifford
1935–1938	Horace G. "Pop" Brown
1939–1951	Emmet R. Fertig
1952–1958	Herman Lawson
1958	Gordon Olvey
1958	Charles Meredith
1958–1959	John R. Neal
1960–1963	Dale Hanshew
1963	John R. Neal
1964–1971	Joe Butler
1972–1975	Max Robinson
1976–1979	Robert V. Wical
1980–1987	Patricia Logan
1988–1995	Mary Sue Rowland
1996 2003	Dennis R. Redick
2004–	John Ditslear

Wical. Of those five, only Moss, Dulin and Wical were actually elected by voters. Olvey was elected by fellow city council members to fill the vacancy left by the death of Herman Lawson. When Olvey himself died after serving only one month, council member Charles Meredith was appointed mayor pro-tem. Meredith served just a few days before another member of the city council, Republican John R. Neal, was elected mayor by the council. (Interestingly, when Dale Hanshew, the man elected to follow Neal as mayor, died before his term was up, Neal was again chosen to fill the mayoral vacancy.)

In the historic election of 1979, Wical, who was not only the first Democratic mayor elected in seventy years but also the city's first full-time mayor, was defeated by city council member Patricia Logan. Logan became Noblesville's first female mayor. She served two terms and was followed by the only other woman to occupy the office thus far, Mary Sue Rowland, who also served two terms.

During the first half of the twentieth century, in addition to supervising the departments and employees of the city government, Noblesville's mayors also presided over the city court. Since the early 1950s, however, an elected city court judge has had jurisdiction over all cases involving traffic and parking offenses and other violations of the city code.

Assisting the mayor in conducting the city's affairs is the Noblesville City Council, also known as the Noblesville Common Council. The council passes ordinances, handles zoning and annexations, and approves budgets and spending.

Originally made up of five members, this body has grown in size as the city's population increased. Two additional members were seated on the council in the late 1970s when Noblesville went from a fifth-class city to a fourth-class city, and two more were added in 2016 as the city's status was raised to second-class. Currently, three members hold at-large seats, while the rest each represent one of the city's six districts.

Lowena Layton became the first woman on the council when she was appointed to a seat in 1972. The first African American council member was C. Murphy White. White served on the council twice (1968–79 and 1988–99) and was elected council president in 1991 and 1999. He also made history in 1979 when he became the first African American to run for mayor of Noblesville.

The Republicans have long been the dominant party in Noblesville, as in all of Hamilton County. These days, that domination is so complete, many local races are decided in the May primaries rather than in November's

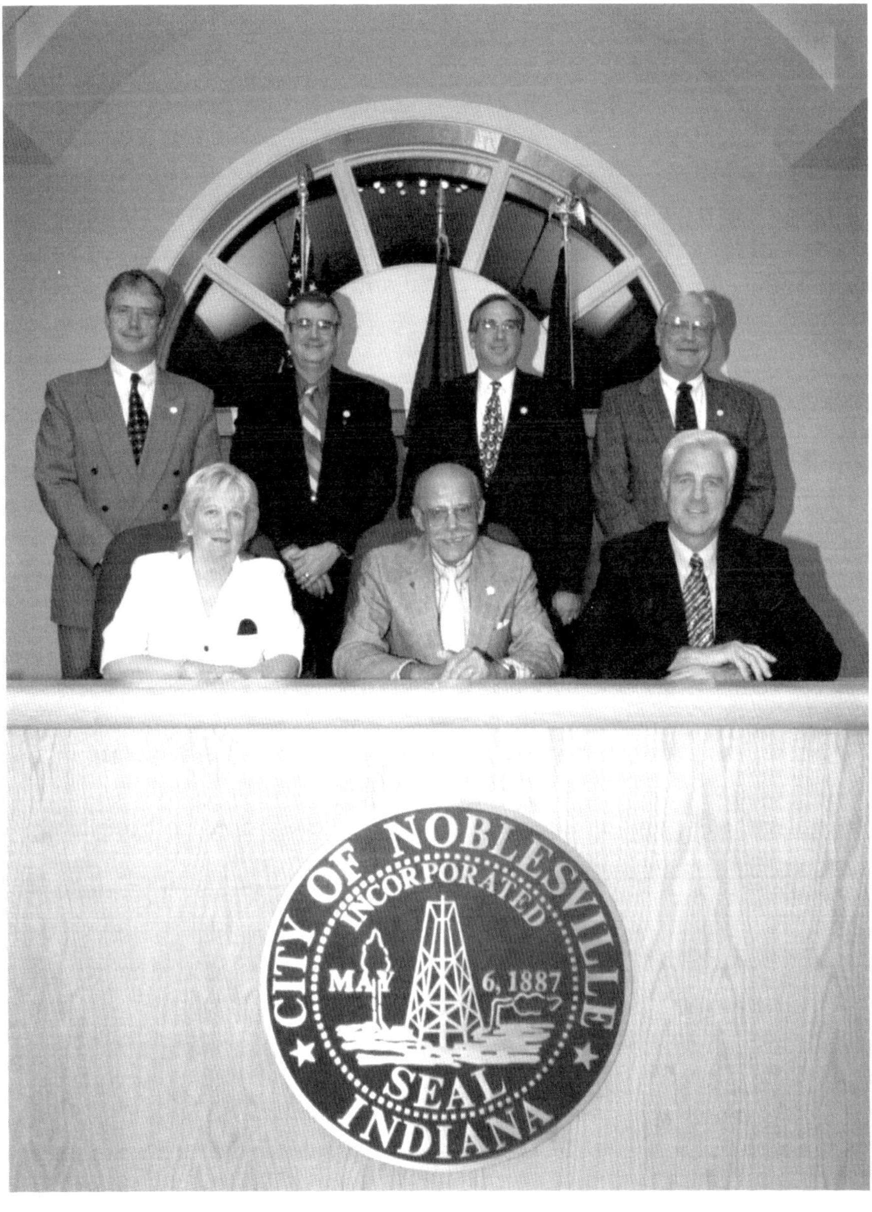

Noblesville Common Council, 1998–99. *Sitting, left to right*: Laurie Hurst, C. Murphy White (president) and Terry Busby; *standing, left to right*: Jack Martin, Rick Moore, Alan Hinds and Dale Snelling. Note the city seal. *Tonja White Goodloe.*

general elections. However, in the past, Noblesville's Democrats were more numerous and active, and during the nineteenth and early twentieth centuries, both parties held conventions in Noblesville to choose candidates for local elections.

The city has been a frequent stop for politicians on the stump and the site of many a political rally or pole raising. Pole raisings were a popular means of mobilizing party members in the nineteenth century. At these events, a long wooden pole, topped by a flag displaying the party emblem or the name of a candidate, was erected in a ceremony marked by speeches, band music, a parade and a barbecue or picnic.

Perhaps the most significant pole raising ever to take place in Noblesville occurred on August 8, 1872. On that day, a throng of African Americans, including two carloads who rode the train from Indianapolis, gathered to raise a 160-foot pole on the courthouse square in honor of Ulysses S. Grant and Henry Wilson, the Republican candidates for U.S. president and vice president. Senator Hiram Revels, the first African American to serve in the U.S. Senate, was among the scheduled speakers, but Revels missed his train and didn't appear.

Several Noblesville politicians have held influential and/or long-running positions in state and national government.

Among those on the state level are William Garver, a member of the Indiana State Senate from 1848 to 1852, and William Winship Conner, who served in both houses of the Indiana General Assembly during his political career. Noblesville teacher Richard Dellinger, a member of the House of Representatives from 1972 to 1992, was the House Majority Leader during the 1980s. Dellinger's successor, Kathy Richardson, represented House District 29 from 1993 to 2018. Howard "Luke" Kenley represented District 20 in the Indiana State Senate from 1992 to 2017. In addition to heading the powerful Senate Appropriations Committee, Kenley made an unsuccessful attempt to become the Republican nominee for governor in 2003.

Two Noblesville men have been elected to the U.S. Congress.

James L. Evans, a member of a prominent Noblesville family (one brother, John D. Evans, served as Indiana State Auditor, while another brother, Walter N. Evans, was a clerk of the Hamilton Circuit Court), was first elected to the U.S. House of Representatives in 1874. Evans served two terms and played an active role in settling a controversy surrounding the 1876 election of President Rutherford B. Hayes.

World War II veteran Richard L. Roudebush was National Commander of the Veterans of Foreign Wars and chairman of the Indiana Veterans

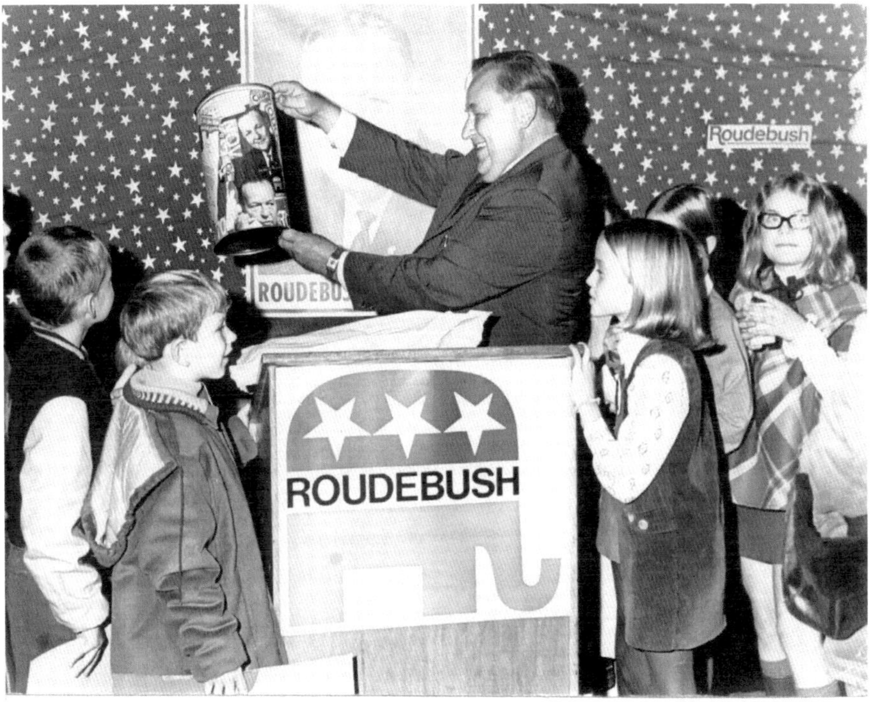

Richard Roudebush celebrating an election victory. *Fred Swift.*

Commission before being elected to the U.S. House of Representatives in 1960. He served from 1961 to 1971 and, due to redistricting, represented three different House districts. After an unsuccessful bid for the U.S. Senate in 1970, he was appointed Administrator of Veterans' Affairs in the Veterans Administration, a post he held until 1977. The Richard L. Roudebush VA Medical Center in Indianapolis is named in his honor.

Noblesville's police and fire departments both have lengthy and interesting histories.

Law enforcement in Noblesville began with a single town marshal charged with executing the orders of the trustees and enforcing the town's bylaws. By the early twentieth century, the force had grown to three members—a chief of police, a day officer and a night officer. In the 1960s, the police chief had ten male officers and one woman who checked the parking meters in the downtown area. More officers continued to be added as the city grew, and today, the Noblesville Police Department consists of several divisions: Patrol, Criminal Investigations, Support and Records. In addition, two community service officers deal with a variety of assignments, from animal complaints to aiding stranded motorists.

Noblesville's earliest known policewoman joined the department in 1916. Although primarily hired to deal with situations involving girls and young women, she was a full-fledged officer, authorized to make arrests. Her name was kept secret at first, but after a few months, the local newspaper identified her as "Mrs. Walter Sanders." When Elma Sanders resigned two years later, the force was left without a policewoman until Laura Dawson was hired in 1922. Dawson stayed on for a year, but she also left, feeling unable to do her job and keep up a household at the same time. It was almost thirty years before Noblesville acquired another female officer, and she was assigned only clerical duties.

Charles Jones became the first African American member of the modern-day Noblesville Police Department in 1971, but he wasn't Noblesville's first African American law officer. Years earlier, before Noblesville incorporated as a city, the April 9, 1880 *Noblesville Ledger* observed that "John Hoard, the colored man," had been elected constable on the Republican ticket by a "handsome majority." (They added, "'Rah for John.")

To date, the only Noblesville policeman to die in the line of duty is Francis W. Castor, who was killed on July 28, 1948. Castor had only been with the department a few days when he was thrown from his motorcycle while on patrol in Forest Park.

In earlier years, the police were headquartered in city hall, but since 1989 the police and fire departments and the city court have been located in the Public Safety Building on the southwest corner of 9th Street and Maple Avenue.

Noblesville's fire department can trace its history back to the Noblesville Hook and Ladder Company, a volunteer organization formed in 1871 with twenty-five charter members. A reorganization by the company in 1901 created the foundation of the fire department of today.

Early fire runs were made with a wagon drawn by a team of horses. (One perfectly matched set was dubbed "Maud and Fraud.") The teams had specially made harnesses constructed by local harness maker John Thom. The harnesses were attached to an overhead pulley, and whenever an alarm sounded, the pulley would drop them directly onto the horses, allowing the horses to be hitched to the wagon quickly, saving time and possibly lives.

Noblesville's horse-drawn fire wagon era came to an end when the city purchased a Rutenber Chemical and Hose fire truck in 1915. The new "auto fire truck," which came equipped with a forty-gallon soda tank, two three-gallon chemical tanks, two six-pound axes and a crowbar, marked the

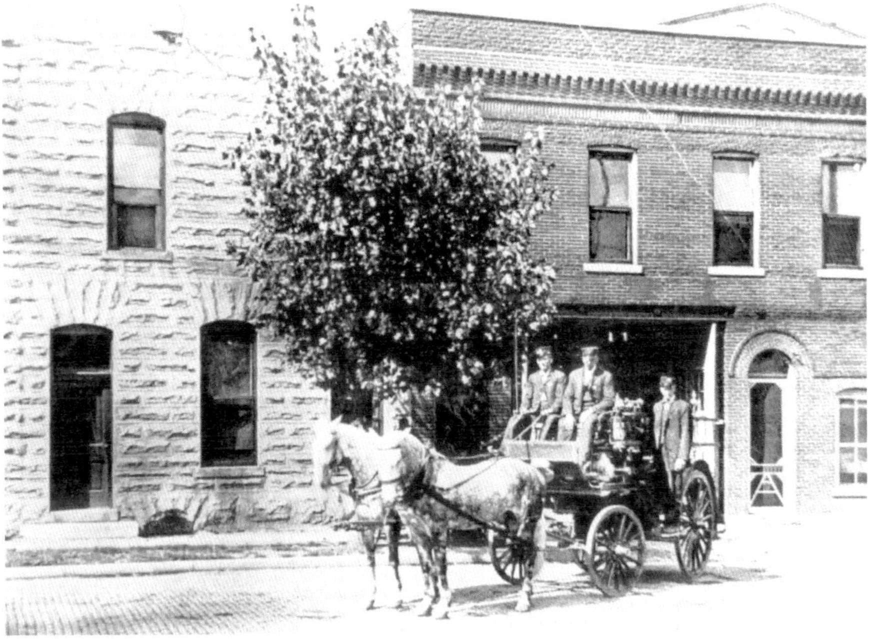

Noblesville Fire Department, about 1913. Pictured here are three men and a team of horses (named Maud and Fraud) pulling the fire wagon in front of the city building and fire station on Maple Avenue between 8th and 9th Streets. Houston Hotel is on the left. *Noblesville Fire Department.*

beginning of a long line of increasingly sophisticated firefighting vehicles acquired by the department over the years.

Today, Noblesville firefighters operate out of six fire stations in addition to the downtown headquarters at the Public Safety Building and they not only battle fires throughout Noblesville and Noblesville Township but also provide emergency medical services. Additionally, specialized teams—a dive team, a hazardous materials team, a water rescue team and a tactical rescue team—have been organized to respond to specific disasters.

The city's first full-time female firefighter, Courtney Wiedenhaupt, joined the department in 1998, but retired from firefighting a few years later due to a health issue.

During Noblesville's first century, the town's many wooden structures made fire an ever-present danger. Several businesses in the downtown area, such as the Evans mill and the first Wild Opera House, were lost to flames before construction around the square was limited to brick or stone. Despite those precautions, Noblesville has suffered several serious fires during the last one hundred years.

Major Noblesville Fires in the Modern Era

January 8, 1942—An overheated furnace was believed responsible for a fire that destroyed Dorman's general merchandise store and Roper's barbershop on the southwest corner of the courthouse square.

August 14, 1951—Volunteer firefighter Byron Galbreath died battling a blaze at the Louis Smith junkyard. Three boys later confessed to setting the fire in order to cremate a dead rat.

March 24, 1957—Firemen from several cities responded to a fire on the north side of the square that destroyed the Sportsmen's Store, Monty's Furniture Market, Todd's Feed Store, the Moose Lodge and several apartments. Syd's Bar and the Noblesville Electric Hatchery suffered water and smoke damage. The blaze was believed to have started in the feed store.

October 13, 1967—The worst fire in Noblesville's history occurred on Friday the 13th. It originated in the paint shop of the Paul Goeke Dodge-Chrysler automobile dealership and devastated half the block west of the courthouse before being brought under control. The Goeke dealership, the Coin-O-Wash Laundry and B&W Pizza were destroyed, and the White Oldsmobile dealership was severely damaged. Raymond Moulder, assistant chief of the Fishers Volunteer Fire Department, was killed when a wall of the Oldsmobile dealership collapsed.

January 18, 1983—The Ruppert Furniture Store, near the intersection of 10th and Conner Streets, burned down in what was later judged a case of arson. Also damaged were the Hudler Press, the Korea Taekwondo Academy, a townhouse and two apartments. Two firefighters were injured, one seriously.

February 2, 1984—The Houston Hotel, on the northeast corner of 8th Street and Maple Avenue, was completely destroyed by a blaze that took the lives of three hotel residents and also threatened Noblesville's city hall next door.

The U.S. Postal Service is another important government agency serving Noblesville residents.

Noblesville has had a post office since 1824, but although it's well established that William Conner's home was the original location, there has been some confusion regarding the first postmaster. While some Hamilton County histories assign that honor to John D. Stephenson, according to the

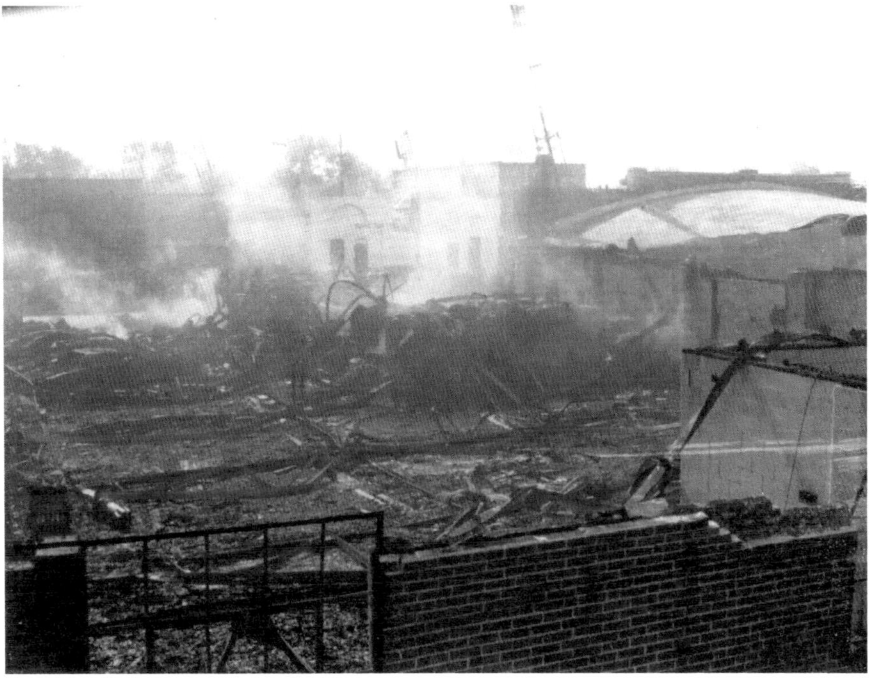

The 1967 Goeke fire on the corner of 6th and Conner Streets. *Noblesville Fire Department.*

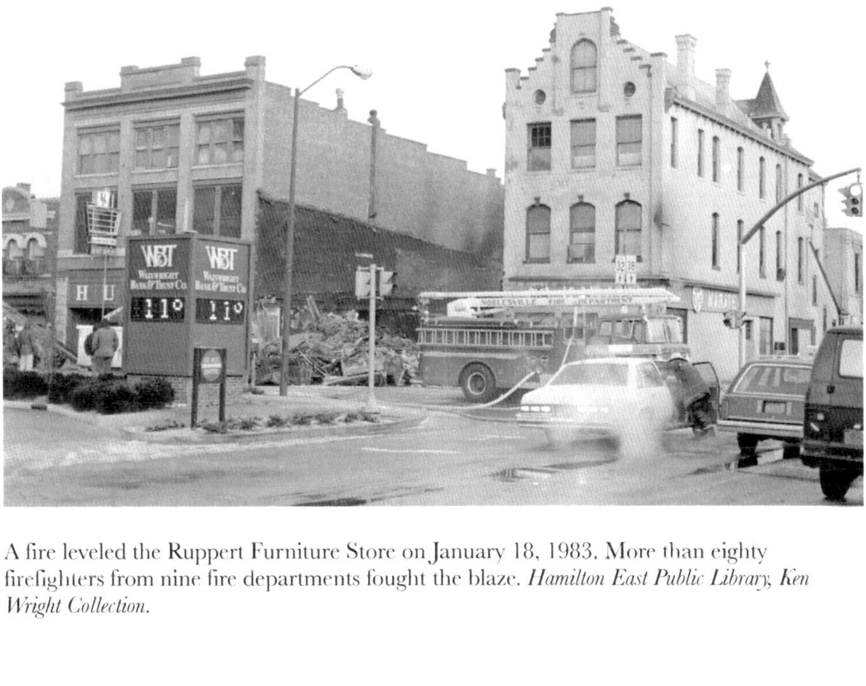

A fire leveled the Ruppert Furniture Store on January 18, 1983. More than eighty firefighters from nine fire departments fought the blaze. *Hamilton East Public Library, Ken Wright Collection.*

federal government's biennial *Register of All Officers and Agents, Civil, Military, and Naval in the Service of the United States*, Josiah F. Polk was Noblesville's first postmaster. Polk held the position for about a year and a half before being succeeded by Stephenson in October 1825.

Perhaps the best known of all Noblesville's postmasters was Gordon Olvey. Olvey, who later served briefly as mayor, developed a reputation as the "Postmaster Poet" during the years he ran the Noblesville post office. A collection of his poetry, *Poems*, was published in 1945.

When the U.S. Postal Service established the ZIP Code system, Noblesville was assigned the 46060 code, but in recent years, it has acquired two more zip codes, 46061 and 46062—yet another indication of the city's growth.

11
THAT'S ENTERTAINMENT

For Noblesville's earliest residents, having fun usually meant just trying to make everyday chores more pleasant. Hunting, fishing and get-togethers such as quilting bees, husking bees and pumpkin peelings might have been enjoyable pastimes, but they also were necessary for survival.

Gradually, that situation changed, as in the case of Muster Day. It was originally a response to an act passed by the state legislature that called for all able-bodied males between the ages of twenty-one and fifty to drill and learn military tactics on one day each year. After the threat of Indian attacks was removed and military preparedness was no longer as important, the day evolved into a holiday rather like the Fourth of July. It came to be marked by picnics, athletic contests and plenty of whiskey.

Music frequently played a role in community gatherings.

During the nineteenth century, Noblesville was known for producing excellent singers and musicians. The Noblesville Choral Union was considered one of Indiana's best musical organizations in its day. Formed in the 1880s with members of the city's church choirs, the group presented operas and cantatas in the old city hall on the southeast corner of 9th and Logan Streets in what the March 27, 1904 *Indianapolis Journal* described as "a manner that would be creditable to more pretentious cities."

During that same century, a succession of brass bands was organized in the city. The most prominent and enduring of these was the Noblesville Military Band, which was created in 1888 with players taken from two earlier companies, the Citizens Band and the GAR (Grand Army of the Republic)

Band. In 1900, the band's first board of directors—Meade Vestal, Emil G. Decker and Jacob D. Hill—filed articles of incorporation with the Hamilton County Recorder's Office. Vestal became the bandleader two years later and went on to hold that position for many years.

In addition to performing many Noblesville concerts, the band appeared in various cities around the state and was invited to play at the 1908 National Republican Convention in Chicago. The evening prior to their departure for the Windy City, band members gave a special performance on the lawn of Vice President Charles W. Fairbanks's Indianapolis home.

A consolidation with the local Elks Band in 1937 brought in new, younger members and kept the group performing right up to the end of the 1930s.

Many years later, Noblesville's musical tradition continued when Deer Creek Music Center, an outdoor amphitheater seating over twenty-four thousand, opened off 146th Street near I-69 on May 20, 1989. The first artist to take the stage was contemporary Christian vocalist Sandi Patty. A wide variety of acts followed over the years, from Frank Sinatra to the Grateful

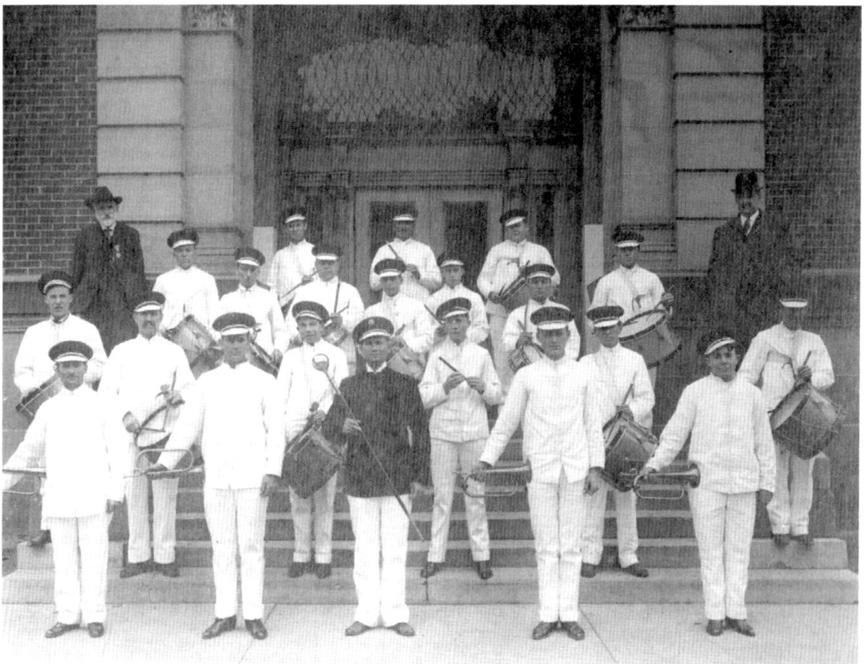

Elks Band in front of courthouse. Organized in 1922, the Elks Band furnished music for Flag Day ceremonies and marched in Decoration Day parades. *Hamilton County Historical Society.*

Dead. Until the Grateful Dead disbanded in 1995, the group's fans, the Deadheads, were noted for their annual pilgrimage to Noblesville to attend the band's concerts.

Verizon Communications bought the naming rights to the venue in 2000 and opened it as the Verizon Wireless Music Center the following year. Twelve years later, under new sponsorship, the name changed again to the Klipsch Music Center, and in 2017, it became the Ruoff Home Mortgage Music Center. For many locals, however, it will always be Deer Creek.

Like the early concerts, Noblesville's first theatrical performances took place in upstairs halls around the square, with attendees forced to climb two or three flights of stairs to sit in a room that was neither comfortable nor particularly safe. For that reason, local theater lovers rejoiced when a new single-story opera house opened on 9th Street between Wayne and Clinton Streets in 1884.

That building burned down in 1891, but four years later, merchant Leonard Wild built a new opera house on 9th Street between Conner Street and Maple Avenue. The new Wild Opera House opened with the play *Charley's Aunt* and went on to provide a variety of entertainment over many years.

The tradition of live theater continues in Noblesville today with organizations such as the Hamilton County Theatre Guild. Formed in 1965 by a group of Noblesville residents, the guild's first production, *Ah, Wilderness!*, was presented in the cafeteria of the 17th Street high school. Three years later, the players moved into the former Emmanuel United Methodist Church on State Road 238, east of Noblesville. The old church, renamed the Belfry, has since become the guild's permanent home.

Motion pictures came to Noblesville as early as 1901 at the Wild Opera House, and they continued to be featured at Wild's Theatre, as it was later known, until 1939. Other early theaters showing motion pictures included the locally owned Home Amusement Company, which opened in 1906 on the north side of the square; the Crystal Theater on 8th Street; and the Star Theatre.

The Star Theatre was located on Logan Street, north of the courthouse. After the Star closed in 1914, the theater underwent major renovations and was renamed the Isis. (An ad promised the theater had been "Cleaned, Deodorized and Disinfected from Street to Sheet.") The Isis was succeeded by the U.S., the American and then the Palace Theaters. The final theater to occupy that space was the Logan, which lasted from 1932 to 1956.

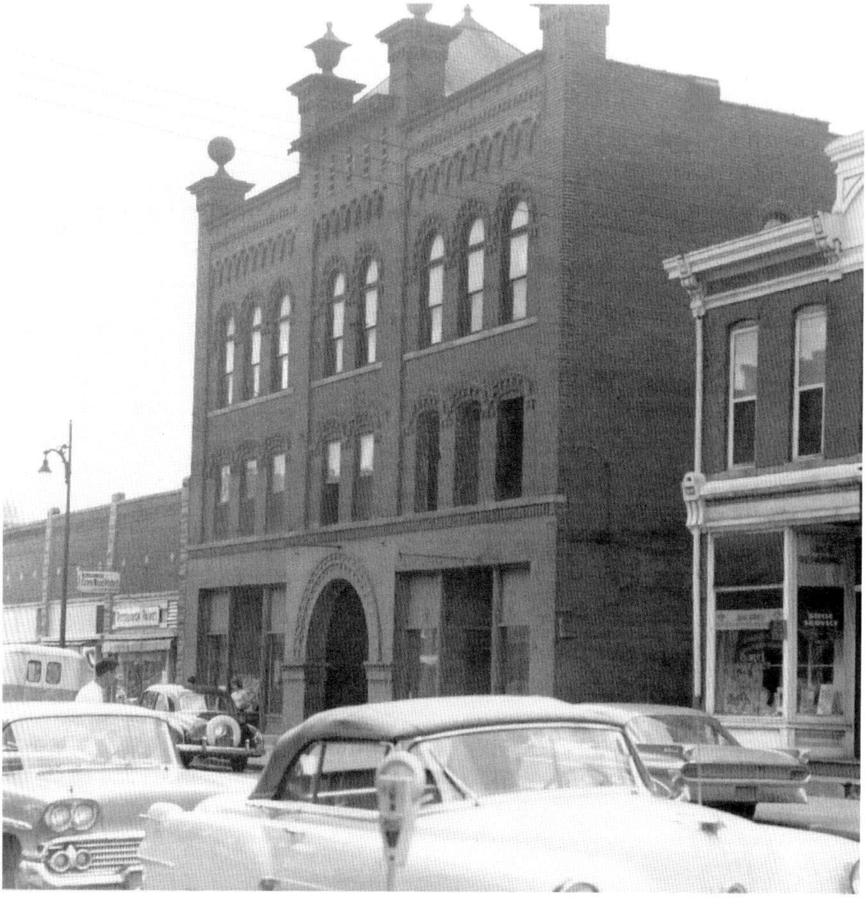

Wild Opera House on 9th Street (formerly Catherine Street) before it was demolished in 1959 to make way for a parking lot. *Hamilton East Public Library, Irv Heath Collection.*

In 1920, the American Theatre opened on 9th Street, just south of Clinton Street. This American (not to be confused with the Logan Street American, which didn't open until 1923) was the first theater in Noblesville specifically constructed for motion pictures. It closed after a few months, however, and was replaced by the Olympic, which was itself later replaced by the State. The last theater in the building was the Diana, which opened in 1938 and closed in 1978.

After the Diana's closing, Noblesville was without an indoor motion picture theater until the Great Escape Theater (currently the Regal Noblesville Stadium 10) opened in the shopping area east of State Road 37 in 2004.

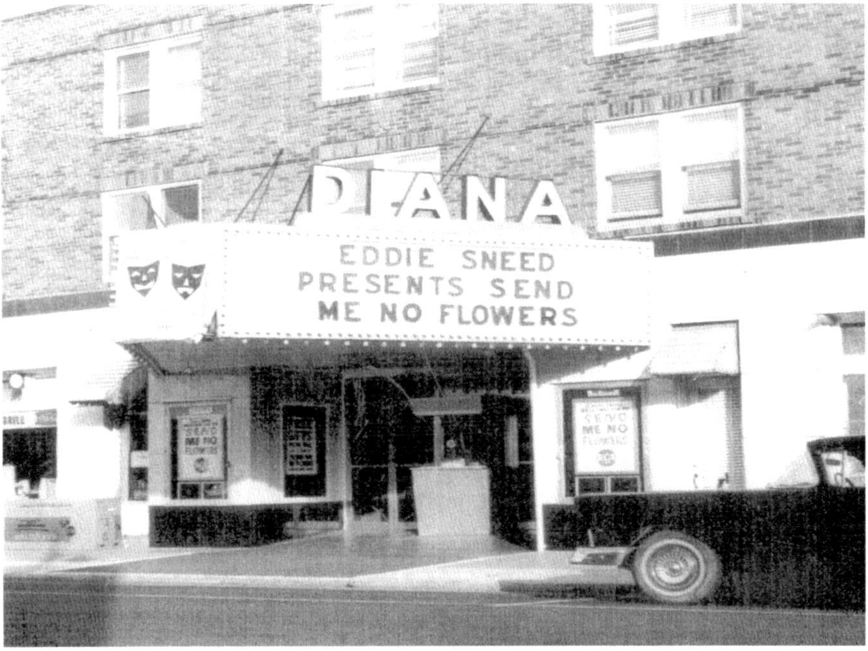

The Diana Theater in 1964, when the show *Send Me No Flowers*, starring Rock Hudson, Doris Day and Tony Randall, was released. *Hamilton County Historical Society.*

The city's only drive-in theater, the Noblesville Drive-In Theatre, opened on May 30, 1951, with the film *Two Guys from Texas*. It was located on County Farm Road (now Cumberland Road), a little south of Monument Street. Later known as the ABC Noblesville Drive-In Theatre, it remained a favorite summer attraction until its closing in 1996.

In the early twentieth century, Noblesville was on a Chautauqua circuit each summer. Chautauqua assemblies traveled from place to place presenting live entertainment and adult education courses in an outdoor setting to people who might otherwise never have had access to such things.

Noblesville's first Chautauqua was held in 1911 at Brown's Woods, just west of what would later become Forest Park. After that, the Chautauquas moved to Hines' Grove, a wooded area at the east end of Christian Avenue. Each year, groups of friends and/or families would camp out during the Chautauqua, pitching their tents on "avenues" laid out on the grounds. Their campsites generally sported creative names such as "Rest-More" and "Lafalot." Lunch and refreshments were available at a concessions tent manned by George Hawkins, the original Gran'Pa of Gran'Pa's candy store.

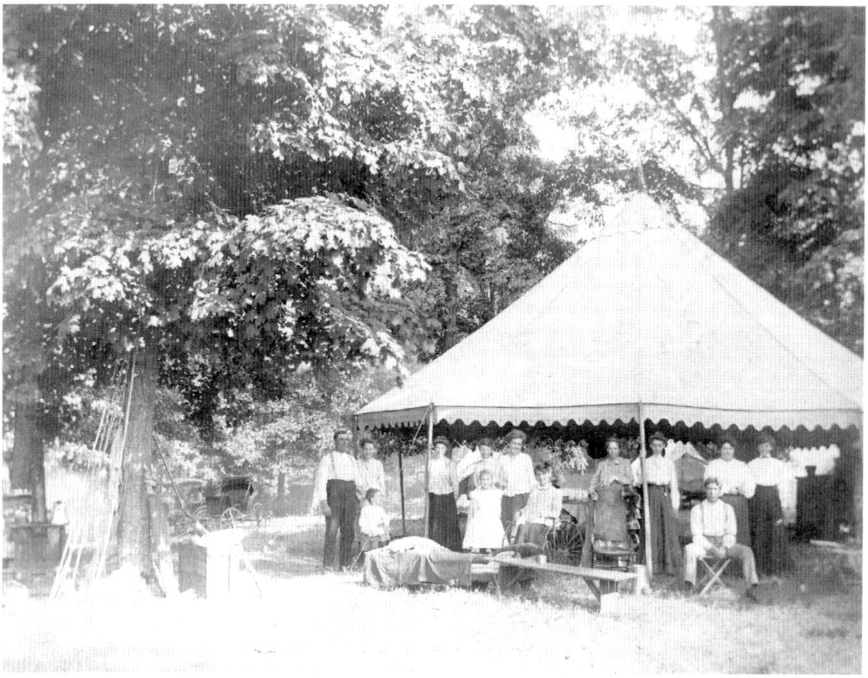

Jacob D. Hill's Chautauqua camp. *Paula Dunn.*

For a season ticket of around two dollars for an adult or one dollar for a child, spectators could attend the entire four to nine days of the Chautauqua and see acts such as Ferrante the Magician and the Royal Welsh Male Singers, hear lectures on useful topics like cooking or raising children and be addressed by nationally known figures. Local talent, such as the Noblesville Military Band, also performed. Among the featured speakers to appear at Noblesville's Chautauquas were explorer Dr. Frederick Cook, Senator (and future president) Warren G. Harding, evangelist Bob Jones and three-time Democratic presidential nominee William Jennings Bryan. (Bryan made three appearances—1912, 1916 and 1922). Perhaps the most memorable speaker of all, however, was Helen Keller, who was featured at the 1915 Chautauqua.

By the early 1920s, competition from motion pictures and radio, and the mobility provided by automobiles left the Chautauqua circuits struggling financially. After 1921, Noblesville's Chautauquas were produced locally rather than as part of a circuit. The city's final Chautauqua in 1926 was moved from Hines' Grove to the Horse Show Grounds, an area between

10th Street and the river, bounded by Harrison Street on the south and Monument Street to the north.

Fairs were another source of outdoor summer entertainment.

There is evidence of a county fair being held in Noblesville as early as the 1860s in the general area that would later become the Horse Show Grounds and the Commons. (The Commons was a largely undeveloped tract bordered by Harrison on the south, 12th Street on the east, Monument on the north and 10th Street on the west.)

The first fairgrounds of which any details are known, however, was located on Ezra Swain's Federal Hill farm in the early 1880s. Swain's fairgrounds contained a half-mile track for horse racing, an amphitheater, several large buildings for animal exhibits and a fine-arts building for displaying baked goods, needlework and other handiwork. The Hamilton County Fair was held there until 1890, when it moved to Sheridan. The Swain family eventually sold the fairgrounds, but later owners continued to hold baseball games, horse races and livestock shows there under the name West Side Park during the first few years of the twentieth century.

Beginning in 1911, the Noblesville Horse Shows ran for several years at the Horse Show Grounds. While the exhibitions focused on horses, they also included competitions in horticulture, sewing and baking. During the 1930s, the horse shows became county-wide affairs and began to be held in conjunction with 4-H exhibits. In some years, they took place at the Horse Show Grounds, in others they were at Forest Park and/or Joseph Field, the high school athletic field at 17th and Conner Streets. The 1933 horse show was even held on the north side of the courthouse square.

The horse shows eventually evolved into 4-H fairs. Throughout most of the 1940s, they were held in different Hamilton County towns, but in 1949, the fair returned to Noblesville at a "temporary" site in the Commons, north of First Ward School.

The following year, a new, permanent Hamilton County 4-H Fairgrounds was established on Pleasant Street, just west of State Road 37, on land that had been part of the old Noblesville Airport. Two new buildings were constructed for animals, while the home economics, garden and entomology entries were housed in what had once been the old airport hangar. More buildings have been added since that time, and today, a wide variety of additional events take place at the fairgrounds throughout the year, from home shows to small business training sessions.

The movement to develop a public park in Noblesville began as early as 1875. The September 3, 1875 *Noblesville Ledger* advocated turning the land

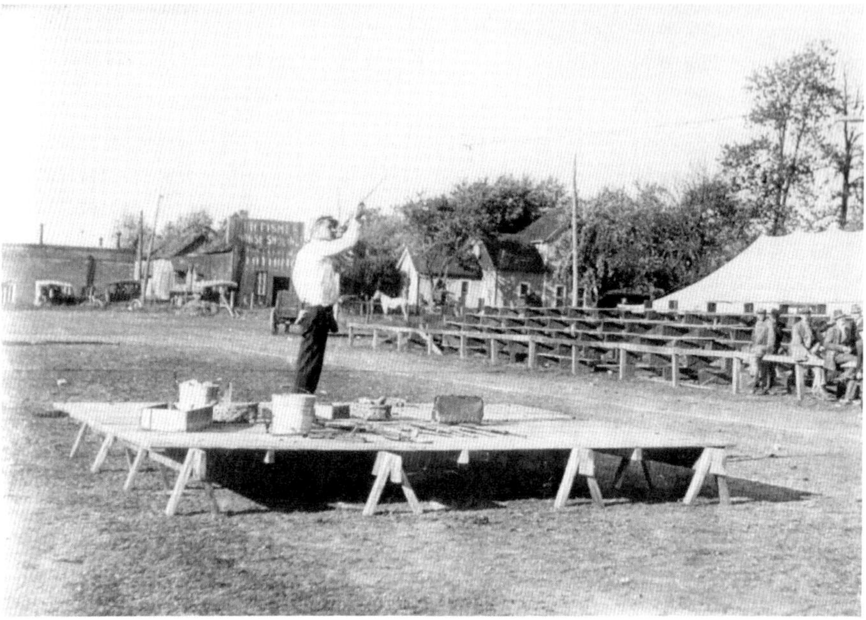

Horse Show Grounds across from First Ward School. *Hamilton East Public Library, Joe Roberts Collection.*

around Llewelyn Spring into a park, declaring, "Nothing that can be done will be more valuable to the reputation of Noblesville." No formal park seems to have ever been dedicated there, however.

In 1920, the idea of a city park gained momentum once again, and several sites were proposed, with most people favoring a location along the White River. When the dust settled, H.G. "Pop" Brown's farm on the Cicero Road (State Road 19) was chosen. The park, dubbed Forest Park, opened in 1926 and has been a popular destination for both residents and nonresidents ever since.

Forest Park has seen a number of changes during its existence.

The park's historic log cabin, dedicated in 1929, was moved there from its former location on Stringtown Pike (Hague Road) to serve as a museum and clubhouse. The museum didn't last, but the cabin was used for parties and meetings for decades, until it deteriorated so badly it was dismantled in 1997. The Forest Park Inn opened as a shelter house and restaurant during the park's first year. Although the restaurant closed long ago, the inn survives as a meeting and banquet facility. Another option for banquets, receptions and other gatherings is the Forest Park Lodge, which opened near the north entrance in 2008. Recreation programs are also held at the lodge.

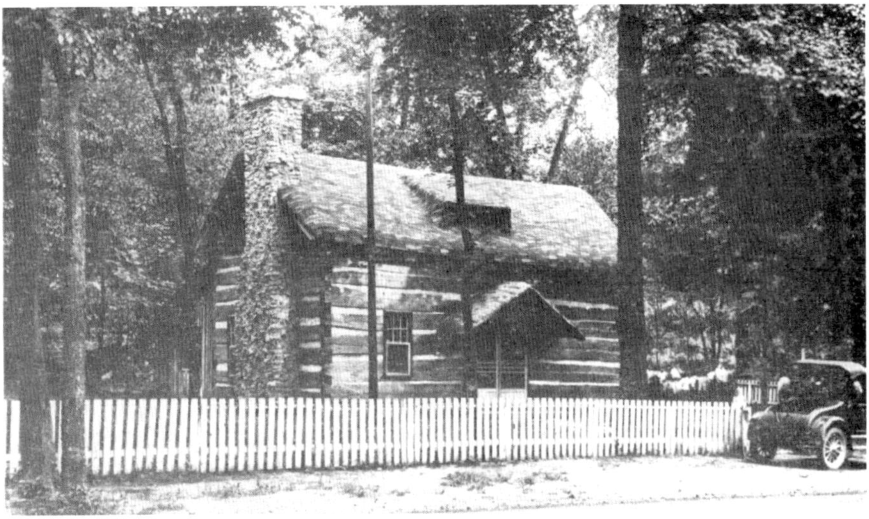

Log cabin at Forest Park. *Hamilton East Public Library, Forest Park Historical Postcards.*

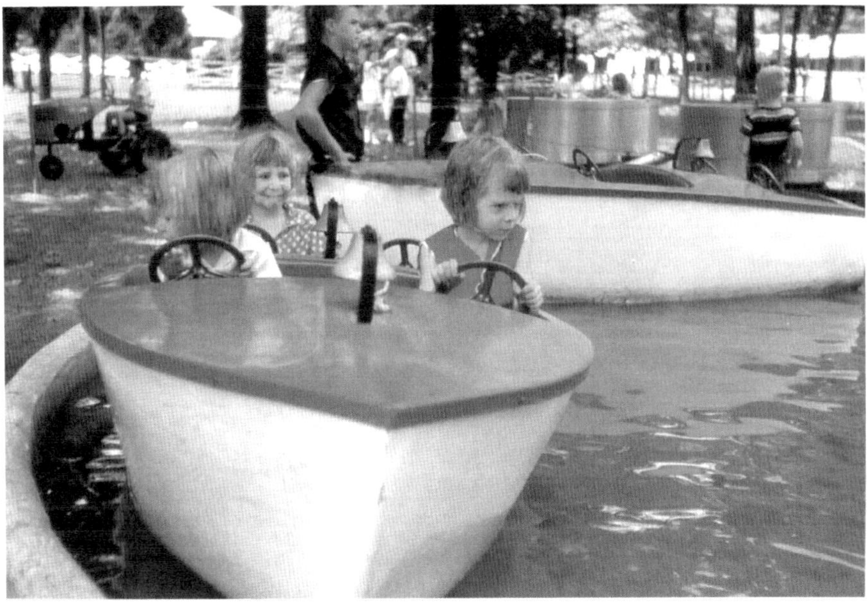

This boat was one of the kiddie rides at Forest Park, which were popular in the late 1950s. Other kiddie rides included a miniature train, a kiddie whip, tractors, a tub-of-fun (spinning tubs) and live pony rides. *Sid Davis.*

The miniature train, boats and other kiddie rides fondly remembered by baby boomers are long gone, and the original playground equipment, including the old corkscrew slide, has been replaced by newer, safer versions, but the Tom Thumb miniature golf course, which dates to 1930, is still there. Nearby are tennis courts, a skate park and the 1920 Little Beauty carousel.

Also at the park are the nine-hole Forest Park Golf Course, the Logan and Emerson Baseball Fields, and the Noblesville Aquatic Center.

The Aquatic Center (originally Central Pool) is the latest of the city's swimming facilities. In 1925, a bathing beach was established on the White River near the end of Monument Street. Two years later, a new gravel-bottomed swimming pool opened next to the river at the park's south entrance, but state board of health rules and a lack of funds closed it in 1930. The following year, a cement pool was constructed at the north end of the park on land previously owned by the Hamilton Chemical Company, manufacturers of anti–hog cholera serum. The building that had housed the company's offices and lab was then converted into a bathhouse. The cement pool served the city until the Aquatic Center was built in 1976.

From 1968 to 2018, Forest Park was the home of the Indiana Transportation Museum (originally the Indiana Museum of Transport and Communication). In addition to interpreting Indiana's railroad history, for many years, the museum ran popular excursions, such as the Indiana State Fair Train and the Polar Bear Express, on the old Nickel Plate railroad tracks.

Today, Forest Park is just one of several Noblesville parks.

The Forest Park Golf Course, dedicated in 1927, was Noblesville's only golf course until the Fox Prairie Golf Course opened on 196th Street in 1970. In the years since, the city has acquired three more public courses: Pebble Brook Golf Course on Westfield Road (opened 1972), Stony Creek Golf Club on 166th Street (1990), and Purgatory Golf Club on 216th Street (2000).

Parades have been a part of countless Noblesville celebrations. While many have been onetime events tied to specific occasions such as political rallies, a few occur annually and deserve special mention.

The oldest annual parade in the city is the Noblesville High School Homecoming parade, which has been taking place since 1949. Floats constructed by each NHS class and several high school clubs are among the parade's highlights. Noblesville's Christmas parade has been kicking off the holiday season since 1962. Many local television celebrities have appeared in the Christmas parades, along with the featured guest, Santa. The city's Fourth of July parade and the accompanying Fireworks Festival date to 1997.

Noblesville's Other Parks

Parks maintained by Noblesville Parks and Recreation:

Southside Park—Opened 1952. Bounded by 3rd, 4th, Washington and Pleasant Streets.

Seminary Park—Opened 1983. Bounded by 10th, 11th, Hannibal and Division Streets (on the grounds of the old Second Ward school).

Dr. James A. Dillon Park—Opened 2007. On Edenshall Lane, near the intersection of Hazel Dell Road and 146th Street.

Federal Hill Commons—Opened 2017. On Logan Street, just west of White River.

Hague Road Nature Haven—In development. At the intersection of State Road 38 and Hague Road.

Finch Creek Park—In development. At 166th Street and Boden Road in Wayne Township.

Parks maintained by Hamilton County Parks and Recreation:

Morse Park & Beach—Opened 1973. By Morse Reservoir at the west end of 196th Street.

Potter's Bridge Park—Opened 1999. On Allisonville Road, just west of Cumberland Road.

Riverwood Canoe Landing—Opened 2005. On Riverwood Avenue, just north of 206th Street.

Bray Family Homestead Park—Opened 2008. On Hinkle Road, just north of State Road 38. (Although technically in Washington Township, it sits on the border with Noblesville Township.)

Roller skating has been a popular local pastime since the late 1800s. Of the several rinks that have been located in the city, the best known is undoubtedly the Rainbo Roller Club, which opened in 1955 on the northwest corner of State Road 32/38 and County Farm Road (Cumberland Road.)

The Rainbo was truly a roller skating palace. When it opened, it boasted an eighteen-thousand-square-foot maple floor, a $3,000 Hammond electric

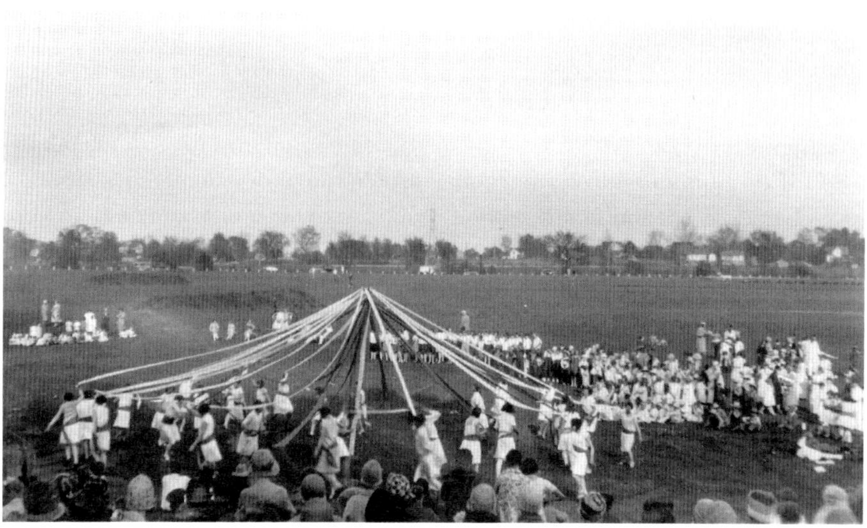

This May Pole Dance by eighth graders closed the May Day 1929 celebration at Forest Park Golf Course on the number 8 fairway. *Hamilton East Public Library.*

organ and one of the top professional skating instructors in the country. The building also served as a community center. The west wing held a drive-in restaurant, and at the east end was a social room available for meetings and banquets.

By the 1980s, interest in roller skating, particularly among teenagers, had begun to wane. The rink closed in 1989 and was torn down shortly afterward.

Noblesville acquired another major recreational facility in 1955 when the Indianapolis Water Company dammed Cicero Creek northwest of the city and created Morse Reservoir (sometimes known as Morse Lake), a body of water stretching from Noblesville to nearby Cicero. Although the reservoir's primary purpose is to provide water to the city of Indianapolis, it quickly became a favorite spot for fishing, swimming, boating and water skiing.

The dam's spillway also proved irresistible to the teens of the 1960s and early '70s, who used it as a gigantic water slide. When Morse Park was established in 1973, authorities put an end to this potentially dangerous sport known as dam sliding.

The fun didn't stop with the end of warm weather.

Years ago, area residents enjoyed riding on bobsleds and in horse-drawn sleighs during snowy winters, and whenever the ice on the White River was thick enough, they also skated and played shinny, an informal hockey game.

In late February or March, when maple trees were tapped, those working the sugar camps treated themselves to wax parties. (Wax was hot maple syrup poured over snow or ice.)

Sledding remains a popular winter pastime, with the hill overlooking Forest Park's golf course a favorite spot, but ice skating disappeared for many years because ice no longer forms on the White River. It wasn't until the Federal Hill Commons Ice Plaza, a portable rink, opened in 2017 that ice skating returned to Noblesville.

12
NOBLESVILLE'S NOTABLES

Noblesville can claim a number of residents whose influence and achievements have been felt beyond the city's boundaries.

One of those people was William Winship Conner (1820–1890.) Although he played an active role in Noblesville's development and was enormously popular in his day, he is all but unknown in modern times, his accomplishments overshadowed by those of his father, John Conner, and uncle, Noblesville founder William Conner.

Conner served in Indiana's state legislature four times—once as a senator (1845–48) and three times as a representative (1843–45, 1850–51 and 1871–72)—and he helped frame the 1851 state constitution. He also was clerk of the Hamilton County Circuit Court from 1859 to 1862. His appointment as Indiana Adjutant General, a position he occupied from 1873 to 1877, earned him the title General Conner. Regarded as one of the best speakers of his day, he was often called upon to deliver addresses at political and social functions.

Another prominent nineteenth-century resident was the man dubbed Noblesville's "Merchant Prince," Leonard Wild (1834–1909.) A native of the German city of Ulm, Wild arrived in Noblesville in 1855. He began as a simple farmhand and eventually saved enough money to enter the milling business. From 1884 to 1887, he and his son, Frank, ran a dry goods store on the east side of the courthouse square. He also served as a director of the Citizens State Bank and was one of the people who persuaded the Strawboard to locate in Noblesville.

It was as a builder, however, that Wild made his greatest impact. According to his obituary in the December 17, 1909 *Hamilton County Ledger*, he was responsible for the construction of more substantial buildings than any other man in the county. Among his projects were Noblesville's two opera houses, the Methodist parsonage, Second Ward School, the Wild Building on the east side of the square and several private homes, including the Robert L. Wilson home and his own Conner Street home.

Two years after Leonard Wild settled in Noblesville, another German immigrant, Newman D. Levinson (1832–1899), arrived. Levinson set up a tailor shop and clothing store in a room on the south side of the courthouse square and for the next forty-two years, was one of the city's most respected and well liked businessmen. His wife, Minnie, was equally well regarded for her charity work.

Newman and Minnie's son, Harry (1867–1930), eventually joined his father in the business. After Newman's death, Harry continued to run the store until 1905, when he moved to Indianapolis and opened a hat shop that became the basis for the Harry Levinson clothing store chain.

The couple's other son, Salmon Oliver (1865–1941), generally referred to as S.O. or "Sol," received a law degree from Yale, then moved to Chicago, where he specialized in corporate law and gained international fame as a peace advocate. His belief that war should be declared illegal led him to establish the American Committee for the Outlawry of War in 1921. In

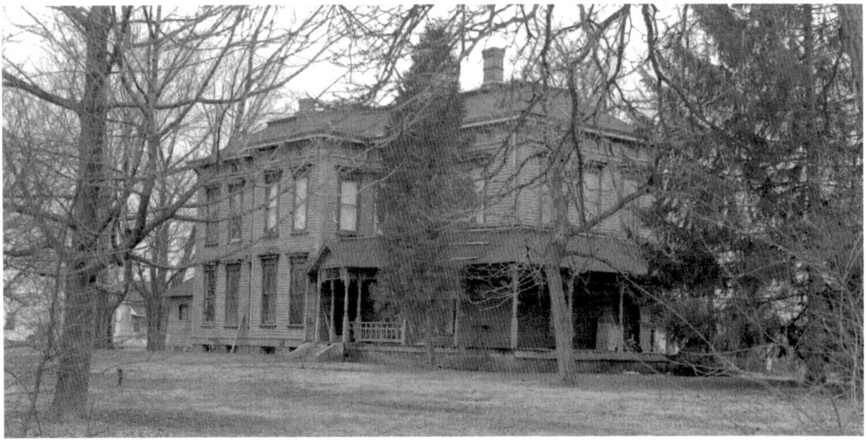

Leonard Wild's first home on Pleasant Street. The two-story Italianate house built in 1880 has had several owners and was divided into four apartments in the 1940s. This imposing house is back to being a single dwelling. It was once considered one of the finest structures in Noblesville. *Hamilton East Public Library, Ken Wright Collection.*

1927, he helped write the Kellogg-Briand Pact, an international agreement that renounces war as a means of resolving conflicts among nations. Those efforts prompted the *Manchester Guardian* to propose him as a candidate for the 1929 Nobel Peace Prize.

Despite having moved out of state, Sol Levinson maintained a lifelong interest in his hometown. The Forest Park Golf Course and the Ladies Aid Society both benefitted from his generosity, as did Noblesville High School. He and Harry donated thousands of dollars toward the construction of the Conner Street high school's gymnasium, and for many years, he funded the Levinson Awards, which were presented annually to the students with the best grades. He took such an active interest in his alma mater that in 1916, the school board announced that the school would be known in the future as Levinson High School as a tribute to his parents. Although the name was primarily used during the first two decades of the twentieth century, references to Levinson High School can be found as late as the 1940s.

Another member of the Levinson family born in Noblesville who went on to fame was Harry Levinson's son, Norman (1900–1972), who grew up to be the award-winning fashion designer Norman Norell. ("Norell" came from combining the first syllable of "Norman" with the "L" from "Levinson.") Norell's simple, classic designs have been favored by numerous Hollywood stars, socialites and politicians' wives—First Lady Michelle Obama wore a vintage Norell dress to the 2010 White House Christmas party—and in 1968, he became the first American fashion designer to introduce his own fragrance, a perfume fittingly called Norell.

Norman Norell isn't the only Noblesville native to have made a name in the arts.

During the early years of the twentieth century, brothers George (1878–1966) and James Ellsworth "Worth" Brehm (1883–1928) both achieved national reputations as illustrators. Although born in Anderson, Indiana, they spent most of their early lives in Noblesville and graduated from Noblesville High School.

Around 1906, the brothers moved to New York, where George's illustrations graced some of the biggest magazines of the day, most notably the *Saturday Evening Post*. He also illustrated advertising for such major American companies as the Ford Motor Company and the National Biscuit Company.

Worth's illustrations also appeared in national magazines. Known primarily for his work in charcoal, his gift for portraying scenes from boyhood led him to illustrate children's books such as Booth Tarkington's

Penrod and Sam and Mark Twain's *The Adventures of Huckleberry Finn* and *The Adventures of Tom Sawyer*.

Award-winning artist Floyd Hopper (1909–1984) originally hailed from Martin County, Indiana. He was on the way to a promising career in art when World War II prompted him to set aside his brushes and take a job at an Indianapolis steel fabricating factory. After the war ended, Hopper helped establish the Noblesville Casting Company and to be near his job, he moved into a home on 126th Street in an area then considered rural Noblesville. (Today, it's in the city of Fishers.) In 1958, he left the foundry and returned to art full-time, painting and conducting classes in the studio in his home.

Although watercolors were Hopper's specialty, he also worked in other mediums. One such piece, an acrylic mural of the Noblesville skyline as seen from Forest Park, was on display at the American National Bank for over a decade. It now hangs in the lobby of Noblesville's city hall.

Rex Stout (1886–1975), creator of the famed fictional detective Nero Wolfe, was born in Noblesville while his father, John Wallace Stout, was part-owner and editor of the *Republican Ledger*. The newspaper's December 3, 1886 edition contained the notice: "Wednesday evening a son was born to J.W. Stout. Mrs. Stout was at the party named above."

Stout's association with the city was brief, however. The family left Noblesville the following year, and by the time Stout's life story was written up in a 1935 *Saturday Evening Post*, none of the local people could even recall them.

African American lawyer, educator and author Cyrus Colter (1910–2002) was born in Noblesville. Like Stout, his family moved away from the city while he was still young, and like S.O. Levinson, he later became a prominent Chicago attorney.

Colter served on the Illinois Commerce Commission for over twenty years and chaired the African American Studies Department at Northwestern University. He is perhaps better known, however, for the writing career he started at the age of fifty. His first book, a collection of short stories titled *The Beach Umbrella*, won the Iowa School of Letters Award for short fiction. He went on to win several other awards for his fiction, which was noted for focusing on characters from the black middle class.

In the early 1890s, stage and silent screen star Richard Bennett (1870–1944), then known as Clarence Bennett, worked as a tailor in Milton Hutto's shop on the south side of the courthouse square. The Cass County native, primarily remembered today as the father of actresses Constance, Barbara and Joan Bennett, enjoyed his time in Noblesville and gladly reminisced about it with Noblesville residents who visited with him in later years.

Singer, songwriter and guitarist Steve Wariner (1954–) was born and raised in Noblesville and graduated from Noblesville High School. At the age of seventeen, he came to the attention of country music star Dottie West, who hired him as a bass guitarist. From there, he went on to a successful career of his own in country music, producing eighteen albums and winning four Grammys, as well as several other awards.

Wariner has worked with some of the country music industry's greats, including the legendary Chet Atkins, who bestowed upon Wariner the title of CGP (Certified Guitar Player), an honor Atkins accorded to only three other guitarists. Wariner is a member of the Grand Ole Opry, the Music City Walk of Fame and the Kentucky Music Hall of Fame.

Noblesville has been well represented in the sports world.

Olympic diver David Boudia (1989–) grew up in Noblesville and is a 2007 graduate of Noblesville High School. A member of the U.S. National Diving Team since 2005, Boudia has competed in three Olympics—Beijing (2008), London (2012) and Rio de Janeiro (2016)—and medaled in two of them. In London, he won a bronze medal in the synchronized ten-meter platform event, and he took the gold in the individual ten-meter platform—the first gold won by an American male diver since Greg Louganis in 1988. At Rio de Janeiro, he earned a silver for the synchronized ten-meter platform and a bronze for the individual event.

Given Noblesville's proximity to Indianapolis, it's not surprising that the city would have several connections to the Indianapolis Motor Speedway.

Race car drivers Conor Daly (1991–) and Bryan Clauson (1989–2016) both called Noblesville home and raced in multiple Indianapolis 500s. Daly, a second-generation driver, was born in Noblesville. (His father, former professional race car driver Derek Daly, is another Noblesville resident.) Although Clauson was originally from California, he grew up in Noblesville and graduated from Noblesville High School. Daly still races, but Clauson died in 2016 as a result of a crash during a race in Belleville, Kansas. The following year, a historical marker honoring him was erected at Forest Park.

Michigan native Preston Tucker (1903–1956) is primarily known as the man who designed the innovative Tucker '48 (sometimes called the "Tucker Torpedo"), but he also spent time at the Indianapolis Motor Speedway and even entered cars in the 1935 race.

In 1937, he moved his family to a farm on State Road 38 (Sheridan Road) just west of Noblesville. During the two years he lived there, Tucker invented a camouflaged antiaircraft combat car, the Tucker Tiger, which he tried unsuccessfully to sell to the U.S. Army. (The car, said to be able to travel at 114 miles per hour, was too fast for the army's use.) Tucker moved back to Michigan in 1939.

In 1937, Earl "Lucky" Teter (1901–1942) entered the first ever locally owned car in the Indianapolis 500. As a car owner, Teter came up short (the "Lucky Teter Special" finished a disappointing nineteenth), but his primary career as a daredevil stunt driver was in high gear that year.

A Noblesville native, Teter grew up on the family farm north of Riverwood and graduated from Noblesville High School. While recuperating from a serious automobile accident, he conceived the idea of the Hell Drivers, a troupe of stuntmen who would perform daring acts with automobiles and motorcycles. From 1934 to 1942, Teter's Hell Drivers traveled all over North America, thrilling crowds with feats such as crashing through flaming barricades and driving cars on two wheels.

In addition to touring, Teter appeared in newsreels and motion pictures. In 1936, Conner Street was closed off south of the courthouse so sportswriter

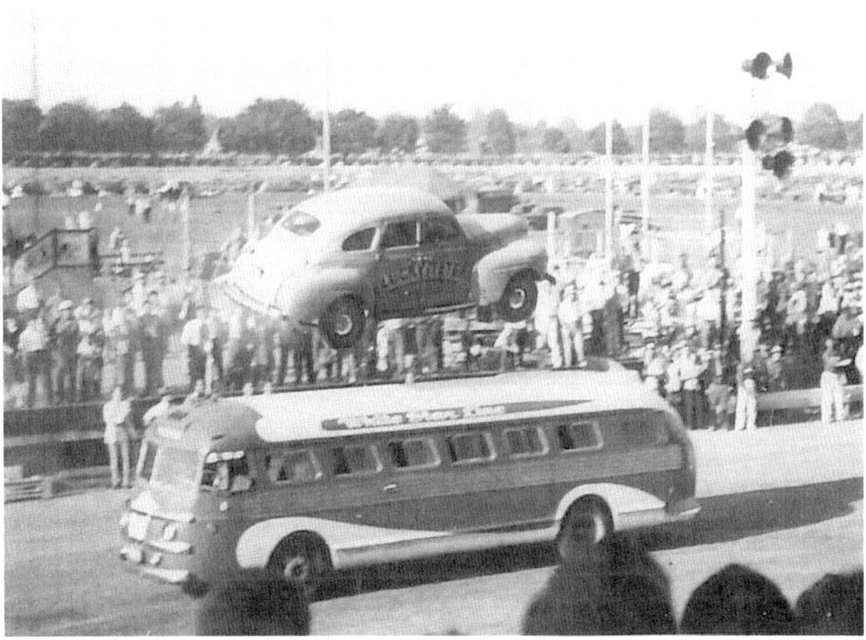

"Lucky" Teter thrilling the crowd at Indiana State Fairgrounds. *Hamilton County Historical Society.*

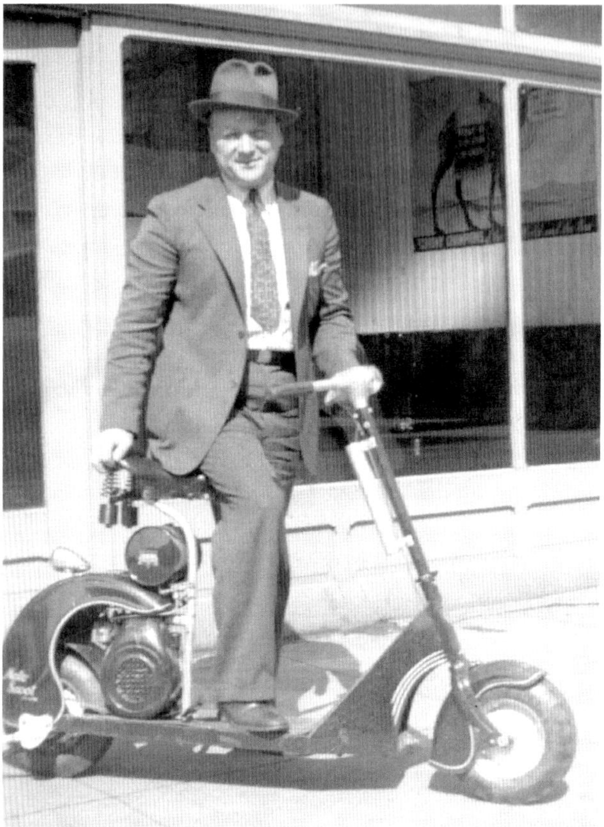

"Lucky" Teter on scooter. *Hamilton East Public Library.*

Grantland Rice could film Teter and his Hell Drivers performing their stunts for one of Rice's "Sport-lights."

Lucky's luck finally ran out on July 5, 1942, when he attempted to jump over a transport truck at the Indiana State fairgrounds during a benefit for the Army Emergency Relief. He crashed into the landing ramp and died shortly afterward.

William J. "Pete" Knight (1929–2004) was a daredevil of a different sort. Born in Noblesville, he lived in the city until the second grade. In 1960, he became one of the few U.S. Air Force test pilots to fly the X-20 Dyna-Soar, which was intended to be the first winged aircraft in space. The program was canceled three years later, but Knight completed astronaut training and was then assigned to fly the X-15, a rocket research craft. On October 3, 1967, while flying the X-15, he set a world speed record for manned aircraft. The record still stands. Knight also is one of only a handful of pilots to earn astronaut wings by flying an airplane in space.

Following his retirement from the U.S. Air Force in 1982, Knight entered California politics. He was elected mayor of Palmdale, California, in 1988 and later served in both the California State Assembly and the state senate.

The first African American child born in Noblesville grew up to be one of its most highly regarded citizens. Nancy Elliott Roberts (1852–1952), affectionately known as "Aunt Nan," was born in a log cabin in a part of southeast Noblesville known as Calamus Swamp. She married Stephen "Steve" Roberts, a stock dealer who was a member of the Roberts family of Roberts Settlement, a rural African American community in the northern part of the county. An excellent cook and manager, Aunt Nan Roberts catered the social functions of some of Noblesville's most prominent residents. The entire community mourned her passing at the age of one hundred.

Reverend Barney Stone (1847–1942), who moved to Noblesville in the early 1890s, was another of the city's most respected citizens. Born into slavery in Kentucky, he ran away from his plantation during the Civil War and joined the Union army, fighting at the Battles of Fort Wagner and Milliken's Bend. White soldiers taught him to read and write, and after the war, he spent three years educating himself at the home of a lawyer. In 1868, he turned to preaching and helped establish churches in Kentucky, Tennessee and Indiana.

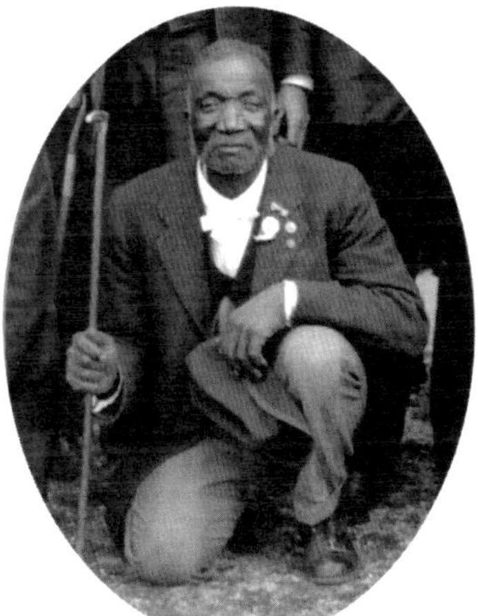

Reverend Barney Stone in front of the Grand Army of the Republic group. *Hamilton County Historical Society.*

In addition to being the pastor of Noblesville's First Baptist Church, Reverend Stone was a teacher, an evangelist, a patriotic orator and, from 1897 to 1903, court bailiff. He was an ardent Republican, who, when too feeble to walk during his last election, had himself carried to the polls so he could vote.

Besides Noblesville's famous citizens, there have been a couple some might call infamous.

Helen Worley Cromell (1886–1969) grew up in Noblesville and neighboring Cicero. (Her last name often inaccurately appears as "Cromwell" because Helen herself eventually used that spelling, explaining that most people thought the name was Cromwell anyway.) Her mother was a member of Noblesville's prominent Joseph family and her uncle Julius X. Joseph was one of the city's mayors, but Helen had other ideas about how to live.

As "Dirty Helen," a madam and the owner of the infamous Sunflower Inn, she was a Milwaukee legend for over thirty years. Her speakeasy turned tavern was a favorite haunt of movie stars, politicians and athletes, and she numbered gangsters such as Al Capone among her friends. Her nickname, "Dirty Helen," came from the salty language she'd unleash on customers who ordered anything but bourbon or scotch.

When Fascist writer and publisher William Dudley Pelley (1890–1965) moved to Noblesville from North Carolina in 1940, he was already notorious throughout the country for his political publications and for forming the Silver Legion, also known as the Silver Shirts, an anti-Semitic paramilitary organization modeled after Hitler's Brown Shirts. That's undoubtedly why he initially used an assumed name when he attempted to find a home in Noblesville for his Fellowship Press. After failing to acquire the Hudler Press, he bought the old box factory at the west end of Pleasant Street and set up shop there.

Two years later, Pelley made national headlines when the anti-Roosevelt, pro-Axis slant of his publications led to his arrest and conviction for criminal sedition. He served half of a fifteen-year sentence before being released in 1950.

Upon returning to Noblesville, he shifted his focus from politics to esoteric and metaphysical matters and established the Soulcraft Press in the former Fellowship Press building. For the next fifteen years, he led a comparatively quiet life, publishing books and other material devoted to Soulcraft, a New Age spiritual philosophy with biblical overtones.

Pelley attracted national attention one final time, however, when a burning cross was discovered outside the mortuary handling his funeral services.

Two other people with Noblesville connections made the national news during the 1960s and '70s.

Charles David Myers (1940–), a member of Noblesville High School's class of 1958, was one of the Freedom Riders, a racially mixed group that rode interstate buses through the South to protest segregation during the civil rights era. He was arrested in Mississippi in 1961 for entering a whites only waiting room at a bus station with six black companions, and chose to work off his fine by doing jail time. During his incarceration, he received national attention from an interview he gave to Pulitzer Prize–winning journalist Westbrook Pegler.

Myers went on to become a photojournalist and was subsequently employed at a Dayton, Ohio television station.

Noblesville native Tim Kraft (1941–) worked on several Indiana Democratic campaigns before volunteering for Jimmy Carter's presidential campaign in 1974. From 1976 to 1977, he was the political coordinator for Carter's transition team, and from 1977 to 1979, he served as Special Assistant to the President for Appointments. In that job, he was charged with setting President Carter's daily schedule and determining who would be allowed to meet with the president.

Kraft left his position in the White House to become the manager of the 1980 Carter/Mondale Re-Election Committee. Following Carter's loss, he returned to his New Mexico home and started a political consulting firm. In the years since, he has been active in both domestic and international politics, serving as an election observer in Central and South America, and as a consultant on Vermont governor Howard Dean's failed 2003 presidential bid.

13

NOBLESVILLE'S NOTABLE VISITORS

In addition to being able to claim a number of celebrated residents, Noblesville has had quite a few famous visitors.

Nowhere is that more evident than in the area of politics. Over the years, the city's proximity to the state capital, its status as a county seat and—in earlier times—its position on the main railroad running north out of Indianapolis, combined to make Noblesville a stop on the itinerary of many a big-name politician.

At least nine past, present or future presidents have paid visits to the Noblesville area. (There may actually have been ten. During the War of 1812, future president Zachary Taylor was part of an army expedition that traveled along the White River in search of hostile Indians.)

The first documented visit of a U.S. president took place on December 9, 1879, when the train carrying Ulysses S. Grant to a large reception in Indianapolis made a brief, unscheduled stop in Noblesville to take on water. A crowd had already assembled along the city's railroad tracks to watch Grant pass by, and when his train came to an unexpected halt, there was a rush to shake hands with the former president. Grant leaned down from the platform of the rear car and obliged his admirers until the train began to move on.

Benjamin Harrison was no stranger to Noblesville even before being elected president in 1888. In earlier years, as an Indianapolis lawyer, he appeared in cases before the Hamilton County court. He also visited at least once while serving as an Indiana senator.

In 1894, former president Harrison undertook a state-wide speaking tour and made Noblesville the first stop on the tour's northern leg. When his train pulled into the city on the morning of October 19, there were flags waving from nearly every home along the railroad tracks, as well as from all the windows of the courthouse. Harrison delivered a short speech to an estimated three thousand people from a platform on the west side of the courthouse, then resumed his journey north.

Four years later, on October 21, 1898, William McKinley became the first sitting president to appear in Noblesville. His train from Chicago was met by a sea of American flags, thousands of yards of red, white and blue bunting and a crowd numbering around eight thousand. The Noblesville schools were dismissed for the occasion and special trains brought in people from Anderson, Lebanon and other nearby cities.

President McKinley was accompanied on his journey by several other dignitaries, including Secretary of the Treasury Lyman J. Gage, Secretary of Agriculture James Wilson and Indiana senator (and future vice president) Charles W. Fairbanks, but it was clearly McKinley the throng came to hear.

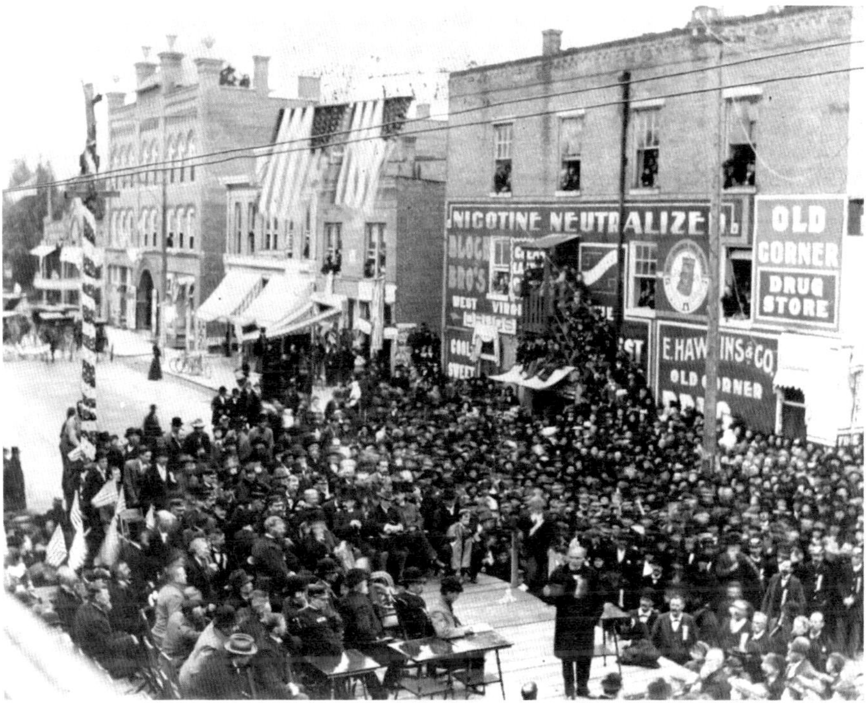

President William McKinley's visit to Noblesville. *Hamilton East Public Library.*

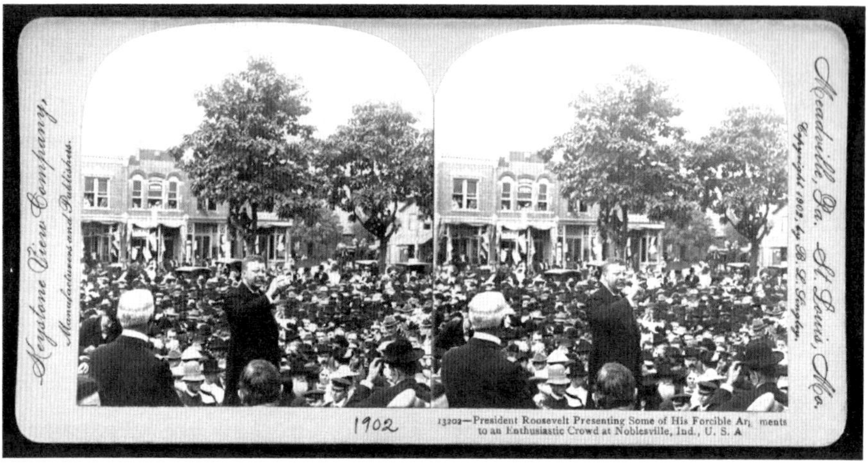

Stereoscopic image of President Theodore Roosevelt on his visit to Noblesville. This image of two photos is viewed by a stereoscope device, making the two images blend as one. *Library of Congress.*

The *Hamilton County Ledger* reported that when the president stood up to address the crowd from a specially erected stand at 9th and Conner Streets, "Hats, umbrellas and handkerchiefs filled the air and the noise was so deafening that it was some time before he could proceed."

The second incumbent president to visit Noblesville was Theodore Roosevelt, who arrived by train on the morning of September 23, 1902. Roosevelt spoke to an audience estimated at around six thousand from a stand just north of the county jail.

A few weeks earlier, Roosevelt had sustained a leg injury when his carriage was involved in a collision with a trolley. Although pain from that injury sent him to St. Vincent's Hospital in Indianapolis later that day, his discomfort must not have been evident during his Noblesville speaking engagement. The *Hamilton County Ledger* noted, "Those famous teeth of the President were easily seen."

On October 4, 1912, Woodrow Wilson made a brief speech from his campaign train when it stopped in Noblesville on the way to Kokomo from Indianapolis.

The featured speaker at the August 1 opening of the 1915 Noblesville Chautauqua was Ohio senator Warren G. Harding, who held forth on the topic of "Alexander Hamilton, the Prophet of American Destiny." The honor of introducing the future president went to Noblesville Milling Company superintendent Charles B. Jenkins. Before Jenkins took the Noblesville job, he'd lived just a few blocks from Harding in Ohio, and the two men were good friends.

One of Harding's opponents in the 1920 election, Democratic vice presidential nominee Franklin D. Roosevelt, broke with the tradition of train travel to arrive in Noblesville via automobile on October 15, 1920. The future president spoke to a large crowd on the west side of the courthouse for nearly an hour, promoting the ratification of the League of Nations treaty, which he described as the predominant issue in the presidential race.

The most recent incumbent president to visit Noblesville was Harry S. Truman, who delivered one of his famous whistle stop speeches from a platform at the rear of his campaign train on October 15, 1948. During the brief visit, Truman was greeted by the Noblesville and Westfield High School bands, and a crowd estimated at around four thousand. Interestingly, his train stopped at the intersection of 8th and Conner Streets—almost the exact spot occupied by Woodrow Wilson's campaign train thirty-six years earlier.

It would be sixty years before another successful presidential candidate visited Noblesville. On May 3, 2008, future president Barack Obama and his family attended a picnic for his supporters at Forest Park during Indiana's hotly contested Democratic primary. While Barack and Michelle Obama spoke to the crowd of several hundred, the Obamas' daughters played in the park.

Unsuccessful contenders for national office have campaigned in Noblesville as well. Perhaps the most notable was Republican presidential nominee James G. Blaine, who was welcomed to the city as enthusiastically and lavishly as if he'd already won the election. Appearing with Blaine on his 1884 campaign stop were Frederick Douglass and two future presidents, Benjamin Harrison and William McKinley. Three-time Democratic presidential nominee William Jennings Bryan made three political appearances in Noblesville several years before his Chautauqua speaking engagements—two during his presidential campaigns of 1896 and 1900 and the third in 1904 on behalf of the state's Democratic ticket. More recently, Republican vice presidential nominee Sarah Palin held a campaign rally at the Verizon Wireless Music Center in 2008 and returned the following year for a book-signing at the Hamilton Town Center mall.

Political issues have also brought celebrities in other fields to Noblesville. During the 1968 Indiana Democratic primary, motion picture actress Myrna Loy stumped for presidential candidate Eugene McCarthy at a reception in a private home, and Morley Safer of the television program *60 Minutes* interviewed members of the local Kiwanis Club on their views on President Richard Nixon and Watergate in 1973 and then again in 1974.

Famed African American author, orator, abolitionist and statesman Frederick Douglass paid three visits to Noblesville. The first took place in 1843 when he and fellow abolitionists came to Noblesville to speak on the evils of slavery and were instead forced to flee the town.

When the "Old Sage" returned on September 1, 1880, to campaign for James A. Garfield, the contrast couldn't have been greater. Douglass's train was met that morning by several bands, an honor guard and a decorated carriage pulled by four white horses. In the afternoon, he attended a pole raising on the courthouse square in honor of Garfield and Albert G. Porter, Indiana's Republican gubernatorial candidate. Later, in an address to a crowd at the old fairgrounds north of the city, Douglass noted the positive changes that had taken place since his first visit, pointing out that thirty-seven years earlier he had appeared in Noblesville as a slave, but on that day, he stood before his audience as "a man among men."

Douglass visited Noblesville again in 1884 to promote the candidacy of James G. Blaine. On that occasion, he spoke on the courthouse square for nearly an hour and a half in what the *Republican Ledger* called "his inimitable and powerful manner" while waiting for Blaine's train to arrive.

Soldier, statesman and author of the novel *Ben Hur* Lew Wallace also visited Noblesville at least three times. In 1897, he was the featured orator at a Grand Army of the Republic ceremony honoring local businessman Henry M. Caylor's service as past state commander, and in 1884 and 1898, he addressed meetings of the Republican Party at the courthouse and Wild Opera House, respectively.

Celebrated Hoosier poet and humorist James Whitcomb Riley, whose works include such classics as "Little Orphant Annie" and "The Old Swimmin' Hole," was a frequent visitor to Noblesville, both as a performer and as a private citizen. During the last decades of the 1800s, he performed several times at the Wild Opera House and once at the city hall.

Riley also often drove to Noblesville to visit his childhood friend, Noblesville mayor Dr. Edgar C. Loehr. The two men had become acquainted through Dr. Loehr's uncle, Daniel Loehr, who had lived near Riley in Greenfield, Indiana, while Riley was growing up. Riley's friendship with Daniel Loehr's family was memorialized in his poem "The Loehrs and the Hammonds," and there is evidence to suggest Riley's poem "Out to Old Aunt Mary's" may have been inspired by Dr. Loehr's aunt, Rachel Loehr.

Before becoming Indiana's best known poet, Riley earned a living painting signs and houses, and one of the earliest homes he painted belonged to Dr. Loehr's father. Whenever Riley visited Noblesville, he made a point of driving by the old Loehr homestead on the northeast corner of 10th and Hannibal Streets. (The structure was razed several years ago.)

In the early years of the twentieth century, Noblesville's Chautauquas brought some big names to the city, such as the previously mentioned William Jennings Bryan and Warren G. Harding. One of the first nationally known figures to appear was Arctic explorer Dr. Frederick A. Cook, who was a featured speaker at the 1911 Chautauqua. Dr. Cook's vehement denunciations of his rival, Robert E. Peary, during his Noblesville speech made newspaper headlines.

The most popular Chautauqua visitor, however, was Helen Keller, who appeared in 1915 with her teacher Anne Sullivan Macy. The woman the *Noblesville Daily Ledger* referred to as "the miracle woman of the age" left her audience as impressed by her quick-witted responses to their questions as they were by her triumph over her handicaps.

One Noblesville man, Colonel Dick Taylor, was particularly interested in seeing Keller so he could tell her of his connection to her family. Years earlier, Taylor had spent several months working for the Alabama newspaper published by Keller's father. When Taylor decided to look for another job, Captain Keller asked him to stay on a few weeks longer to run things while Keller got married. The woman Keller married was Helen Keller's mother.

In 1853, the Children's Aid Society was formed in New York City with the goal of helping the city's homeless children. Between 1854 and 1929, agents of the society gathered up thousands of children from streets and orphanages and sent them out on trains to new—and hopefully better—homes in the West. This later became known as the Orphan Train Movement, although not all the children were orphans. Some were simply victims of poverty or abusive relationships.

On August 4, 1859, a train bearing a group of these children and their sponsor, Henry Friedgen, arrived in Noblesville. The youngsters were given lunch at the Ferguson Hotel, then taken to the Christian Church and lined up so prospective foster parents could get a look at them.

John Brady, later known as John Green Brady, was picked out of the lineup by Judge John Green of Tipton. The judge decided to take Brady home with him because he thought Brady was "the homeliest, toughest, most unpromising boy in the whole lot." Judge Green wanted to see what could be made of the boy.

Brady justified the judge's faith in him. After graduating from Yale and the Union Theological Seminary, he went to Alaska as a Presbyterian missionary and became such a prominent advocate for the territory that President William McKinley appointed him Alaska's territorial governor in 1897. He held the post until 1906.

Brady's good friend and companion on the train ride to Noblesville, Andrew Burke, remained in Noblesville and lived with three different families while growing up. When the Civil War broke out, he enlisted as a drummer boy for the Seventy-Fifth Indiana Regiment. After the war, he went west like Brady and settled in the Dakota Territory, where he got into politics. In 1890, he was elected the second governor of North Dakota, an office he occupied until 1893.

Notorious bank robber John Dillinger never robbed a Noblesville bank, but a member of his gang, Harry Pierpont, did—or rather attempted to.

On December 16, 1924, Pierpont and five other young men ran into the Citizens State Bank with revolvers drawn. Staring down the barrel of a gun, the bank's president, William E. Dunn, coolly slid his foot onto a burglar alarm just as bookkeeper Wesley Affenback also stepped on a hidden button. It's not clear which button was hit first, but the alarm went off immediately, sending the would-be bandits flying out of the bank empty-handed. They jumped into a stolen getaway car, which had been kept running by a seventh gang member, and sped off.

Although Pierpont escaped the law on that occasion, a few months later, he was caught robbing a Kokomo bank and sent to the Indiana State Reformatory in Pendleton, Indiana. It was there he encountered Dillinger and embarked on a fatal friendship that ultimately led to his execution in an Ohio reformatory in 1934.

During the 1960s and '70s, the stars of some popular television shows visited Noblesville on behalf of local charities.

From 1967 to 1971, the annual United Fund (now known as United Way) campaign was kicked off each fall with an appearance on the courthouse square by a different celebrity. The first to help light the United Fund torch was Michael Landon of *Bonanza*. He was followed by Peter Graves of *Mission Impossible* in 1968, Barbara Eden of *I Dream of Jeannie* in 1969, Fess Parker of *Daniel Boone* in 1970 and James Brolin of *Marcus Welby, M.D.* in 1971.

In 1977, Mary Frances Crosby and her mother, Kathryn, came to downtown Noblesville to promote the special performance of a play at Beef 'n' Boards dinner theater in Indianapolis. The production was a benefit for a proposed Lions Club Eye Center at the I.U. Medical Center. Mary Crosby later joined the cast of the program *Dallas* and became famous as the woman who shot Larry Hagman's character, J.R. Ewing.

Last, but certainly not least, no account of famous Noblesville visitors would be complete without mentioning the many giants of the entertainment and music industries who have performed at the Noblesville amphitheater currently known as Ruoff Home Mortgage Music Center. Bob Hope, Elton John, Bon Jovi, Garth Brooks, Phish, the Dave Matthews Band, the Grateful Dead, Jay-Z and Jimmy Buffett are just a handful of the big names who have appeared there to date—and the list continues to grow.

14
MAKING HEADLINES

A few events in Noblesville's history have so significantly impacted the community as a whole that they merit special attention.

Noblesville has been fortunate to have avoided widespread tornado damage such as that which proved deadly to the nearby towns of Sheridan and Arcadia on Palm Sunday 1965. The same can't be said for flooding, however. Noblesville was hit hard by the Great Flood of 1913.

On March 23—Easter Sunday of that year—rain began to fall across the Midwest and parts of the East and didn't let up for three days. With the ground still partially frozen, there was no place for extra water to go. Rivers and creeks soon spilled over their banks.

For the first time in Noblesville's history, the city's business district was threatened by the White River. To the north, west and south of the public square, little could be seen but water. The March 26 *Noblesville Daily Ledger* noted that the county courthouse offered the best view of the devastation and advised readers to slip the janitor a little money to persuade him to take them up in the courthouse tower for a look. Binoculars were recommended.

Noblesville was essentially cut off from the rest of the world for several days. The trains and interurban stopped running, roads were impassable, and any bridges not destroyed by the torrent were barely holding together. Few telephone lines remained in service, which had the local Western Union telegraph office working overtime to pick up the slack.

No deaths occurred, but the damage wrought by the flood was extensive. A three-foot-high levee of sandbags and banked earth constructed on 9th

Street broke, sending six feet of water into the pumping station of the city's waterworks, forcing it to close. Hundreds of homes were left without water, and the fire department had no means of fighting fires. Floodwaters completely covered Riverside Cemetery, knocking over fences and monuments, washing out the drives and disturbing some of the graves. Even the neighboring towns of Cicero, Westfield and Arcadia were affected. Their electricity, generated in Noblesville, was cut off when the wires supplying them broke after a pole was swept away by the deluge.

The hardest-hit section of Noblesville was an already flood-prone area in the southwest part of the city dubbed "Johnstown" after the Pennsylvania city devastated twenty-four years earlier by a historic flood. Everything west of 5th Street was under water, leaving 100 to 150 families destitute. One well-known Johnstown resident, described as a "character" by the local newspaper, vowed to remain in his home rather than evacuate, but after one night in the flooded area, he changed his mind and gratefully accepted a rescue by boat the following morning.

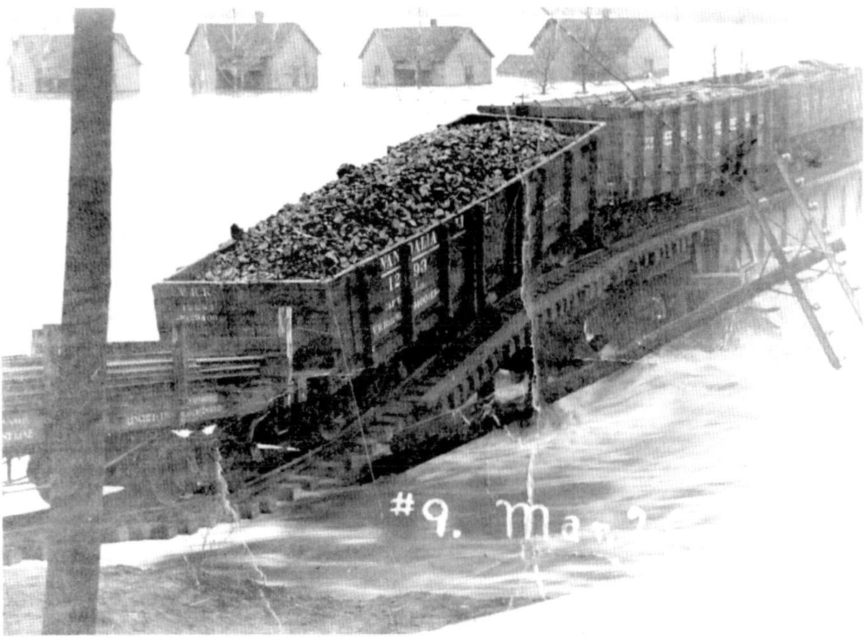

The flood of 1913 washed out the Lake Erie and Western Railroad bridge, knocked down power lines and left carloads of coal hanging over the water. The cars filled with coal were an attempt to weigh down and hold the bridge. This failed. *Hamilton East Public Library, Joe Roberts Collection.*

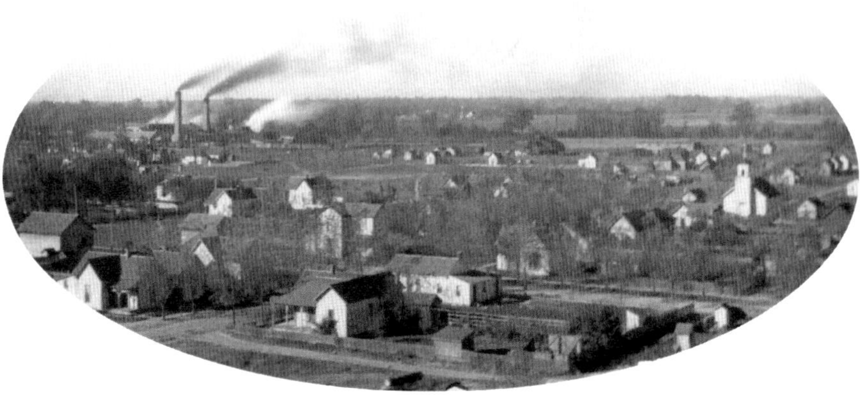

View of "Johnstown" before the 1913 flood. *Hamilton County Historical Society.*

Relief efforts began almost at once. Dr. Samuel Harrell opened his hospital to people forced from their homes, while a store set up by the Ladies Aid Society in the Hare building on Conner Street met victims' immediate needs for food, clothing and other necessities. Women of the local churches provided meals, grocers donated baskets of food and a fund started by the *Noblesville Daily Ledger* brought in cash donations, as did two benefit performances at the Star Theatre.

By the end of the week, the river was back to its normal level, but the cleanup went on for some time, and for many years afterward, the citizens of Noblesville became uneasy any time there was excessive rainfall.

Another memorable weather-related event was the Blizzard of '78, which began on Wednesday, January 25, 1978, and, like the Great Flood of 1913, continued for three days. During that period, Noblesville received fifteen inches of fresh snow on top of five inches already on the ground, the wind gusted as high as fifty miles per hour and the temperature dipped to zero.

The entire city shut down as drifts—some up to eight feet high—began to pile up. The *Noblesville Daily Ledger*, the county's only daily newspaper, suspended publication for two days—the first time in the paper's ninety-year history. Emergency shelters were opened in the Hamilton County jail, the National Guard Armory and in the United Auto Workers and United Rubber Workers halls. Citizens band radio groups played a vital role in alerting authorities to stranded travelers and others in need of aid, while

Noblesville's National Guard unit mounted rescue missions in heavy vehicles. The guard also transported Riverview Hospital personnel to the hospital.

Riverview was itself the scene of considerable drama. From late Wednesday until noon on Saturday, every able-bodied person in the building helped in every way possible to keep things running smoothly. Dr. Doyle Manhart delivered three babies during that period, but he also assisted in the kitchen, as did the hospital administrator, Peter Mariani. Some dedicated hospital employees trudged a mile through the snow to get to work, and Dr. Paul Waitt rode in on a snowmobile from Sheridan, about twelve miles away.

It was nearly a week before streets and roads were cleared and life began to return to normal. When it was all over, there was one local casualty of the blizzard. An elderly man died of a heart attack while attempting to rescue a neighbor he'd seen fall into a drift. Ironically, in the blinding snow, the gentleman had failed to notice the neighbor had gotten herself out and was safely back in her house.

One of the worst interurban wrecks in county history occurred on the courthouse square in downtown Noblesville.

On the evening of May 24, 1919, a railcar traveling from Cicero crossed the river and roared down 9th Street at an estimated thirty-five or forty miles per hour—well over the speed limit for a populated area. When the interurban hit the traction switch on the east side of the square, its front wheels jumped the tracks, sending it careening into the stone curbing around the courthouse lawn. (Cracks and gouges left by the impact are still visible south of the steps leading to the east entrance of the courthouse.)

Several parked vehicles were crushed by the out-of-control railcar, including one belonging to the Wiggins family. Mr. and Mrs. Harry Wiggins had left their three children in their automobile while they stepped across the street to buy ice cream cones for the ride home. The Wiggins's two daughters survived the crash, but eight year-old Robert was killed and over twenty others in the interurban were injured.

Traction company officials spent the night clearing away the wreckage. They laid the blame on the city, claiming oil spread on 9th Street to control the dust had gotten onto the interurban's rails, making the railcar uncontrollable. Noblesville mayor Jack McCoun and other city officials mounted their own inspection of the rails, however, and found no oil anywhere except that rubbed off by passing automobiles at the Harrison Street crossing. Nor was any oil found on the interurban's wheels.

Three weeks later, after interviewing several witnesses, an investigation headed by Hamilton County coroner William Rhoades determined the

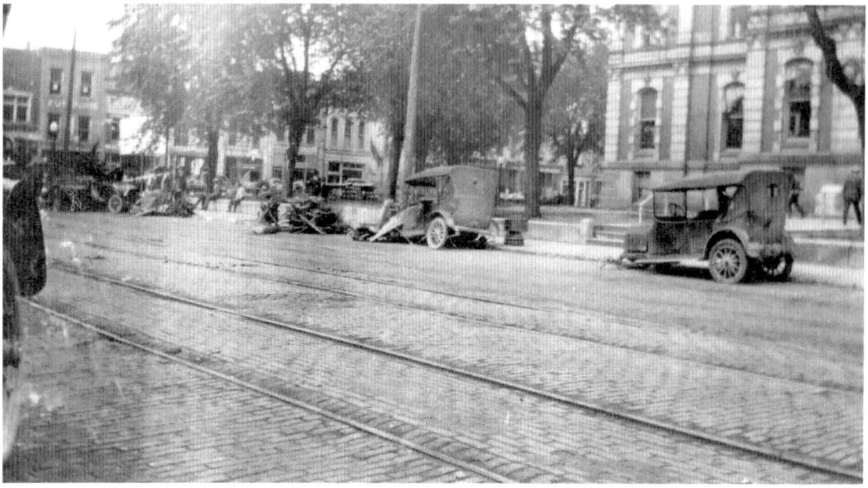

Interurban wreck shows the exterior damage to cars crushed by the runaway interurban car. *Hamilton County Historical Society.*

accident was caused by speed and negligence. Rhoades believed the car was in such bad shape it should never have been in service that evening. It was September before the Indiana Public Service Commission issued its official findings, but the commission agreed with Rhoades's conclusions.

The company settled out of court with most of the injured parties and paid for the ruined automobiles, but the following year Harry Wiggins filed suit seeking $10,000 for the death of his son. Before the trial started, a settlement was reached, and the lawsuit was dismissed. Wiggins received $1,800, and the company paid all costs associated with the case.

Perhaps the most sensational event to take place in Noblesville was the 1925 murder trial of Indiana Ku Klux Klan Grand Dragon D.C. (David Curtis) Stephenson.

In March of that year, Stephenson forced Madge Oberholtzer, a young Indianapolis woman whom he'd dated a few times, to accompany him to Chicago. During the train ride, he brutally assaulted her. Afterward, instead of traveling on to Chicago, they disembarked in Hammond, Indiana, where Oberholtzer convinced Stephenson to allow her to go into a drugstore to buy some rouge. She came out with a box of mercury bichloride and, upon returning to their hotel, swallowed several tablets in an attempt to commit suicide. The mercury made her so ill, the alarmed Stephenson took her back to her home in Indianapolis, where she died in agony almost a month later.

Stephenson and his bodyguards, Earl Klinck and Earl Gentry, were indicted for Oberholtzer's murder. The defense attorneys, believing a fair trial in Marion County wasn't possible, requested a change of venue, and the case landed in the Hamilton County court of Judge Fred Hines on May 23. In August, however, the defendants claimed bias on the part of Judge Hines, and he was replaced by Judge William Sparks of Rushville.

The trial finally got underway on October 12 in the second-floor courtroom of the Hamilton County courthouse and continued until November 14. On that day, a jury made up mainly of local farmers acquitted Klinck and Gentry of the charges, but Oberholtzer's dying declaration, dictated to her family lawyer, helped get Stephenson convicted of second-degree murder.

It was a stunning turn of events for the man who'd repeatedly told Oberholtzer, with some justification, that he was the law in Indiana. During the early 1920s, the KKK was a power to be reckoned with in the state, and D.C. Stephenson ran the Klan. His conviction essentially broke the organization.

That Stephenson's downfall took place in Noblesville is significant, for the city had a reputation for being a stronghold of the "Invisible Empire." Three large KKK parades took place there between 1922 and 1925,

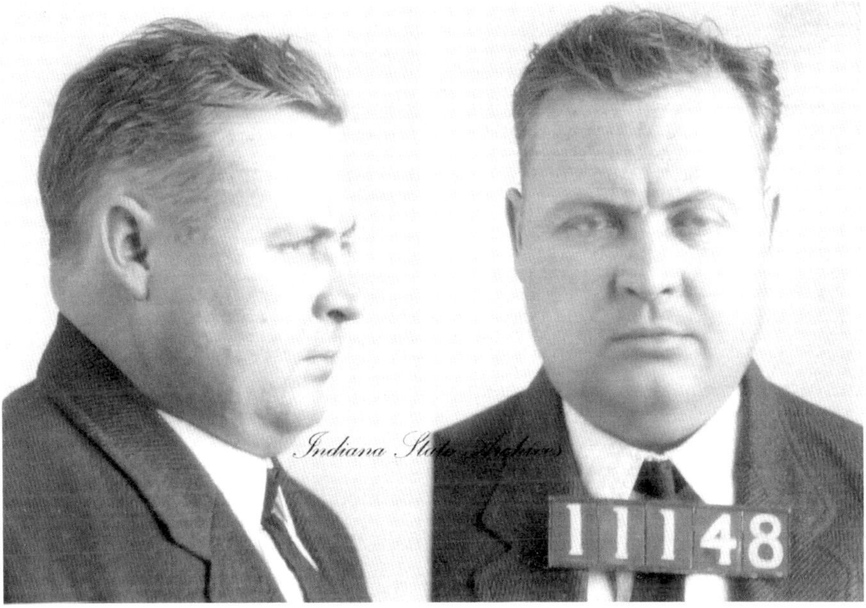

Mug shot of D.C. Stephenson. *Indiana State Archives.*

and the final day of Noblesville's Independent 1925 Chautauqua was designated "Klan Day," with Imperial Wizard Hiram Wesley Evans the featured speaker.

In order to understand Noblesville's association with the Klan, it's important to note that the Klan of the 1920s differed from the Klan in the South during the Reconstruction period or the 1960s civil rights era. The 1920s version of the KKK was spread across the entire country, not just the South, and its main targets were foreigners, especially Catholics and Jews, rather than African Americans. The country was still reeling from the recent world war, and as people watched the rising tide of immigrants, many of whom were Catholic, some worried that the United States could be taken over by a foreign power, such as the pope. That apprehension ran especially deep in predominantly Protestant Indiana.

From June to August 1925, while Stephenson was awaiting trial, a series of Klan Komment! columns appeared in the *Noblesville Daily Ledger*. In the articles, the Klan promoted patriotism, Christianity, Prohibition, good morals and obedience to the law, which provides an explanation as to why some people were swayed into signing up. Others joined because they were threatened with economic ruin if they didn't. Of those who did become members, many paid their dues, then had nothing more to do with the organization.

After the Stephenson trial, KKK membership dwindled all over the country. The Klan was largely forgotten in Noblesville until a small group of Klansmen attempted to hold a march in the city in 1973. The violence that local authorities feared didn't materialize, but the number of anti-Klan counterdemonstrators who showed up made it clear the KKK wasn't welcome in Noblesville.

The city wasn't quite done with the Klan, however. In 1995, contractor Don Roberts discovered a trunk full of old KKK membership cards from the 1920s on a property he'd acquired. Some people felt the records should be destroyed, but instead, Roberts gave them to the Hamilton County Historical Society, which restricted access to family members and serious researchers. Although the membership cards remain a delicate subject, they have their value—they prove that the local Klan organization didn't solely consist of Noblesville residents. The membership roll contains names and addresses from nearly *all* the cities and towns of Hamilton County, as well as from a few communities just outside the county.

The biggest economic development in Noblesville's history was launched in October 1886 by a group of local businessmen who organized a company

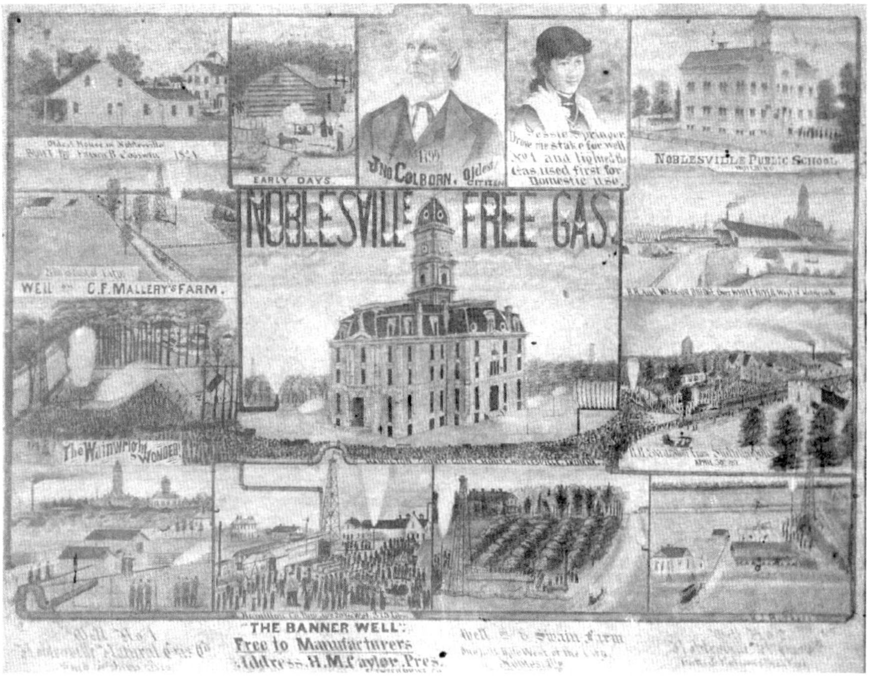

Gas boom postcard depicting several of the gas wells in the area, including the Wainwright Wonder, the Banner Well, the well on the Swain farm and the well on the C.F. Mallery farm. *Hamilton County Historical Society.*

to drill for natural gas or any other valuable substance they could find. It was a gamble that paid off in a big way—Noblesville had the good fortune to be located on a large, seemingly inexhaustible gas field.

On the night of January 22, 1887, a crew of men drilling a well at the southeast corner of 11th and Pleasant Streets struck pay dirt. The flow of gas from the well was so strong, the men felt it wise to stop drilling. When they resumed two days later, they quickly realized they had one of the best natural gas wells in the state, if not the entire country. Once ignited, light from the well was visible as far away as Atlanta and Westfield, leading some country folk to think there was a major fire in town.

The first well was soon followed by others with names like the "Pioneer," the "Mallery Boomer," the "Banner-Enterprise," the "Volcano" and the biggest of all, the "Wainwright Wonder." By January of the following year, there were over twenty-five natural gas wells in the Noblesville area, and more were in the process of being drilled, not just in Noblesville, but across the county. Special excursion trains brought thousands to Noblesville from

Indianapolis just to hear the deafening roar of the gas and witness the spectacle of the flames lighting up the sky.

The entire city was giddy with gas boom fever, a sentiment expressed somewhat graphically in the January 28, 1887 *Noblesville Independent*: "Now let the croakers croak, we have the Boom. It is spelled with a big B. It has come to stay. The little word of three letters 'Gas' has opened possibilities; the fortunate spot was touched, and good Mother Earth vomited up her riches in our lap."

Noblesville entered a new era of prosperity. Not only were residents' homes and businesses well supplied with gas for lighting and fuel, but several factories such as the Strawboard, the Foundry and Machine Works, and the Novelty Works were lured to the city as well. Many new buildings were constructed, including most of those still standing around the courthouse square.

By the early years of the twentieth century, however, the seemingly inexhaustible supply began to dwindle, largely due to wastefulness. After the gas ran out, the growth of some of Noblesville's neighboring towns stagnated, but Noblesville was more fortunate. Since much of its reserves were piped to Indianapolis, it hadn't invested as heavily in the gas industry and didn't suffer a serious decline.

One of the largest crowds ever to assemble in Noblesville came together to celebrate the joint Centennial of Noblesville and Hamilton County in 1923. In honor of the occasion, the entire city was decked out in patriotic colors, and the windows of various businesses displayed donated heirlooms and artifacts from the county's pioneer past.

The two-day celebration was kicked off on October 3 by speeches, songs and a homecoming on the courthouse square. Some of the county's oldest residents were honored at the event, as was a special guest, Margaret Ellen Conner Crans, the only surviving child of Noblesville founder William Conner. That afternoon, a parade featuring floats and exhibits from all the townships marched through the city streets. Dancing and various contests followed, and later that evening, a pageant depicting events from the county's first one hundred years was presented at the Horse Show Grounds.

The second day began with more contests, and then at noon, an enormous pitch-in dinner took place on Logan Street between 10th and 14th Streets. Clarke Millikan and Anna Gascho, the oldest man and woman present, were the guests of honor at the feast, which featured a 150-pound birthday cake decorated with one hundred pink candles. In the afternoon, a skirmish was held at the Horse Show Grounds by Battery B of the 139th Indiana

Field Artillery. The festivities were capped off that evening by music and a fireworks display, also at the Horse Show Grounds.

The historic celebration was filmed for a motion picture that was later shown at the American Theatre. Unfortunately, although the two-reel *Centennial Year in Hamilton County* was intended to be preserved for future generations, its current whereabouts are unknown.

Fifty years later, the Noblesville and Hamilton County Sesquicentennial was observed with a weeklong series of events held at several sites in Noblesville from June 30 to July 7, 1973. Like the Centennial, there were various contests, bands and music, dances, dinners, fireworks (on the Fourth of July) and a large parade featuring entries from all the townships. Added to that list were a Kiwanis pancake fry, a food auction, style shows, a queen contest and ball, a bluegrass festival and a special ancestor-descendants recognition program.

The Sesquicentennial's biggest attraction, however, was a pageant produced by the Hamilton County Theatre Guild, *Hamilton County through the Years*. The second night of the three-day event was rained out, but the two other performances filled the main bleachers at Noblesville High School's football field. Among the enormous cast of county residents helping to tell

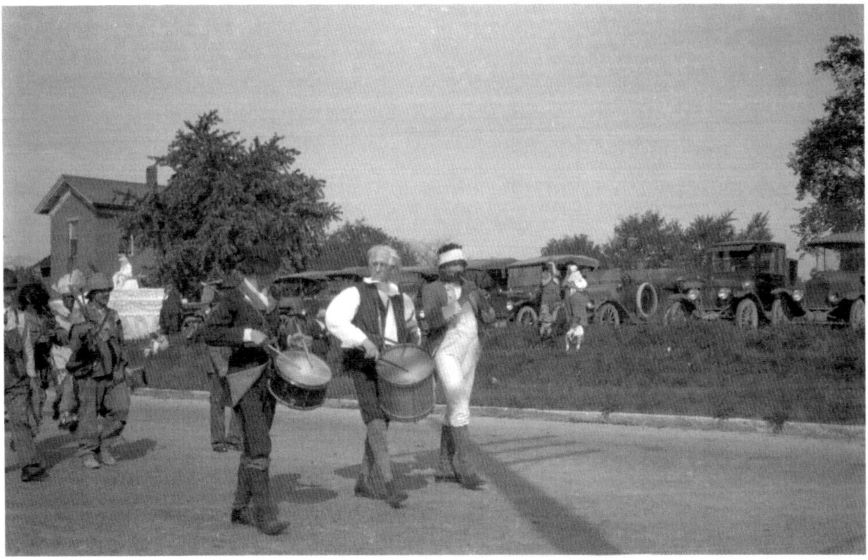

One of the units in the 1923 Centennial parade was the personification of the *The Spirit of '76* as portrayed by Earl Wild, Will W. Hare and Elwood Wilson. *Hamilton County Historical Society, Brooks Collection.*

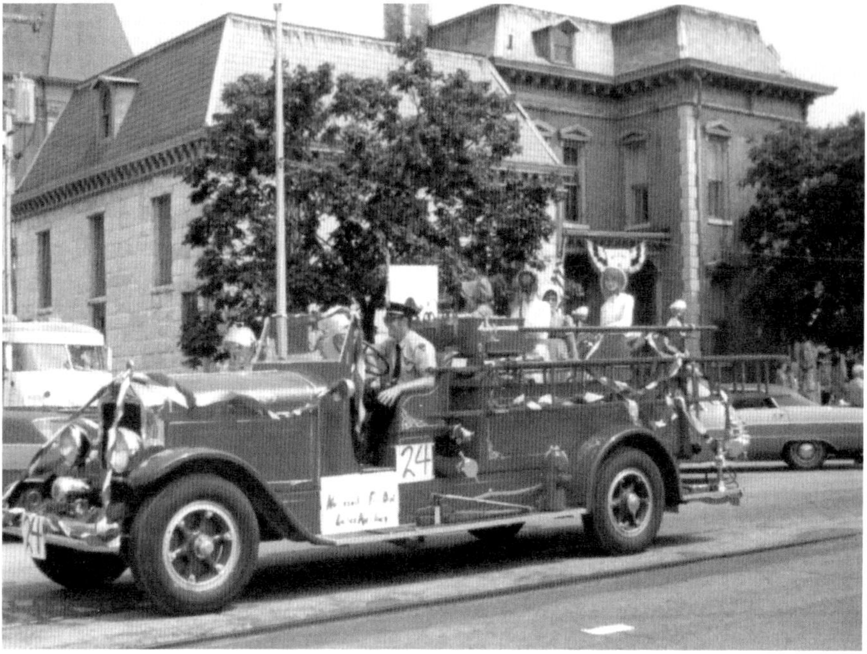

The Noblesville Fire Department drove the 1935 American LaFrance pumper truck in the 1973 Sesquicentennial parade. The Ladies Auxiliary of the fire department were on board. *Sherry Faust.*

the story of Hamilton County's first 150 years were over a dozen World War I veterans; Amel Walton Mongold, who won a "Miss Noblesville" popularity contest in 1915; and a group of children who portrayed the vegetables that spelled out Lavina Noble's name in Josiah F. Polk's garden (from the legend of how Noblesville acquired its name).

The week ended with the Hamilton County Birthday Party, an ice cream social sponsored by the First Christian Church. Church members in old-fashioned costumes served cake and ice cream to over two thousand people during a three-hour period.

Like the Centennial, the festivities of the Sesquicentennial were preserved on film. Fortunately, copies of that film still exist to serve as inspiration for the upcoming Bicentennial in 2023.

On May 25, 2018, Noblesville made national news when Noblesville West Middle School became the site of the first school shooting in Indiana.

Thanks to science teacher Jason Seaman, who heroically tackled the student shooter, no lives were lost, but Seaman and student Ella Whistler were shot multiple times. Both survived and recovered in time to serve as co-grand marshals of the city's Fourth of July parade that year.

The incident inspired displays of support from people around the country, including singer-songwriter Taylor Swift and the Indianapolis Colts, who wore #NOBStrong T-shirts at one of their practices. It also prompted many Indiana schools to review their security procedures.

15
NOBLESVILLE TODAY

If William Conner and Josiah F. Polk were alive today, they would be amazed by the changes in the land they once called home.

The dense forest and many of the wild animals they knew are long gone. Only a few clumps of woods remain scattered throughout the township. The rest of the countryside, which was initially converted into acres of productive farmland, has been altered yet again and is now covered by numerous subdivisions and shopping areas. The wild animals the early settlers once trapped and hunted have either moved on to less populated territory or adapted to an urban lifestyle.

Horseshoe Prairie, the site of the county's first settlement, is home to a gravel pit and no longer inhabited. William Conner's historic 1823 brick home, two miles south of Horseshoe Prairie, has been restored and currently serves as the centerpiece of Conner Prairie Interactive History Park, a living history museum with a national reputation. The museum originally had a rural Noblesville address, but it is now located within the city limits of nearby Fishers.

And that small town Conner and Polk laid out on the banks of the White River in 1823? It's the seat of government for what has become Indiana's fastest growing county *and* one of the fastest growing counties in the entire country.

The city of Noblesville has itself seen considerable growth. After spending most of its existence with fewer than eight thousand inhabitants, it is now one of the fifteen largest cities in Indiana, with a population currently estimated at over sixty thousand. The greatest part of that increase has come in the last thirty years or so, a trend initiated in the early 1970s when the Shorewood Corporation constructed North and South Harbors. Today, Noblesville can count nearly three hundred other subdivisions.

Population Statistics for Noblesville Town and Noblesville City

Population of Noblesville Town

1850	**1860**	**1870**	**1880**	**1890**
664	1,115	1,435	2,221	*

Population of Noblesville City

1900	**1910**	**1920**	**1930**	**1940**	**1950**
4,792	5,073	4,578	4,811	5,575	6,567
1960	**1970**	**1980**	**1990**	**2000**	**2010**
7,664	7,548	12,253	17,655	28,590	51,696

*1890 census figures were destroyed in a fire

Noblesville's current boundaries extend well beyond the original plat, running north to 216th Street, west to the Noblesville/Washington Township line at Gray/Moontown Road, south to 136th Street and as far east as Atlantic Road at the Hamilton/Madison County line. The city not only covers most of Noblesville Township, but it takes in portions of Wayne, Fall Creek and Delaware townships as well. It touches both Morse Reservoir in the north and I-69 in the south and shares borders with the neighboring cities of Fishers, Carmel and Westfield.

The heart of the city, an area often called "Old Town" because it existed before most of the subdivisions were established, is a blend of both the old and the new. The public square is bounded on three sides by buildings constructed during the gas boom years of the nineteenth century, while on the west side sits the modern Hamilton County Government and Judicial

Center. Federal and Greek Revival buildings and magnificent Queen Anne and Italianate residences mix with homes built during the post–World War II housing boom or later. The iconic old brick sidewalks can still be seen on some streets but are slowly being replaced by modern cement slab walks. (In a nod to the city's historic past, however, in recent years, sections of the old bricks have been retained in some of the new sidewalks.)

The map of Old Town remains unchanged for the most part, but a few streets have been altered. Among them are Chestnut Street between 9th and 10th Streets, which disappeared years ago when Kenley's supermarket expanded into a small strip mall, and 6th Street between Conner and Logan Streets, which was sacrificed for the construction of the Hamilton County Judicial Center. Conversely, Logan Street, which once ended on the west bank of the White River at State Road 19, now extends to River Road, while Presley Drive, which was a mere access road, was recently expanded to connect with Pleasant Street.

Presley Drive's new route takes it through two roundabouts, the most recent and radical development in local road construction. Noblesville's first roundabout appeared at the intersection of 136th Street and Brooks School Road in 2007. Since then, over twenty additional city intersections have been converted into roundabouts—including the five-point junction of 10th Street, Greenfield Avenue and Christian Avenue—and more roundabouts are planned.

Also relatively new to the city are the "Zones of Significance" signs affixed to some street signs. The zones were created in 2008 to highlight Old Town Noblesville's history and architecture. Their names and arbitrarily drawn boundaries were inspired by both actual historic areas of the city and by the city's development during different time periods.

Noblesville's business district was once confined primarily to streets around the courthouse square. Today, there are a number of shopping areas spread out all over the map, some of which include outlets of the country's biggest chains. The largest of these commercial districts is the Noblesville Corporate Campus. Located along 146th Street between State Road 37 and I-69, it combines office, retail, medical and light industrial space with housing. Hamilton Town Center, an open-air mall containing shops, restaurants and a sixteen-screen movie theater with the county's only IMAX, opened there in 2008.

Downtown Noblesville is far from dead, however.

When most of the stores dedicated to providing items necessary for everyday living disappeared from the courthouse square, the downtown area adapted by switching its focus to attracting a different kind of trade. The few longtime town square stalwarts that remain, such as Syd's Bar, Sunrise Cafe @ Uptown (the Uptown Cafe), Kirk's Hardware and Smith's Jewelers, have been joined by a number of antique stores, boutiques, art galleries and locally owned restaurants. Visitors now come from all over to shop and take in the local cuisine in buildings in which prescriptions were once filled or shoes were sold.

These days, when someone mentions "Dirty Helen," they probably aren't talking about infamous Milwaukee madam and Noblesville native Helen Worley Cromell but rather the craft beer named in her honor by the local brewpub, Barley Island, which is located just off the square.

The newest feature of downtown Noblesville is the recently completed Riverwalk, a paved pathway that follows the east bank of the White River. Constructed in three phases from 2008 to 2017, the joint city-county project runs from Logan Street, past Riverside Cemetery, to Division Street and offers an impressive view of the river and its wildlife not previously available.

Near Logan Street, at the Riverwalk's northern end, is a pedestrian bridge over the White River and State Road 19. The bridge, constructed in 2001, allows those on foot or on bicycles to safely travel between downtown Noblesville and Forest Park. It also connects the Riverwalk with two of Noblesville's popular trails, the White River Greenway and the Forest Park/Morse Beach Trail. Both routes wind together through Forest Park, then split off, with the White River Greenway heading northeast to Potter's Bridge and the Forest Park/Morse Beach Trail traveling northwest to Morse Park on the reservoir.

Just west of the Hamilton County Judicial Center and adjacent to the Riverwalk lies the future location of the Hamilton County Fallen Firefighters Memorial. The memorial, which is dedicated to the three county firemen who have died in the line of duty (Byron Galbreath, Cyrus Clark and Raymond Moulder), will include a piece of a steel beam recovered from New York's World Trade Center after its destruction on September 11, 2001.

In addition to Noblesville's everyday attractions, several local organizations sponsor festivals and special events that draw visitors and residents alike to the city's Old Town each year. Among the annual activities are Noblesville Main Street's various First Friday events, Farmers Market, Old Mill Festival and Street Dance; the Noblesville Preservation Alliance's historic homes tours; the Noblesville Cultural Arts Commission's Shakespeare in the Park and summer band concerts; the Hamilton County Artists' Association's Art Fair on the Square; the Lions Club's Pork Chop Dinner and Pancake Breakfast; the Nickel Plate Arts Maker Faire (held in conjunction with the

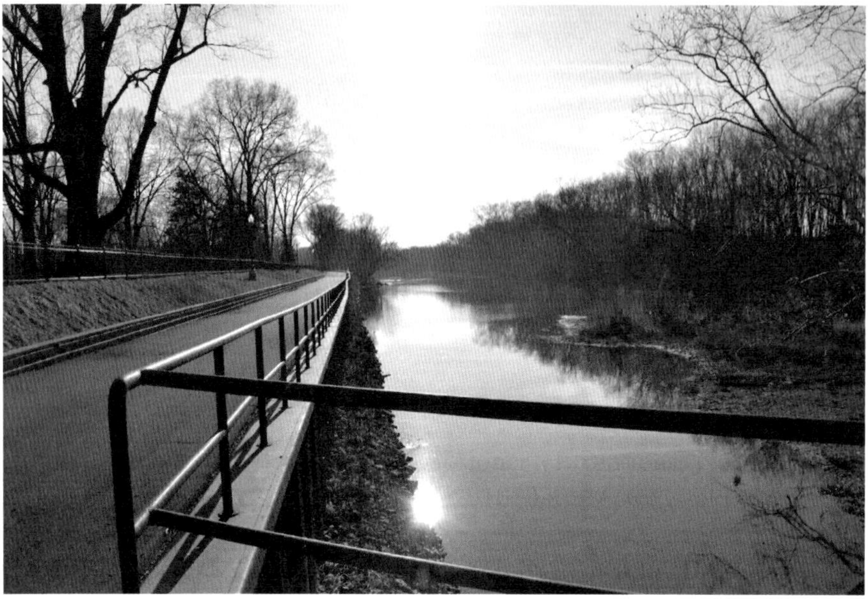

Riverwalk looking south from Riverside Cemetery. *Michael Kobrowski.*

St. Michael's Episcopal Church Strawberry Festival); the Hamilton County Parks and Recreation Department's Potter's Bridge Fall Festival and the Hamilton County 4-H Fair.

The list of events continues to grow as the city continues to grow.

Noblesville's journey from Conner and Polk's small settlement of hardy pioneers to modern metropolis has been an eventful one. Along the way, the city has survived setbacks and adversities that might have destroyed another community. It has endured the collapse of the Central Canal project, the fizzle of the gas boom and four dark years of the Ku Klux Klan's influence. Yet Noblesville is still standing and thriving, and throughout it all, despite a skyrocketing population, it somehow manages to retain its small-town charm.

In 1896, a promotional brochure produced during the gas boom included the following assessment: "Noblesville is a progressive and up-to-date city and one that is alive to the great opportunities of the age."

Those words could easily have been written today. Twenty-first-century Noblesville is a city with both a rich history and a promising future, a city that looks forward to its upcoming Bicentennial in 2023 and is ready to take on the new challenges that lie ahead.

BIBLIOGRAPHY

General References

Campbell, Frank S. *The Story of Hamilton County Indiana.* Noblesville, IN: Hudler Press, 1962.

Foland, John A. *Remembrances*. Noblesville, IN: Rowland Printing Company, 1976.

Haines, John F. *History of Hamilton County: Her People, Industries and Institutions.* Indianapolis: B.F. Bowen & Company, 1915.

Hamilton County, Ind. 175 & Counting. Noblesville, IN: Noblesville Daily Ledger, 1998.

Hamilton County vertical files, Hamilton East Public Library, Noblesville, Indiana.

Helm, T.B. *History of Hamilton County, Indiana*. Chicago: Kingman Brothers, 1880.

Noblesville city directories, various years.

100th Anniversary tabloid. *Noblesville Daily Ledger*. September 29, 1988.

Sanborn Fire Insurance Map from Noblesville, Hamilton County, Indiana. Sanborn Map Company. Various years.

Shirts, Augustus Finch. *A History of the Formation, Settlement and Development of Hamilton County, Indiana: From the Year 1818 to the Close of the Civil War.* Salem, MA: Higginson Book Company, 1901

Chapter 1

Duncan, Robert B. *Old Settlers*. Indianapolis: Bowen-Merrill Company, 1894.

Finch, J.G. "James G. Finch, Pioneer Boy of Horse-Shoe Prairie" Ed. John P. Metzger. *Noblesville Daily Ledger*, March 28–April 8, 1969.

———. "Settlement of Noblesville, Hamilton County." *Indiana Magazine of History* 6, no. 2 (June 1910): 75–80.

Fletcher, Reverend J.C. "Early Days." *Indianapolis News*, May 11, 1881.

Lasselle, Charles B. "The Old Indian Traders of Indiana." *Daily State Sentinel* (Indianapolis), January 25, 1858.

Noblesville Daily Ledger. "Courthouse; Beauty Spot Is in Discussion." August 25, 1933.

Noblesville Ledger. "Valuable Spring." July 9, 1875.

Shirts, Augustus Finch. "'Horse Shoe Prairie' Settlers." *Indianapolis News*, April 2, 1896.

Thompson, Charles N. *Sons of the Wilderness*. Indianapolis: Indiana Historical Society, 1937.

Chapter 2

Blackburn, Glen A., comp. Nellie Armstrong Robertson and Dorothy Riker, eds. *The John Tipton Papers*. Vol. 1, *1809–1827*. Indianapolis: Indiana Historical Bureau, 1942.

Burgess, Joe H. *Hamilton County and the Civil War*. [United States: s.n., 1968?].

Cline and McHaffie. *The People's Guide: A Business, Political and Religious Directory of Hamilton Co., Ind.* Indianapolis: Indianapolis Printing and Publishing House, 1874.

Daily American Organ (Washington, D.C.). "Removal of J.F. Polk, Esq." May 1, 1855.

Dempsey, Charles. "Invasion of Cuba." *Hamilton County Ledger*, October 7, 1898.

Evening Star (Washington, D.C.). "The Late Josiah F. Polk." October 15, 1860.

Gay, Sydney Howard. "The Hundred Conventions." *Liberator* (Boston, MA), October 20, 1843.

Haimbaugh, Frank D., ed. *History of Delaware County, Indiana*. Indianapolis: Historical Publishing, 1924.

Hamilton County Ledger. "History." September 26, 1890.

———. "Reaping Rewards!" September 26, 1890.

Helm, T.B. *History of Carroll County, Indiana.* Chicago: Kingman Brothers, 1882.

Metsker, John P. "Swain Family Bought New Hospital Site." *Noblesville Daily Ledger*, May 7, 1951.

The Newspaper (Noblesville, IN). "Our Village." February 2, 1837.

Noblesville Daily Ledger. "A Marker to Be Placed at Grave of Gen. Conner." May 14, 1926.

Noblesville, Hamilton County [map]. Scale not given. Andreas, Alfred T. *Illustrated Historical Atlas of the State of Indiana*. Chicago: Baskin, Forster & Company, 1876, 95.

Papenfuse, Edward C., et al. *Archives of Maryland, Historical List, New Series*. Vol. 1. Annapolis: Maryland State Archives, 1990.

Polk, J.[osiah] F. to United States Commissioner of Pensions, November 21, 1855. Fold3. Accessed March 25, 2018. https://www.fold3.com/image/1/305367898.

———. Advertisement. *Public Ledger* (Richmond, IN). April 17, 1824.

———. "Mr. Polk's Report." *African Repository and Colonial Journal*, no. 6 (1831): 71–81.

Tucker, E. *History of Randolph County, Indiana*. Chicago: A.L. Kingman, 1882.

U.S. Department of State. *Register of All Officers and Agents, Civil, Military, and Naval, in the Service of the United States*. Washington, D.C.: 1825–51.

Warner, C.S. Map of Hamilton County, Indiana [map]. Scale: 1½ inches to the mile. Waterloo City, IN: C.A.O. McClellant and C.S. Warner, 1866.

Chapter 3

Indianapolis News. "A Building Boom." March 4, 1901.

Loehr, E.C. "Patriotic Proclamation." *Noblesville Daily Ledger*, April 9, 1917.

Noblesville Daily Ledger. "City in Frenzy of Unrestrained Noise Making." November 8, 1918.

———. "City Quiet as Surrender Is Announced." May 8, 1945.

———. "Council Starts Work Numbering the Residences." March 28, 1922.

———. "How Our County Has Helped in Winning War." November 9, 1918.

———. "Patriotic Demonstration a Big Success." April 14, 1917.

———. "A Wrecked Car and Machine Gun Are Found." April 7, 1934.

Noblesville Morning Times. "City's Celebration Has 500-Mile Race Flavor on Square." August 17, 1945.

Ohio State Moose Association. "Lodge History by Number." Accessed January 6, 2017. http://www.ohiomoose.com/pdf/LodgeOps/LodgeHistory-ByNumber-ALL-Lodges.pdf.

STATS Indiana. "Indiana City/Town Census Counts, 1900 to 2010." Indiana Business Research Center at Indiana University's Kelley School of Business. Accessed December 1, 2016. http://www.stats.indiana.edu/population/PopTotals/historic_counts_cities.asp.

Chapter 4

Enterprise (Noblesville). "The Old Store and the New Bank Building. Their History and Owners." September 24, 1909.

Indianapolis News. "New Noblesville." January 18, 1893.

Noblesville Daily Ledger. "American Strawboard." December 6, 1913.

———. "A Building with History." July 3, 1914.

———. "Business Firms of Long Ago." August 10, 1914.

———. "City's Oldest Businessman Dead." June 22, 1915.

———. "Dissolution Noblesville Milling Co." January 18, 1944.

———. "Noblesville Milling Co." December 4, 1913.

Phillips, John. "A Dealership for the Ages." *Car and Driver Magazine* (February 2009): 88–93.

Times (Noblesville). "Clancy's to Celebrate 50th at Noblesville Street Dance." July 10, 2015.

Chapter 5

Evans, Madison, A.M. *Bibliographical Sketches of the Pioneer Preachers of Indiana*. Philadelphia: J. Challen & Sons, 1862.

Finch, J.G. "Settlement of Noblesville, Hamilton County." *Indiana Magazine of History* 6, no. 2 (June 1910): 75–80.

Fletcher, Calvin, and Gayle Thornbrough, ed. *The Diary of Calvin Fletcher*. Vol. 1, *1817–1838*. Indianapolis: Indiana Historical Society, 1972.

F.W. Emmons Addition to the Town of Noblesville. *Hamilton County Deed Record Book F, April 1837–June 1839*. 308. Hamilton County Courthouse, Noblesville, Indiana.

Hamilton County, Indiana School Directory. various years.

Hamilton County Ledger. "High School Dedication." December 18, 1900.

Hamilton County Register. "City and County." November 9, 1870.

Indiana State Sentinel. "Notice to Builders." October 29, 1846.

Noblesville Daily Ledger. "'Aunt Nan' Roberts, Nearing Century Mark, Recalls Noblesville History." April 4, 1947.

———. "An Interesting History of School Houses in Noblesville Township." August 16, 1917.

———. "Two Schools to Be Closed by the Trustee." August 11, 1941.

Noblesville Topics. "Noblesville Became 'Millers' in 1925." January 29, 1975.

Shirts, Augustus Finch. "Early History." *Noblesville Democrat*, December 9, 1892.

———. "'Horse Shoe Prairie' Settlers." *Indianapolis News*, April 2, 1896.

State of Indiana to Earl S. Stone. *Hamilton County Deed Record Book M, May 1848–Aug. 1849*, 145–47. Hamilton County Courthouse, Noblesville, Indiana.

Chapter 6

Burgess, Joe H. et al., comp. *Centennial History of First Friends Church Noblesville, Indiana*. [United States: s.n.], 1992.

Cole, Barton W. *A Historical Sketch of the Christian Church of Noblesville, Indiana: 75th Anniversary, November 7, 1909.*

Correll, James. L. *Crownland Cemetery, vol. 1.* [United States: s.n., 1995?].

"First Christian Church, Noblesville, Indiana Centennial Celebration of Present Location, 1834–1955." Unpublished pamphlet. Hamilton East Public Library, Noblesville, Indiana.

Gascho, Mr. and Mrs. Clarence., comp. *First Methodist Episcopal Church, 1822–1939, First Methodist Church, 1939–1968, First United Methodist Church, 1968–1978*. [United States: s.n., 1978?].

Herrington, Robert. "Firmly Planted: Bethel AME Church Celebrates Its 150th Anniversary." *Current in Noblesville*, August 6, 2013.

Indiana Genealogical Society, comp. *Indiana Cemetery Locations*. Vol. 2. CD-ROM. Fort Wayne: Indiana Genealogical Society, April 1, 2006.

Moore, A.Y. *History of the Presbytery of Indianapolis*. Indianapolis: The Presbytery, 1876.

Noblesville Daily Ledger. "Estimate of Bob Jones." December 26, 1914.

———. "Old Cemetery Abounds with Early History." May 25, 1946.

———. "Stone Marks First Burial in Riverside." May 29, 1942.

"Our Lady of Grace Catholic Church. Dedication." September 8, 1991. Unpublished pamphlet. Hamilton East Public Library, Noblesville, Indiana.

Records of the Sessions of the Noblesville Presbyterian Church.
Wheeler, Marcia Lee. *A Journey of Faith in the Hoosier Heartland: A History of the First Christian Church, Noblesville, Indiana, 1834–1999*. [United States: s.n., 1999?]

Chapter 7

Garmel, Marion. "Marion Garmel." *Indianapolis Star*, December 19, 1991.
Hensley, Joanna, and Katherine Lewis. "New Owner, Name Revitalize TV Channel." *Noblesville Ledger*, June 28, 2002.
Hudler, Daily M. "My Personal Column." *Noblesville Morning Times*, January 23, 1942.
Indiana State Library. "Hamilton County Newspapers." Accessed June 14, 2017. http://www.in.gov/library/2794.htm.
Inman, Julia. "On the Air." *Indianapolis Star*, May 29, 1987.
———. "TV Scene." *Indianapolis Star*, June 5, 1979.
Latzke, Paul. "Fighting the Telephone Trust." *Success Magazine* 9, no. 143 (April 1906): 245–46.
Miller, John W. *Indiana Newspaper Bibliography*. Indianapolis: Indiana Historical Society, 1982.
Montgomery, Gregg. "Tuning in to Hamilton County on Channel 19." *Noblesville Daily Ledger*, January 9, 1996.
The Newspaper (Noblesville). January 12, 1837.
Noblesville Daily Times. "Adding a Page in History." June 2, 2003.
Times (Noblesville). "Catholic Radio Station WSQM-FM Signs On in Noblesville." October 13, 2011.
Wellman, Faith. "Switchover Was Success as First DDD Call Cleared at 2:06 a.m." *Noblesville Daily Ledger*, August 18, 1958.

Chapter 8

Birchfield, Roger. "Residents Fight Bridge Closing." *Indianapolis News*, March 25, 1977.
Hamilton County Ledger. "The First Car Here." November 3, 1903.
Indianapolis Journal. "Midland's Remarkable History." August 30, 1902
Indianapolis News. "Noblesville Bridge Open Again." June 24, 1987.
———. "Protests Save Historic Bridge." October 15, 1938.

———. "Troubles of a Railroad." November 28. 1899.

Indiana State Sentinel. "Railroad Celebration." March 12, 1851.

Neal, Georgianne. "River Fords Important in Pioneer Road System." *Noblesville Daily Ledger*, March 31, 1980.

Noblesville Daily Ledger. "Aunt Nan" Roberts, Nearing Century Mark, Recalls Noblesville History." April 4, 1947.

———. "City Contracts for Three Stop and Go Signals." September 23, 1924.

———. "Last Traction Car Operated Sunday Night." September 12, 1938.

———. "Many Witness Program at the New Airport." August 21, 1944.

———. "Old Tollgate of Other Days." March 19, 1920.

———. "Police Enforce Signal Rules." September 27, 1924.

———. "Roads Should Be Named." April 24, 1914.

———. "Three Young Men Buy the Local Flying Service." April 17, 1947.

———. "Two Men Acquire Land for New Noblesville Airport." October 30, 1985.

Noblesville Morning Times. "Noblesville Airport to Close Flying Activities." July 29, 1949.

Young, Captain Noel. "State Guard, C.A.P. Join in an Exhibition." *Noblesville Daily Ledger*, August 22, 1944.

Chapter 9

Brodt, Duane A. "Controversy Never Far from Courthouse." *Noblesville Daily Ledger*, June 26, 1992.

Gifford, Bill. "One Hundred Eleven Years of History." *Noblesville Daily Ledger*, May 19, 1955.

Hamilton County Ledger. "New Harrell Hospital Will Be Opened Saturday." June 18, 1909.

Hamilton County Register. "City Hall." July 6, 1870.

Metsker, John P. "Swain Family Bought New Hospital Site." *Noblesville Daily Ledger*, May 7, 1951.

Metzger, John P., ed. "James G. Finch, Pioneer Boy of Horse-Shoe Prairie." *Noblesville Daily Ledger*, April 8, 1969.

Miesse, Lulu. "A Trip on Parnassus." *Library Occurrent* 6, no. 3 (July 1921): 96–100.

Noblesville Daily Ledger. "Beautiful New Structure Given Name, Riverview." September 3, 1952.

———. "Formal Opening of City Building Tuesday." March 28, 1955.
———. "Large Crowd at the Corner Stone Laying." September 23, 1914.
———. "Parking Corp. Purchases Opera House." July 5, 1959.
Noblesville Ledger. "County Commissioners." June 4, 1875.
———. "The Court House Proposition." March 19, 1875.
———. "An Old Landmark Gone." June 18, 1875.
Ruthhart, Bill. "Putting Energy into Restoration: Group Raising Money to Fix Up 1922 Power Plant on White River." *Indianapolis Star*, June 11, 2005.
Wikipedia. "National Register of Historic Places in Hamilton County, Indiana." Accessed September 30, 2017. https://en.wikipedia.org/wiki/National_Register_of_Historic_Places_listings_in_Hamilton_County,_Indiana.

Chapter 10

Bishop, Reginald. "'Nothing to Keep Young People in Noblesville.'" *Indianapolis News*, January 1, 1976.
Guthrie, Wayne. "Fire Houses of Old Had Tom-Jerry Team." *Indianapolis News*, November 27, 1961.
Hamilton County Register. "Organization of Hook and Ladder Company." February 22, 1871.
Hinds, Alan Philip. *A Capsule History of the Noblesville Common Council, Noblesville Indiana*. [United States: s.n. May 10, 2005.]
Indianapolis Journal. "Death of James L. Evans." May 29, 1903.
———. "Excursion to Noblesville." August 8, 1872.
Indianapolis News. "The City." August 8, 1872.
Indiana State Sentinel. "Indiana Legislature." January 9, 1851.
Local Laws of the State of Indiana Passed at the Thirty-Fourth Session of the General Assembly. Indianapolis: John D. Defrees, State Printer, 1850.
Noblesville Daily Ledger. "Council Accepts Resignation of Fire Department." August 28, 1923.
———. "Fire Fighters Grow from Pioneers to Efficient, Modern Department." July 8, 1955.
———. "Mrs. Chas. Dawson Appointed Police Woman for City." September 5, 1922.
———. "One of the Guys." October 9, 1998.
———. "Police Woman Is on Duty." June 22, 1916.
Noblesville Ledger. April 9, 1880.

Noblesville Town Council. *Clerk's Record, Vol. No. 1.* April 5, 1851–December 5, 1873. Noblesville City Clerk's Office, Noblesville, Indiana.

Republican Ledger. "It Is Yes." May 6, 1887.

U.S. Department of State. *Register of All Officers and Agents, Civil, Military, and Naval, in the Service of the United States.* Washington, D.C.: Government Printing Office, 1825.

Chapter 11

Enterprise (Noblesville). "New Attraction." April 17, 1908.

Hamilton County Ledger. "Band Going to Chicago." June 12, 1908.

———. "Passion Play Coming." January 18, 1901.

Indianapolis Journal. "Noblesville Women Who Are Artists in Music." March 27, 1904.

Noblesville Daily Ledger. "Auto Horn Kills Music of Bells." December 17, 1917.

———. "Board Decides Not to Operate Bathing Pool." May 10, 1930.

———. "Enjoying Camp Life at Chautauqua." August 4, 1915.

———. "4-H Exhibit Entries Break All Records." August 2, 1950.

———. "Horse Show Came to an End Saturday." October 5, 1914.

———. Isis Theater ad. April 25, 1914.

———. "Large Crowd at Opening of the Bathing Beach." July 29, 1925.

———. Noblesville Chautauqua ad. July 31, 1922.

———. "Noblesville Drive In Theatre" ad. May 29, 1951.

———. "Rainbo Roller Club Plans Opening." September 1, 1955.

———. "Samuel B. Mott's Idea of a City Park." August 10, 1920.

———. "Snow Spoils Most Skating." December 27, 1935.

———. "Wednesday Large Day at Hamilton County Free Fair." August 21, 1930.

———. "Will Open Bathing Beach on Tuesday." June 20, 1927.

Noblesville Democrat. "A Grand Opening." November 29, 1895.

Noblesville Independent. "Opera House." September 26, 1884.

Noblesville Ledger. "A Park." September 3, 1875.

Program of the Hamilton County Chautauqua, Aug. 10–18, 1912. Unpublished pamphlet. Hamilton East Public Library, Noblesville, Indiana.

Snyder, Jerry. "A Journey Fraught with Peril." *Noblesville Daily Times*, July 23, 2004.

Chapter 12

Baker, Ronald L. *Homeless, Friendless and Penniless: The WPA Interviews with Former Slaves Living in Indiana*. Bloomington: Indiana University Press, 2000.

Beekman, Scott. *William Dudley Pelley: A Life in Right-Wing Extremism and the Occult*. Syracuse, NY: Syracuse University Press, 2005.

Couts, Shirley. "Dirty Helen: The Naughty Lady from Noblesville." *Hamiltonian County Magazine* (November 1978): 35–41.

Hamilton County Ledger. "Another Pioneer Gone." May 23, 1890.

———. "Mr. Leonard Wild Is Dead." December 17, 1909.

———. "Mr. N.D. Levinson." June 20, 1899.

"Indiana Man Is Well-Known Illustrator." *Rainbow of Delta Tau Delta* 66 (May 1943): 136–38.

Noblesville Daily Ledger. "Harry Levinson Succumbed to a Stroke Apoplexy." June 16, 1930.

———. "Invention of a Local Man." November 2, 1938.

———. "Levinson High School." June 7, 1916.

———. "'Lucky' Teter Died in Stunt at Army Show." July 6, 1942.

———. "Noblesville Is Honored by a Movie Star." June 10, 1937.

———. "Noblesville Man Is Listed with Who's Who." October 24, 1935.

———. "Rev. Barney Stone Dies at Ripe Old Age." November 21, 1942.

———. "Start Today on the Lucky Teter Movie." May 26, 1936.

Pegler, Westbrook. "Fair Enough." *Logansport (IN) Press*, June 13, 1961.

Republican Ledger. "Additional Local." December 3, 1886.

Tim Kraft Papers: A Guide to His Papers at the Jimmy Carter Library. Jimmy Carter Presidential Library and Museum. Last modified October 2013, accessed March 18, 2018. https://www.jimmycarterlibrary.gov/library/findingaids/Kraft_Tim.pdf.

Truitt, Mrs. Arza W. "Tribute to Mrs. Nan Roberts." *Noblesville Daily Ledger*, August 29, 1938.

Chapter 13

Brazil (IN) Daily Times. "Peary Gets Easy Money." July 6, 1911.

Hamilton County Ledger. "Faithful Services Rewarded." August 13, 1897.

———. "Matchless McKinley!" October 25, 1898.

———. "The President's Visit." September 26, 1902.

Indianapolis Journal. "Gas Belt Is Awake." October 20, 1894.
Indianapolis News. "Tour of the Ex-President." October 19, 1894.
Noblesville Daily Ledger. "Auspicious Opening of Chautauqua." August 2, 1915.
———. "Bank Robbery Frustrated." December 17, 1924.
———. "Comment." October 8, 1936.
———. "Helen Keller's Appearance Awe Inspiring." August 7, 1915.
———. "The Hoosier Poet Calls on Mayor Loehr." May 15, 1915.
———. "Knew Helen Keller's Father." July 19, 1915.
———. "Most Exciting Contest Since '96 is Expected." July 2, 1940.
———. "Noblesville Mecca for Orphans in Mid-1800s." July 22, 1976.
———. "Pres. Truman Greeted by Huge Crowd Here; Urges All to Vote." October 16, 1948.
———. "Roosevelt Talked About the League." October 15, 1920.
———. "State—Movie Star On Stage." September 23, 1936.
Noblesville Ledger. "Town Brevities." December 12, 1879.
———. "The Two D.D.'s." September 3, 1880.
Republican Ledger. "Blaine." October 24, 1884.

Chapter 14

Indianapolis News. "Noblesville's Natural Gas." January 7, 1888.
Leibowitz, Irving. *My Indiana*. Englewood Cliffs, N.J.: Prentice-Hall, Inc., 1964.
Noblesville Daily Ledger. "Case Compromised." December 10, 1920.
———. "Citizen Band Radios Play Major Role." January 28, 1978.
———. "City Exonerated from All Blame." September 18, 1919.
———. "Completes One Investigation—Begins Second." June 19, 1919.
———. "County Slowly Recovers from Blizzard of '78." January 28, 1978.
———. "Crowds Testify to Success of Parade." July 9, 1973.
———. "Drama at Riverview Was All Heroics." January 30, 1978.
———. "Echo of Traction Wreck in This City." January 3, 1920.
———. "Klan Komment!" June 20–August 22, 1925.
———. "Klan Walk Uneventful." April 9, 1973.
———. March 26, 27 and April 1, 1913.
———. October 1–4, 1923.
———. "Onc Killed and 23 Hurt in Traction Accident." May 26, 1919.
———. "Rushville Judge to Preside in the Stephenson Case." August 11, 1925.

———. "Sesquicentennial Schedule of Events." June 29, 1973.
———. "Sesqui-Week to Wind up with Huge Parade Saturday." July 6, 1973.
———. "War on Snow Goes On; Another Inch Tonight." January 30, 1978.
Noblesville Independent. "Boom! Boom!! Boom!!! Gas! Gas!! Gas!!!" January 28, 1887.
———. "'The First Shall Be Last and the Last First.'" June 17, 1887.
———. "Hurrah! Hurrah!! Hurrah!!! Noblesville to the Front." October 29, 1886.
Safianow, Allen. "'You Can't Burn History': Getting Right with the Klan in Noblesville, Indiana." *Indiana Magazine of History* 100, no. 2 (June 2004): 109–54.

Chapter 15

Cline & McHaffie. *The People's Guide: A Business, Political and Religious Directory of Hamilton Co., Ind.* Indianapolis: Indianapolis Printing and Publishing House, 1874.
Jarosz, Francesca. "Carmel Defends Roundabouts: Despite Fatal Crash, Interchanges Are Safer, Well-Marked, Officials Say." *Indianapolis Star*, October 3, 2007.
Noblesville Daily Ledger. "Population of Hamilton County." September 10, 1880.
Noblesville Through a Camera. N.p.: Daulton & Scott, 1896.
STATS Indiana. "Indiana City/Town Census Counts, 1900 to 2010." Indiana Business Research Center at Indiana University's Kelley School of Business. Accessed December 1, 2016. http://www.stats.indiana.edu/population/PopTotals/historic_counts_cities.asp.

INDEX

D

E

F

G

H

M

N

T

U

V

W

Z

ABOUT THE AUTHORS

PAULA DUNN is a Noblesville native. A lifelong history lover, one of her first jobs was as a costumed interpreter at Conner Prairie Pioneer Settlement, a living history museum near her home. She has a BA in history and German, and a master's in library science from Indiana University, and has held professional positions at the Speedway (Indiana) Public Library and the *Indianapolis Star/News* library. She currently writes a weekly column dealing with life in Hamilton County, past and present, for the *Times* of Noblesville.

NANCY A. MASSEY moved to Noblesville in 1983 with her husband and two sons. As Indiana Room Coordinator at the Hamilton East Public Library, Nancy works with local history researchers and genealogists, and maintains the Local History and Genealogy Collection at the library. She serves as a director on the Hamilton County Historical Society Board of Directors. The Indiana Genealogical Society appointed Nancy as the Hamilton County Genealogist. This past year, Nancy began serving on the Hamilton County Cemetery Commission. She received a BA in history from the University of North Carolina at Charlotte. She is coauthor of Images of America: *Noblesville.*